Ministerial Ethics

Being a Good Minister
in a Not-So-Good World

4210-56

IBSN: 0-8054-1056-2

Dewey Decimal Classification: 253
Subject Heading: MINISTERS // CHRISTIAN ETHICS
Library of Congress Catalog Number: 92-36921
Printed in the United States of America

Unless otherwise indicated, all quotations of the Scriptures are from the Holy Bible, *New International Version,* copyright © 1973, 1978, 1984 by International Bible Society. Scripture quotations marked NRSV are from the *New Revised Standard Version of the Bible,* copyright © 1989 by the Division of Christian Education of the National Council of Churches of Christ in the United States of America. Used by permission. All rights reserved. Scripture quotations marked NKJV are from the *New King James Version.* Copyright © 1979, 1980, 1982, Thomas Nelson, Inc., Publishers. Scripture quotations marked GNB are from the *Good News Bible,* the Bible in Today's English Version. Old Testament: Copyright © American Bible Society 1976; New Testament: Copyright © American Bible Society 1966, 1971, 1976. Used by permission. Scripture quotations marked KJV are from the *King James Version* of the Bible.

Library of Congress Cataloging-in-Publication Data

Trull, Joe E.
  Ministerial ethics: being a good minister in a not-so-good world
  Joe E. Trull & James E. Carter.
     p.   cm.
  Includes bibliographical references.
  ISBN 0-8054-1056-2
  1. Clergy—Professional ethics.   2. Clergy—Conduct of life.
I. Carter, James E., 1935–   .   II. Title.
BV4011.5.T78   1993
241'.641—dc20
                                                    92-36921
                                                    CIP

**To All Good Ministers
Who Faithfully Serve
Jesus Christ and His Church
with Integrity**

Wide was his parish, houses far asunder,
But never did he fail, for rain or thunder,
In sickness, or in sin, or any state,
To visit to the farthest, small and great,
Going afoot, and in his hand a stave.
This fine example to his flock he gave,
That first he wrought and afterwards he taught;
Out of the gospel then that text he caught,
And this figure he added thereunto—
That, if gold rust, what shall poor iron do?
For if the priest be foul, in whom we trust,
What wonder if a layman yield to lust?

—Geoffrey Chaucer, *Canterbury Tales*

PREFACE

After half a century of relative silence on the subject, the last decade has witnessed a renewed interest in ministerial ethics. One reason for this attention is our rapidly changing culture—clergy ethics are more complex in today's society. Another contemporary factor is the seeming increase of moral failures in the ministry.

Rightly or wrongly, churches formerly assumed Christian ministers were persons of integrity who could be counted on to be ethical. No longer is this presumption possible.

As a result, theological seminaries and church-related colleges are reexamining their responsibilities for spiritual formation and rethinking their curriculum. The teaching of ministerial ethics to ministerial students is a new priority in many schools.

The purpose of our text is twofold. First, this study intends to teach Christian ministry students the unique moral role of the minister and the ethical responsibilities of that vocation. A second purpose is more practical: to provide for new and established ministers a clear statement of the ethical obligations contemporary clergy should assume in their personal and professional life.

This work is the joint effort of two persons who have been friends since seminary days and who feel uniquely bonded by their Christian faith, their love of ministry, and their like-mindedness. We have spent most of our adult lives as pastors, an aggregate of more than fifty-five years of ministry in rural, small-town, suburban, university, and downtown churches. The two of us now serve by guiding and training other ministers in their vocation.

Although the seminary teacher authored the more foundational chapters of the book (1,2,6,7) and the denominational worker the more practical ones (3,4,5), the entire work is the product of both of our minds, as we have labored together throughout the project.

We have also worked very hard at inclusiveness. Aware of our own white-male-Baptist-pastor perspective, we have intentionally tried to address all ministers: male and female, pastors and associate ministers, generalists and specialists, ethnic groups and various Christian traditions. Although our theological approach is from the evangelical tradition, we hope clergypersons of every persuasion may find in this book encouragement and assistance for their own ministry.

Like all good ethical choices, this book is the result of the broad influence of many people. Numerous colleagues, friends, and other ministers have made significant contributions. Each topic brings to mind many "good ministers" we have known across the years. We wish to thank each of them.

In particular, Joe E. Trull is grateful to New Orleans Baptist Theological Seminary for sabbatical leave in 1991-1992 to complete this book, to Union Theological Seminary in Virginia for inviting him to be a Research Fellow on their campus during that time, to the T. B. Maston Foundation for providing a grant to assist in this project, and to the late T. B. Maston himself, beloved mentor and teacher whose life and lessons are often reflected in this work.

James E. Carter is particularly grateful to the churches he has served as pastor through the years, to the Executive Board of the Louisiana Baptist Convention for its encouragement to write, to the Southern Baptist churches and ministers in Louisiana with whom it is his privilege to work, and to T. B. Maston, who though not his major professor, was also a major influence in the formation of his ethical thinking.

Both of us wish to give special recognition to these laypersons, teachers, and ministers who read our manuscripts and gave invaluable advice along the way: John Alley, Larry Baker, Wayne Barnes, Cynthia Beal, Cheryl Burns, Robert Parham, Allen Reasons, and Nell Summerlin.

For that unique support and counsel which only a spouse can give, our personal gratitude to Audra and Carole.

CONTENTS

INTRODUCTION 9

1. THE MINISTER'S VOCATION: Career or Vocation? 18
   The Call to Ministry
   The History of Professions
   The Meaning of Professional
   The Crisis in Professional Life Today
   The Minister as a Professional

2. THE MINISTER'S MORAL CHOICES: Endowed or Acquired? 42
   Being Good—The Ethics of Character
   Doing Good—The Ethics of Conduct
   Living Good—The Ethics of Integrity

3. THE MINISTER'S PERSONAL LIFE: Incidental or Intentional? 67
   In Relation to Self
   In Relation to Family
   In Relation to Finances
   In Relation to Sexuality

4. THE MINISTER'S CONGREGATION: Friend or Foe? 94
   Ministerial Leadership—Authority and Power
   Ministerial Duties—Roles and Responsibilities
   Ministerial Transitions—Beginning and Closure
   Ministerial Success

5. THE MINISTER'S COLLEAGUES: Cooperation or Competition? 129
   Local Church Leaders
   Church Staff
   Other Ministers
   Other Churches
   Other Professionals

6. THE MINISTER'S COMMUNITY: Threat or Opportunity? 155
   Basis for Ethical Involvement
   Community Service
   Political Involvement
   Public Morality
   Legal Responsibilities

7. A MINISTERIAL CODE OF ETHICS: Help or Hindrance? 182
   Codes in the Professions
   A Ministerial Code of Ethics
   How to Write a Code of Ethics

APPENDIXES 220
   I. Early Denominational Codes
   II. Contemporary Denominational Codes
   III. Ministerial and Parachurch Group Codes
   IV. Sample Codes of Ethics: Pastor or Senior Minister Code
                                Associate Minister Code
                                Pastoral Counselor Code
                                Military Chaplain Code

INTRODUCTION

Ours is an age of ethical uncertainty. In Walker Percy's novel, *The Thanatos Syndrome*, a minister faces an ethical dilemma. Percy capsules his moral confusion and ours in one line: "This is not the Age of Enlightenment, but the Age of Not Knowing What to Do."[1] One writer calls this quote an apt aphorism for our age, and adds,

> Politicians, scientists, physicians, business leaders, everyday citizens, and our clergy increasingly find themselves in situations where they really do not know what to do. As a result, ethics has become a boom industry, and moral failure a regular front-page phenomenon. Conventional wisdom seems glaringly inadequate in the face of our environmental, technological, political, economic, and social situations.[2]

Ministerial ethics can no longer be assumed, if ever they were. The question suggested in the front line of this book, "How to be a good minister?", is as relevant as the morning news. In a city not far from where one of us lives, the pastor of one of the fastest growing churches in the South was arrested for drug smuggling. He confessed to flying cocaine from Colombia for $50,000. The minister, whose church had led the state in baptisms for several years, was sentenced to three years in prison and fined $10,000.

A regional magazine in a metropolitan area in the Southwest recently featured a cover story, "Thy Neighbors' Wives," which chronicled the sexual affairs of a megachurch pastor. The article claimed the charismatic leader was obsessed with wealth, power, and status. "One beautiful woman was not enough," said a deacon, referring to the minister's wife. "He was set up as an ideal man. He was adored and he ate it up."[3]

The saddest chapter in these two tragic stories was the final one. Neither fallen minister seemed remorseful when exposed, nor did they appear repentant when sanctioned. After a brief absence, they both established new independent congregations in the same cities where they had previously pastored.

Moral failures in the ministry are all too common today. Chaucer asked, "If gold rust, what shall poor iron do?" Obviously, it too rusts. Perhaps more rapidly. "For if the priest be foul, in whom we trust," continued the author of *Canterbury Tales*, "What wonder if a layman yield to lust?"

The present crisis in ministerial ethics is both a reflection of our times, as well as an influence on our society. Ethical failure in the pulpit affects the pew. At the same time, clergy morals seem to mirror the general decline in morality among the laity. Our day is fraught with political coverups, insider trading on the stock market, savings-and-loan scandals, and illegal gambling by sports figures. Numbed by it all, people are seldom shocked when they hear of an immoral minister.

A few years ago the academic dean of a seminary asked one of us to develop a course in ministerial ethics. Although I had been teaching for only a short time, I was very interested in pastoral ethics, due partly to the fact that I came to the seminary from the pastorate. For twenty-five years I had served congregations as varied as a rural mission in southern Oklahoma, a small community church in North Texas, a suburban congregation in Richmond, Virginia, and the downtown First Church of El Paso, Texas. (The other one of us has served similar size congregations in Louisiana and Texas for over thirty years before becoming Director of Church Minister Relations for Louisiana Baptists in 1988.) Both of us knew from our own experience that pastors needed help in personal and professional ethics.

The dean of the seminary had additional concerns beyond the normal help ministers need in pastoral ethics. Moral scandals involving televangelists and prominent religious leaders had recently made the pages of *USA Today*, *Time*, and *Newsweek*. These embarrassing stories created an atmosphere of distrust and disgust toward all ministers. Yet, even more alarming was the crisis in our churches. It seemed that each week brought another Shakespearean tragedy to the stage, as the curtain rose to reveal a new tale of a fallen minister and a forced termination.

A study of the dismissals of Southern Baptist pastors by Norris Smith, a Southern Baptist Sunday School Board specialist in the area of forced terminations, revealed "immorality" as a leading cause of their dismissals, second only to "lack or abuse of communication." The survey defined "immorality" as "sexual misconduct, substantive lying, and the misuse or embezzlement of church funds." Smith pointed to a lack of accountability and of clear professional guidelines among individual pastors as contributors to ethical failure.[4]

These events, as critical as they were, did not of themselves justify a new course in the seminary curriculum. More positive reasons were needed. Like an archeologist searching for clues to Pharoah's secret burial chamber, I began to sift through the academic artifacts of pastoral ethics. Three significant facts emerged which verified the crucial need to teach professional ethics to today's ministers.

The first discovery actually became the basic rationale for the ministerial ethics course and for this book. Discovery one: the Christian minister occupies a unique role among all vocations. This is true not only in relation to other occupations, but also among the traditional service professions. No other vocation is as ethically demanding as is the Christian ministry. No other professional is expected to model morality as is a minister.

Today's ministers walk an ethical tightrope. At one moment they may serve as prophets, priests, or educators; in the next, they may be administrators, counselors, or worship leaders. Each of these roles raises ethical dilemmas and exposes moral vulnerability not faced by doctors, lawyers, or other professionals.

For example, most church members trust without hesitation those "called of God" to minister. Yet this intimate relationship, which often involves sharing a parishioner's soul, makes a church minister vulnerable to many subtle temptations. The most obvious danger is sexual misconduct. Many clergy catastrophes involve romantic affairs, sexual liasons, homosexual acts, and other sexual transgressions.

Equally immoral, though often overlooked, are certain ministerial habits that may be accepted as part of the "job description." Pulpit exaggeration is accepted as a normal trait of preachers. How often does a church member say, "Oh, he's just preaching!"

More serious is the unethical conduct of an autocratic leader who misuses power, manipulates people, and practices deception and dishonesty. Pascal warned that "men never do evil so completely and cheerfully as when they do it from religious convictions." Our American culture stimulates in many preachers the desire to be a success. To be called as pastor of a large, prestigious church is the goal that has led many good ministers to sacrifice their integrity at the altar of success.

A second surprise I encountered as I explored the ministerial ethics wilderness was the lack of literature on this subject. A decade ago in his classic *A Survey of Recent Christian Ethics*, Edward Leroy Long, Jr., noted that "practically no attention has been given to the ethical problems arising from the practice of ministry, though the role of the church with respect to social issues has been hotly debated."[5] Other than Nolan Harmon's *Ministerial Ethics and Etiquette* (a 1928 publication in its twelfth reprinting) and Clark Hensley's booklet *Preacher Behave!* (now out of print), little was available as a practical manual for ministers. Professor Karen Lebacqz's *Professional Ethics*, which is an excellent academic text dealing with basic concepts in pastoral ethics, was the only contemporary book available, other than two works dealing with professional ethics in general.[6]

Fortunately, in the last few years three new books and several journal articles have appeared.[7] Although helpful in many ways, all of the new texts seem hesitant to give specific guidance and fail to deal in a practical way with many pertinent areas of ministerial ethics. As we were writing this book a compilation of essays written by members of the Chicago Area Ethics Study Group appeared.[8] The authors of this latest work chose a "terrain-mapping model," explaining that specific issues facing the modern clergy "are simply too numerous and too varied."[9] All four clergy ethics books were also written from a liberal Protestant tradition, whose theology and ecclesiology no doubt influenced their content and method.

As New Orleans Baptist Theological Seminary initiated a course titled "Professional Ethics for Ministers" in 1988, a third reality emerged which underscored the critical need for this discipline. As both of us talked to our colleagues and surveyed other seminaries, we were surprised to learn that few divinity schools listed a course in ministerial ethics. Catalogs of only one of six Southern Baptist seminaries listed a course in ministerial ethics.[10] A representative sampling of twenty other Protestant seminaries revealed only three offering a course in pastoral ethics (two of those were taught by the authors of the newest texts in this field).[11] Strangely enough, law, business, and medical schools are adding courses in professional ethics.[12]

Little wonder, then, that ours is a critical day for pastoral ethics. With seminary training in ministerial morality seldom available and with a minimal amount of adequate literature on the shelf, church ministers are left to flounder without aid in an ethical sea full of moral snares and malevolent sharks.

Ministers ask many difficult ethical questions. What does being a minister require of me morally? What does confidentiality mean and is it always expected? How is pastoral authority abused? When is preaching plagiarized? Is there a code of ethics that all ministers should follow? These and many other queries from clerics deserve an answer.

Introduction

Because of this need, a course in professional ethics for ministers was created. After three years and over two hundred enrolled students, it became apparent that an adequate ministerial ethics text was also needed, one designed with the evangelical Protestant minister in mind.

This is the rationale behind this book—we wanted to create a text to help ministers resolve the complex professional problems they face daily. This volume is by no means exhaustive. It is an attempt to provide basic ethical guidance for all persons involved in local church ministries—not only pastors but also ministers of education, ministers of music, youth ministers, church counselors, and other similar church professionals.

New Orleans is swampy, spongy, and unstable, mainly because the city exists below sea level. Whenever a building of any size is erected, the contractor must first bring in a large pile-driving machine to pound long telephone poles into the ground. These treated pillars become the foundation on which the structure sits. Otherwise, the edifice would slowly disappear into the delta mud, having no adequate support.

Both authors of this text hold certain basic assumptions, foundation pillars upon which the structure of this book is built. Since ethics is about "oughtness," we plan to discuss with you what persons called to be ministers of Jesus Christ ought to be and do. But before we can do that, you the reader need to understand our basic theological perspectives on the minister, the ministry, and the world they live in. As the Apostles' Creed expresses the essence of Christian belief, so these six affirmations state our basic convictions about ethics in ministry. If ministers are to be ethically sound and soundly ethical, it is our conviction that these pillars of truth must stand sturdy and deep.

1. We are convinced that *most ministers want to be persons of integrity*, persons whose professional lives uphold the highest ethical ideals. Christ's moral imperative in the Sermon on the Mount, "Be perfect, therefore, even as your heavenly Father is perfect" (Matt. 5:48), is a call for Christian maturity in all disciples. This "impossible possibility," as Reinhold Niebuhr calls it, is especially challenging for the Christian minister. The goal of this book is to give the clergy assistance in fulfilling this command of Christ to be mature followers, both in their personal and professional life, as ministers of the gospel.

2. Being good ministers suggests that *developing moral character and conduct is a difficult process*. Neither a salvation experience nor a call to ministry ensures ethical uprightness. All major books on ethics in ministry echo a common theme: the necessity for trustworthiness, prudence, truthfulness, and integrity in the life of the person called

to share God's message. Developing these traits requires diligent effort.

The front line of our book suggests that an ethical ministry does not come quickly or easily. We live in a ". . . Not-So-Good World" which, like Ulysses's Songs of the Sirens, lures us away from our station. Discerning the dangerous obstacles lurking in this less-than-ideal world, like spotting fallen boulders on a mountain road, requires keen eyesight and constant vigilance.

3. Although the basic moral character of ministers has been formed before they enter seminary or begin serving a church, *every cleric needs training in ethics and spiritual formation.*[13] If personal character and conduct has a place in ministerial ethics, vocational training should at least address the issue. In the 1970s the Association of Theological Schools became convinced that "the spiritual development of persons preparing for ministry" is "a priority issue of major dimensions."[14] The association initiated two special studies designed to meet this need. The result was the development of a new holistic model of theological education which integrated spiritual formation into the seminary curriculum and community. Spiritual formation has become a topic of major concern among[15] religious institutions of higher education.[16]

All of this does not mean ministers must be intellectuals in order to be moral. Walker Percy, physician and novelist, had one of his characters say: "I made straight A's and flunked ordinary living."[17] Nevertheless, ethical training can help.

For some preachers, theological education is not an option; these ministers must turn to other resources for the wisdom in ethics they need. A wise prophet taught both of us, years ago, that most pastors do not fail in ministry because of faulty doctrine or poor preaching. Success in the ministry, he said, depends on how well you get along with people and how Christlike you are. Both of these traits are learned skills, not natural endowments.

4. Since ethics can be improved through diligent study, there is an art to *doing ethics,* one which *can also be learned.* Before entering the gospel ministry, every ordained church leader must be examined by some responsible group to determine moral and spiritual fitness.

Christians rightly assume a person set apart by a church or denomination measures up to the biblical standards enumerated in 1 Timothy 3:1-7. The descriptive term translated "bishop" or "pastor" in this passage is *episkopos* (v. 1), a Greek word meaning "overseer." The title stresses the administrative role of the church leader. This pastoral function is not limited to skillful management of church business affairs; it also includes the ability to analyze facts, discern judgments,

Introduction

and make good moral choices. It is our conviction that doing ethics is, in part, a skill that can be learned and one that must be practiced by a capable minister.

5. The central moral choice facing the Christian minister is the same one confronting all professional persons: *Will I be an enabler or an exploiter?*[18] As we will explain in the first chapter, it is the nature of a professional to render services that pose the possibility of life or death (doctor), poverty or wealth (lawyer), and salvation or damnation (minister). The client-parishioner is in a dependent position and is vulnerable to exploitation by the professional who holds this "dangerous knowledge." Ministers, like doctors and lawyers, must be sure the service they render is given to enable, not in order to manipulate financially, sexually, or in any other way.

6. This final affirmation may surprise you: *A ministerial code of ethics, if used appropriately, can be beneficial*, both to ministers and to the churches they serve. If a life of moral integrity is the goal of every shepherd of God's people, and if the Christian community desires to encourage and support that intent, a written ethical covenant can enhance that purpose. Yes, there are risks involved in an established code of ethics for ministers; but there are also hazards if the clergy has no clearly stated standards of conduct. The final chapter will discuss these issues and propose that every minister who reads this book, as a beginning, write a personal code of ethics. This code of conduct is not meant to be a moral creed set in concrete, but a personal, dynamic document that challenges ministers to maintain the highest ethical life-style in every aspect of their calling. It also will inform the church and community of the professional ethics they can expect from ministers.

From biblical times to the present, the moral character of the proclaimer of the gospel was expected to be exemplary and "above reproach" (1 Tim. 3:2). Being a good minister has always meant more than just maintaining minimal standards. It is a call for maximum discipleship. To be an evangelist of the kingdom of God involves lordship—the rule and reign of God over every area of your life.

Ministerial ethics does not end when you walk out your office door—in many ways it just begins. A pastoral code of ethics includes personal habits, financial decisions, family commitments, pastoral responsibilities, congregational relationships, community involvements, and much more. We will look at these traditions and try to explain how Christian ethical ideals impact the world of the contemporary minister.

Of course, our effort to answer these questions is relative to our own traditions and perspectives, and we do not claim to have all the answers.

To give ethical meaning to the ministerial pilgrimage, we have drawn a few maps. As cartographers know well, maps need constant updating, as do our limited observations.

The stars by which we set our sextant, however, have been fixed in the heavens since creation. If you will take regular bearings with the Creator's divine compass, keeping your eyes fixed on "the bright Morning Star" (Rev. 22:16), you shall arrive at your destination without destruction or detour.

Suggested Readings

Marty, Martin E. "Clergy Ethics in America: The Ministers On Their Own." In *Clergy Ethics in a Changing Society*, eds. James P. Wind et.al., Louisville: Westminster/John Knox Press, 1991, 23-36.

"Ministry Ethics" in *Review & Expositor* 86 (Fall, 1989): 505-73.

Noyce, Gaylord. *Pastoral Ethics: Professional Responsibilities of the Clergy*. Nashville: Abingdon, 1988, 15-28.

Trull, Joe E. "Ministerial Ethics: A Matter of Character, Conduct or Code?," *Theological Educator* 43 (Spring, 1991): 5-10.

Notes

[1] Walker Percy, *The Thanatos Syndrome* (New York: Farrar, Straus & Giroux, 1987), 75.

[2] James P. Wind, "Clergy Ethics in Modern Fiction," in *Clergy Ethics in a Changing Society: Mapping the Terrain* (Louisville: Westminster/John Knox, 1991), 99.

[3] Glenna Whitley, "The Second Coming of Billy Weber," *D Magazine* (July, 1989), 94.

[4] Joy Jordan-Lake, "Conduct Unbecoming a Preacher," *Christianity Today* 36 (10 February 1992), 29.

[5] Edward Leroy Long, Jr., *A Survey of Recent Christian Ethics* (New York: Oxford University Press, 1982), 151.

[6] Darrell Reeck, *Ethics for the Professions: A Christian Perspective* (Minneapolis: Augsburg, 1982); and Dennis Campbell, *Doctors, Lawyers and Ministers: Christian Ethics in Professional Practice* (Nashville: Abingdon, 1982).

[7] See Gaylord Noyce, *Pastoral Ethics: Professional Responsibilities for the Clergy* (Nashville: Abingdon, 1988); Richard Bondi, *Leading God's People: Ethics for the Practice of Ministry* (Nashville: Abingdon, 1989); Walter E. Wiest and Elwyn A. Smith, *Ethics in Ministry: A Guide for the Professional* (Minneapolis: Fortress Press, 1990); and "Ministry Ethics" in *Review & Expositor* 86 (Fall, 1989): 505-73.

[8] James P. Wind, Russell Burck, Paul F. Camenisch, and Dennis P. McCann, eds., *Clergy Ethics in a Changing Society* (Louisville: Westminster/John Knox Press, 1991).

[9] Ibid., 13.

[10] Southern Seminary in Louisville, Kentucky. Southwestern Seminary in Ft. Worth, Texas, had discontinued teaching a course previously offered, but reestablished it in 1990.

[11] Richard Bondi of Chandler School of Theology and Walter Wiest of Pittsburgh Theological Seminary. The other school was Union Theological Seminary of Virginia.

[12] See Nita Sue Kent's "One Choice at a Time" in *The Baylor Line* (September, 1991), 18-23, for a summary of one university's efforts at teaching ethics in schools of nursing, business, law, journalism, and various disciplines.

Introduction

[13]See Urban T. Holmes II, *Ministry and Imagination* (New York: Seabury, 1981) and *Spirituality for Ministry* (San Francisco: Harper & Row, 1982); Alfred Hughes, *Preparing for Church Ministry: A Practical Guide to Spiritual Formation* (Danville, N.J.: Dimension, 1979); and Adrian van Kaam, *Formative Spirituality*, vol. 1 (New York: Crossroad, 1983).

[14]"Report on the Task Force on Spiritual Development," The American Association of Theological Schools, *Theological Education* VIII (Spring, 1972): 3.

[15]We are indebted to our colleague Dan Holcomb and his paper, "The Spiritual Formation of the Minister," for this summary.

[16]See Anne Davis and Wade Rowatt, Jr., eds., *Formation for Christian Ministry*, 3d ed. (Louisville, KY: *Review and Expositor*, 1988).

[17]Walker Percy, *The Second Coming* (New York: Farras, Straus, Girous, 1980), 93.

[18]Reeck, 38, where the author defines enablement as "the devotion of professional skills to meeting the needs of client groups and ultimately, to the common good."

1

THE MINISTER'S VOCATION:
Career or Profession?

Oliver Sacks began his book, *The Man Who Mistook His Wife for a Hat*, with the fascinating story of a person suffering from agnosia.[1] Dr. P. (the patient) was a distinguished musician and teacher in Berlin. His students first recognized his strange behavior when he was unable to identify people he knew. In addition, he often mistook objects like parking meters and fire hydrants for young children. At the close of one session with Dr. Sacks, Dr. P. started looking for his hat. Finally, he reached toward his wife's head and tried to put it on his own.

Agnosia is the psychiatic term for loss of the ability to recognize familiar objects. Dr. P.'s illness prevented him from recognizing persons, for he saw faces only in bits and pieces. Although he retained a highly abstract cognitive ability, he could see beings only as partial shapes. Incredible as it seems, Dr. P. got along well despite his disability and was able to work until the end of his life.

Amusing and yet tragic, the case of Dr. P. resembles ministry and ministerial ethics.[2] Today's minister must wear many "hats." Every seminarian knows that a call to become the minister of a church is a call to various tasks. Preaching, teaching, counseling, visiting, administrating, promoting, recruiting, leading worship, and community service are just a few of the roles. The unseen danger for the busy religious worker is "clerical agnosia," becoming the minister who mistook a parishoner for one of his hats! In short, persons can be lost in the midst of an active ministry.

What has caused this multiplication of roles which increases the risk of contracting clerical agnosia and overlooking persons? James Gustafson has observed three primary developments during this century which have precipitated this role change for ministers:

The first is the voluntary character of religion in the United States, which in its various dimensions makes the clergy unusually responsive to the desires and needs of the laity and to changes in the culture. The second is the breakdown of a sense of independent authority in the clergy; in the absence of wide acceptance of the traditional bases of their authority, clergymen seek substitute ways to make themselves legitimate. The third is the effort of the clergy to find new ways to make religious faith relevant to changing social and cultural patterns.[3]

These changes have led to clergy confusion and a condition Gustafson calls *anomie*, a lack of clear delineation of authority.[4] The typical minister is bewildered, not only about what to do, but also about whom to serve. Who has the final word: the individual member, the congregation, the denomination, or God? Like a circus juggler, the nervous minister tries to keep these competing authorities balanced.

The Dr. P. story is a parable of what can happen to any church overseer. Without realizing it, pastors and other ministers can slip into believing that all is well as long as the "bits and pieces" of people are visible. Ministry can become very impersonal. Church members begin to look like consumer-oriented clients, and the church itself takes on the appearance of a corporation whose chief executive must work to keep "profits" high and "customers" happy. Amidst this busy-ness, the real purpose of ministry can be lost.

Recently one of us was reading an article in a denominational paper from another state that featured a seminary student. The story identified him as pastor of "one of the fastest growing churches in Louisiana." Both of us know very well the small mission church where he pastors. The caption did not seem to fit. A check of the denominational records for the past three years verified our fears. The church membership numbered only a few more than one hundred. During a previous year church records reported a large percentage decrease, followed by a similar increase the next year. While this was "growth," overall attendance appeared about the same as it had been for several years.

There is nothing wrong with numerical increases in a church. However, if ministers become so obsessed that they worship their own success rather than God, they exaggerate statistics and rationalize unethical practices. Church leaders must tell the truth!

As we shall propose in the next chapter, the moral ideal for the minister is integrity, a life of ethical wholeness and moral maturity. How does the person called of God to serve the church achieve integrity of character and conduct?

The most naive believe that since the minister is set apart by God, ethics will take care of itself, for God calls only good people. Others assume that those who preach the gospel must surely live by the Bible's precepts and principles. Most laypersons admire the dedication of those who devote their lives to a Christian vocation and suppose this commitment ensures a Christian life-style. Yet ministerial integrity is neither simple or automatic. Clergy ethics, however, does begin with a proper understanding of the minister's vocation.

The purpose of this chapter is to reexamine the vocational role of the clergy. This begins with the minister's understanding of "calling"—is it to a career or a profession? To answer this basic question, we must also define what we mean by "profession." A brief review of the history of professions, which originated in the religious orders (who originally "professed" something), will aid our understanding of the term.

Another feature we explore is a significant change in cultural values in our society, which has precipatated a crisis for professionals. Many believe because of a change in professionalization in American society, the professional ethics model is fundamentally inappropriate for today's clergy. Finally, we shall attempt to determine if the minister is indeed a true professional, and, if so, how the professional ethics model can be a tool for "doing" clergy ethics.

The Call to Ministry

A basic prerequisite for an ethical ministry is a clear understanding of the minister's calling. How does a person enter vocational Christian service? Does a candidate receive a divine calling from God or simply choose a career? Is the ministry an occupation or a profession? What does the office itself require of the ordained: an inspiring moral life, effective church leadership, polished ministry skills, sound theological beliefs, unerring professional conduct, or some combination of these ministerial attributes?

H. Richard Niebuhr called the ministry of his generation a "perplexed profession." The situation today has not improved, for contemporary clerics are equally puzzled. Like butterflies newly hatched, seminary graduates flutter away from ivy-covered campuses planning to fly high, only to crash into the brick wall of Old First Church. Young ministers quickly discover that pastoral ministry is more like running a secular business than the spiritual enterprise they expected. The weekly calendar is crammed with financial meetings, publicity decisions, personnel problems, and client complaints. When will there be time for theological discussions, spiritual disciplines, or the real mission of the church?

A survey of recent graduates by two seminary faculty members surprised the researchers. It revealed the major concern of these first-time ministers was coping with the uncertainties as to who they were in ministry. "We found beginning clergypersons almost completely at the mercy of the expectations of their first parish without counterbalancing claims from denomination or profession. Formation of clerical identity depended on satisfying the first congregation."[5]

If this be true, how important it is for first-time clergy to have a clear understanding of their role. Every church has an unwritten list of expectations for its ordained, and, similarly, each new church shepherd arrives with a notebook filled with plans and priorities. The two sets seldom match. Much disappointment and many tensions during the first years arise from such misunderstandings. The result can be catastrophic: increasing conflict, ministerial fatigue, and even forced termination. Yale professor Gaylord Noyce asserts, "Clergy 'burnout,' so publicized, results more from a blurred pastoral identity than from overwork. Professional ethics well taught counteracts that kind of haziness."[6]

So the question arises again: To what is the minister called, a career or a profession? An occupation or a unique vocation? Each cleric must also ask, Whom do I serve, Christ or the congregation? Or to put it another way, Am I serving Christ as I serve the congregation? To build a ministry based upon integrity requires that a minister's sense of calling and concept of service be biblical, ethical, and Christlike.

Most evangelical ministers would identify with Jeremiah's account of his calling:

> The word of the Lord came to me, saying,
> "Before I formed you in the womb I knew you,
> before you were born I set you apart;
> I appointed you as a prophet to the nations"
> (Jer. 1:4-5).

This messenger to Israel believed the Sovereign Lord graciously planned for him to be a spokesman for God from the beginning of his existence. Christian ministers should likewise be confident of God's plan for their lives as revealed in their call to the Christian ministry. This conviction about the will of God is more than a choice of careers according to personality inventories; it is an acknowledgment of a divine appointment.

As Yahweh chose Abraham to lead a new people (Gen. 12:1-3) and sent Moses on a redemptive mission (Ex. 3:10), so God calls and sends the modern minister. Our response to God's calling must be like that of Isaiah, "Here am I. Send me!" (6:8).

Jehovah's prophets are not only called, they are given a message and a mission, as was Deborah (Judg. 4—5), Isaiah (6:8-9), Amos (7:15), and John the Baptist (John 3:1-3). The apostle from Tarsus was so convinced that God appointed him as a missionary to the Gentile world that he wrote, "I am compelled to preach. Woe to me if I do not preach the gospel!" (1 Cor. 9:16).

There can be no doubt, the minister of the gospel of Jesus Christ is set apart and sent forth by God to fulfill a divine mission. The ministry is a *vocatio*, a "calling" from God.

At the same time, the minister usually fulfills this calling through service to a congregation of God's people. This body of believers pays the salary of the church leader and expects some type of ministerial service in return. How does a person set apart by God to minister to the Christian community interpret his or her relationship to the church?

Another early church leader, Simon Peter, wrote a clear word about pastoral responsibility to the *ecclesia* of Christ:

> Be shepherds of God's flock that is under your care, serving as overseers—not because you must, but because you are willing, as God wants you to be; not greedy for money, but eager to serve; not lording it over those entrusted to you, but being examples to the flock (1 Pet. 5:2-3).

It is impossible to discuss ministers and what they do apart from the church, for what the clergy most needs is a function of what the church most needs.[7]

> [A]t a very early date, from among the ranks of the baptized, the church found it good to call some if its members to lead, to help the congregation nurture within itself those virtues needed for the life and work of the colony. Call these leaders preachers, priests, pastors, prophets, or just plain Jane—this is their particular vocation: building up a congregation.[8]

Although the minister's primary loyalty is to God, this devotion must never be an excuse for avoiding pastoral duties. Ministry involves both privilege and responsibility. The minister's calling always must be fleshed out in some kind of community, usually a local congregation. One cannot serve Christ without serving people, for to serve people is to serve Christ (Matt. 25:31-46).

As we seek a clear understanding of the minister's calling, it should also be noted that the terms "vocation," "profession," and "career" have multiple meanings. William F. May, of Southern Methodist University, has suggested that this confusion of terminology has created tensions. He first points out that every Christian has a vocation, which traditionally has meant a commitment to God and neighbor. A career, however, is a more selfish thing; it is a means to pursue one's own private aims and purposes. Instead of asking what is the need of the community, a career person asks what do I want to be and where do I want to go?[9] If this last question is uppermost in your mind, does that not mean you are pursuing a career, and not answering a call?

In the biblical sense, as Luther and Calvin both emphasized, all Christians are "called" to serve God in and through their vocation. The authors of this book contend that the minister, as a professional, stands somewhere between this generalized concept of vocation for all Christians and a specific career. She or he is fulfilling a calling and not just choosing a career. Yet, something more is involved. This unique calling to be a Christian minister has features which result in unusual obligations.

As we are about to see historically, the word *profess* originally meant "to testify on behalf of," or "to stand for something." Being a professional carried implications about knowledge and moral responsibility. "The professional knows something that will benefit the wider community, and he or she has a responsibility to use that knowledge to serve the wider human community."[10] Let us now explore how this traditional concept of a professional relates to the vocation of the minister.

The History of Professions

The chapel speaker during a special series of lectures on evangelism was appealing to seminary students for wholehearted dedication and sacrificial service. "You are not a professional," he concluded, "you are a servant of Jesus Christ." One of us who was in that service felt a little uncomfortable, for only an hour earlier the listener had taught a seminary class the meaning of being a professional minister.

The misunderstanding is common. The term "professional" is considered by some as a secular title reserved for reverends who are more concerned with status and prestige than spiritual ministry. Not so. In fact, the very opposite should be true.

In order for us to understand the true meaning of the word *professional*, it is important to review briefly the history of professions, how professionalization began and what changes have occurred over the years. This is especially crucial for our comprehension of the present-day crisis facing all professionals, including ministers.

Darrell Reeck believes the roots of our contemporary professions can be traced back to those early priests, healers, and chiefs who promoted human values in primitive societies. Unlike the modern version, these "prototypical professionals" were unspecialized and usually perpetuated themselves through inheritance rather than achievement. Nevertheless, these traditionalists did use their basic skills to meet basic human needs in their cultural groups.[11]

In early Israel a special class of religious professionals developed, namely priests and prophets. These two groups became the supreme authorities in law and religion, as well as performing some medical functions. The wealthy commercial and political "professionals" were castigated by prophets like Amos for crushing the poor through dishonest and unethical business practices. The concept of the prophet in ancient Israel is a "religious-cultural creation of the highest order," because it "presupposes the very source and meaning of the life of the individual and of the covenanted community."[12]

By the time of Jesus, a variety of professions had emerged: priests, teachers, lawyers, physicians, and professional soldiers. Although Christ often denounced the clerics and legal experts of His day as hypocritical and legalistic, He Himself became known as a rabbi from Galilee, a member of the teaching profession. In the Gospels and the Book of Acts we also meet another professional, the "beloved physician" Luke, who ministered to Paul and wrote two books of the New Testament.

During the period of the Middle Ages, particularly in Northern Europe, very little change occurred. With the established church in control, the clergy became the dominant professional group. Through control of education, the religious leaders of the medieval period wrote the rules governing the practice of all other professions. There were some benefits of this control. Medicine, law, business, and teaching all existed within a common framework of shared values and beliefs.

It was also during this time and afterward that many occupations and commercial groups organized into guilds. The guilds served to maintain standards, train recruits, and discipline the wayward. After the Industrial Revolution, some guilds evolved into professions.

Important to our understanding of modern professions and the ministry was the revival of a key doctrine during the Reformation period. Two key religious Reformers of the sixteenth century were Martin Luther and John Calvin. Before this period it was generally concluded that the only persons receiving a "divine calling" were those chosen by God to enter the spiritually superior monastic way. This "calling" (vocatio) was reserved for religious professionals alone.

Luther and Calvin challenged this tradition, based on the biblical teaching of "calling," which was prominent in Pauline Epistles (1 Cor. 7:20f; 12:28; Eph. 4:11; Rom. 12:6-8). Both Reformers asserted that every worthwhile form of work was a "divine calling." The farmer, the merchant, and the cobbler, not just the priest, also had a call from God to serve the world in their work.

Luther, being a bit more conservative, felt each person should labor *in* the same occupation as the worker's forebears. Calvin disagreed. He taught that the call to serve God and people was *through* whatever vocation best suited that person. This added emphasis from Calvin was extremely significant, for it meant admittance to a profession would be based not on inheritance, but achievement. The importance of this teaching for professional life is difficult to overestimate.

> [T]he Judaeo-Christian culture from Biblical times through the Reformation imbued the concept of *profession* with the moral principle of service grounded in a religious vision of God working together with people for the improvement of all creation. The doctrine of the *vocation* or *calling* became the religious and moral theme that most illuminated the meaning of the professions and professional work.[13]

After 1500 the professions stagnated, remaining small and exclusive. Members of the professions led the "good life" of leisurely gentlemen, gaining high social status through attachment to the king and his court. Work that required labor was for the trades; the professional lived the life of refinement among the upper classes.

Even as late as the eighteenth century, the education and competence of professionals was deplorable. Physicians knew Latin and the Greek classics, but very little about science or how to treat sick people. The law profession had actually deteriorated since medieval times, as barristers primarily served the gentry.

The clergy was not unaffected by these social trends. In eighteenth century England, the minister's role was mainly "an occupational appendage of gentry status."[14] By the nineteenth century many of the clergy were anxious to be regarded as professionals with specific functions and duties. Regrettably, this desire was difficult to achieve, since the minister's role included many functions not a part of ordination, but more related to his social position as patriarch of his rural parish. Often the local English pastor was also judge, doctor, lawyer, magistrate, and teacher.[15]

The professions in colonial America, however, took on a new character. Unhampered by the social class restrictions and institutional inheritance so rigid in England, the American professional "blithely ignored such hallowed distinctions as that between barrister and attorney, or between apothecary and physician. Professionals were judged by the competency of their performance and not by the impressiveness of their credentials."[16]

This unique development of the professions in America also had significant impact on religion. At first there were relatively few professions, the major ones being medicine, law, and clergy. As in rural England, in many towns in the new colonies the minister was the only professional, the one called upon to help in matters of law and medicine, as well as religion. At this time all professions not only held a sense of service to the entire community, but they also believed their service was to God.

For the minister, this sense of calling, of being chosen by God for this work, was even more intense. Yet Protestantism, with its Reformation tradition, also insisted every occupation was a holy calling. This generalization of the idea of calling led many in America to adopt an attitude of anti-professionalism.

> Lay preachers who were truly called by God could be seen as superior to an educated but spiritually tepid ordained ministry. The growth of the Baptist churches, which began to outnumber the older established Protestant denominations . . . offers an indication of this trend.[17]

The different social situation in America created a different history for professionals. Lacking a true noble class, doctors, lawyers, and ministers attached to the middle class and offered to the young an avenue of expression and achievement.

The twentieth century has witnessed an explosion of the professions in the United States. One of the positive results has been a high degree of specialized knowledge and skills, which has created high standards of living through multiple choices of professional services. Orthodontists straighten teeth, neurosurgeons correct spinal injuries, and ministers of music direct church choirs. However, with the market orientation of American capitalism, the services of professionals have sometimes been seen as one more commodity for sale to the highest bidder. Lawyers often feel like "hired guns"; doctors appear more preoccupied with technology and economics than patients; ministers view themselves as slaves to laity expectations.

In 1991 a large Southern Baptist seminary surveyed laity and clergy in eight southeastern states concerning the role of pastors. About thirty-two hundred persons responded. The results indicated unreasonably high expectations for pastors by laity, as well as wide differences of opinion between the two groups.

> Lay respondents showed a strong preference for a direct, aggressive, program-oriented leadership style, whereas professional ministers said they valued "shared, caring relational styles," . . . [P]eople in the pews expect pastors to be equally competent in virtually all aspects of ministry. . . . when laypeople were asked 108 questions about qualities

for pastoral ministry, "they basically said all 108 are important. So there is nothing unimportant, which is in a way quite unrealistic."[18]

This is part of the crisis the clergy face today as they seek to clarify their role and define their ministry in the modern world.

What conclusions can be drawn from this brief history of the professions? The earliest use of the word *profession* was in relation to those who "professed" vows in a religious order. The essential services provided to society by these religious commmunities included both the sacred and the secular, as monasteries became centers of culture and education. Thus these religious orders provided society with artists and educators, experts in law and medicine, and political advisors and leaders, as well as theologians, priests, and ministers.[19]

Gradually the three vocations of medicine, law, and divinity came to be regarded as unique. The term "laity" originally referred to those untrained in these three professions, because of their clerical foundations. By the late Middle Ages, physicians and lawyers who took no religious vows were practicing their craft. However, the original qualities the clergy "professed" continued to define the true professional.[20]

One ideal that emerges from this moral heritage of professional life is a theme which Darrell Reeck terms *enablement*, "the devotion of professional skills to meeting the needs of client groups and ultimately, to the common good."[21]

The opposite of enablement is exploitation. Reeck believes a critical question for all contemporary professionals, and especially for the modern minister, is this one: Am I, in my professional life, an enabler or an exploiter? Before that question can be fully addressed, however, we must first understand very clearly what it presently means to be a professional, and if that term really fits the minister's role today.

The Meaning of Professional

In popular language the word *professional* is used in careless ways which confuse. Athletes call themselves "pros" and occupations like exterminators and beauticians advertise their work as "professional." This common usage of the term intends to elicit from the public both respect and confidence, but it actually conceals the true meaning of professional.

Sociologists have written extensively about the true nature of professions, professionalization, and professionalism. Two major schools have developed: the "Harvard school" exemplified by Talcott Parsons and the "Chicago school" represented by Eliot Friedson. The Harvard school is functionalist in approach, seeing a profession as a distinct occupation, characterized by complex knowledge, social importance, and a high degree of responsibility. The Chicago school assumes the category of professional is a "semi-mythic construct," created by members of an occupation to obtain social and economic advantage.[22]

The functional definition of a profession has been accepted by most researchers as basic and conceptually more substantial. Using Talcott Parsons' definition as a basis, James Adams characterized a profession this way:

> [I]t performs a unique and essential social service; it requires a long period of general and specialized training, usually in connection with a university; it presupposes skills that are subjected to rational analysis; service to the community rather than economic gain is supposed to be the dominant motive; standards of competence are defined by a comprehensive self-governing organization of practitioners; a high degree of autonomy . . . ; some code of ethics . . . [23]

Sociologist Parsons also argued for certain moral obligations, such as competence and lack of self-interest, as essential to performance of the social function of a profession.

Concerned about the moral drift in medicine, a health practitioner contends there are four unchangeable characteristics of the helping professions:

> The four features that are fundamental to a true profession are: 1) the nature of the human needs it addresses, 2) the vulnerable state of those it serves, 3) the expectations of trust it generates, and 4) the social contract it implies. Taken together, these features set the traditional ideal of a profession apart from other occupations that lay claim to the title.[24]

In a contemporary text on professional ethics, Michael Bayles outlines three central features that are necessary for an occupation to be a profession: (1) extensive training; (2) a significant intellectual component in the training; and (3) the trained ability provides an important service in society. The university professor also notes there are other features common to many professions, namely credentialing, an organization of members and autonomy in his or her work.[25]

Other functional definitions of a professional by sociologists are similar, emphasizing four traits: specialized training, a sense of calling to serve the public, self-regulation including a code of ethics and autonomy.[26]

To compare these lists of professional characteristics with the vocation of minister is to recognize many points of identity. The clergy seem to fit all of these requirements except two, a code of ethics and autonomy, both of which are partially met in some denominations.[27]

Concerning the first, a code of ethics, some Christian groups have developed this document for their ministers, while others have not. The reasons for this inconsistency and the difficulty a code of ethics poses for ministers will be explored in chapter 7.

The second characteristic is the most critical dimension in the analysis of professions, the variable of autonomy, which is especially plaguing for the clergy. Professional autonomy is rooted in an authority based on superior competence. It is assumed, for example, that an orthopedic surgeon is competent in his or her area of specialized knowledge, and therefore will assume responsibility for professional decisions. This issue of professional autonomy has become a major area of conflict between professionals and the organizations in which they practice.[28]

The autonomy of the Protestant minister is much more limited than other professionals because in most churches the clients (members) are also the directors and owners of the organization in which the clergy practice. There has been no small amount of church conflict over pastoral authority and congregational control.

One of the reasons many sociologists are reluctant to include clergypersons as professionals is because the pastoral role has become an occupational conglomerate. Not only are there various specializations like education minister, church counselor, church administrator, and youth minister, but also a multiplicity of tasks in each category.

> The job means different things to different people, depending upon who these people are and what they do. In fact, the overall image of the clergy appears confused, and to many, both in and outside the ministry, unattractive.[29]

Another research team, Carr-Saunders and Wilson, in a standard volume on the professions, exclude the church from consideration because "all those functions related to the ordinary business of life ... which used to fall to the Church, have been taken over by other vocations. The functions remaining to the Church are spiritual, ..."[30]

One critical significance of an adequate definition of professions is the fact that "one of the most revealing ways of grasping the character of any civilization is precisely through discerning the ultimate orientation and the types of leadership which the civilization adopts."[31] Our culture could be judged by the way professional life exists today. A widening gap is developing between the traditional definition of a profession and the way professions function at the close of the twentieth century.

Before we can attempt to determine if the minister is a true professional, then, one other task remains. To understand the cultural crisis which threatens professional life today is necessary. It may very well be, due to the shift of values in modern American society, that the possibility for a minister to be a professional is no longer an option.

The Crisis in Professional Life Today[32]

Michael Bayles began both editions of his contemporary and much-quoted book *Professional Ethics* with this opening paragraph:

> The ethics of professional conduct is being questioned as never before in history. Lawyers, physicians, engineers, accountants, and other professionals are being criticized for disregarding the rights of clients and the public interest. Perhaps society is reconsidering the role of professions and professionals. In any event, many difficult ethical challenges are being faced by both professionals and the public. Given the important roles professionals are playing in society during the last decade of the twentieth century, everyone is concerned with professional ethics.[33]

Between the Reformation and modern professionalization, the twin Christian doctrines of vocation and covenant changed decisively. The sense of "calling" was broadened to the "priesthood of all believers" and eventually included every individual. The doctrine of covenant encouraged the forming of religious communities of discipline, who believed they served the purposes of God by serving others.

> In recent years, however, the idea of vocation has been replaced by the idea of career as the governing notion of professional life. And the idea of covenant has been replaced by the idea of contract. "Career" comes from a word that referred to the race course in the ancient Roman world. It is a word that refers to achievement by competitive combat, getting ahead, and triumphing over others—even if such achievement involves merely going abound in circles. . . . The word "contract" refers to the utilitarian agreements between parties whereby we establish a give-and-take relationship in which goods or services are exchanged on a tit-for-tat basis.[34]

This secularization of vocation and covenant into career and contract has seriously threatened the recovery of the traditional virtues of professionalism. A physician, Edmund Pellegrino, is alarmed that the central idea of a profession, altruistic service and effacement of personal reward, are today downgraded. The shift is in the direction of self-interest and away from moral commitments. Dr. Pellegrino believes the present moral character defections of many doctors, lawyers, scientists, and even ministers constitutes a grave danger to professional life and to our present society.[35]

The crisis has both a personal and a social dimension. On the personal side, contemporary professional life poses certain risks. A researcher who has studied the professions in American history has recently warned of the perils of modern professional life. Teachers, doctors, lawyers, and pastors, he wrote, face three present dangers: to become more self-reliant, more success oriented, and more convinced of how deserving they are. The Notre Dame professor concluded:

> The church of Christ does not need smug professionals, preoccupied with managing their own careers. The church does not need success-oriented members who reach out only to other winners. The church does not need those who expect the good life because of how hard they work. Instead, Christians are to live out the original ideal of the professions: to serve rather than to be served.[36]

On the other hand, Dennis Campbell has analyzed some new realities in American society which threaten a Christian approach to professional practice. Three major movements in Western culture which deteriorate the underpinnings of professionalism are secularization, pluralism, and relativism.[37]

The United States, like most other nations in our Western world, is dominantly secular. Life is no longer informed by a vision of God or the church. There are many competing views of reality in the marketplace of ideas, and thus, no one view commands the ultimate loyalty of a majority of Americans.

During the Middle Ages when the professions were emerging, a Christian world view prevailed. All aspects of personal and social life were defined by the church and a religious interpretation of life. Society was unified by common religious beliefs and shared values. Concepts of professionalism developed during a time when Christian moral values were widely accepted.

Secularization, like weeds in an unmanaged garden, gradually outgrew the Christian monopoly of Western civilization. As new views challenged the traditions of the past, a pluralism of ideas about the meaning and value of life emerged. This pluralism created many problems for the common life of Americans because it bred another cultural monster, relativism. Relativism contends that there is no one absolute view of reality, therefore all perspectives are equal in value.

With nothing of ultimate meaning to believe in, the average American must turn to material reality for salvation. Religious affirmations make no sense for people who believe that only "what is, is now, and there is no more." When it comes to values and virtues, modern Americans are diverse, divided, and often disinterested. Columnist Ann Landers put it in language we all can understand: "As for standards of morality, I'm sorry to say, forget it. That train left a long time ago."[38]

This absence of shared values is a serious problem for the professions. If America encourages a pluralism of world views and if all of these views and their ethical teachings are of equal value, how can anyone make judgments about moral actions?

> Unless judgments can be made about moral decisions, they are not *moral* decisions, but simply decisions of individual idiosyncrasy. Ethical reflection requires clearly stated assumptions to which one can appeal when reasons for action are examined.[39]

To develop guidelines for ethical conduct among professionals requires some consensus about values. The social crisis facing all professionals today is the increasing lack of shared values in American society.

Professional ethics also faces a crisis that has both personal and social dimensions. In many ways it is an outgrowth and reflection of the social changes discussed above. The authority and identity of the professional person is in jeopardy as never before. Traditionally the authority of doctors, lawyers, and ministers was never questioned, due to their vocational competence and their dedication to serve.

In our contemporary world, however, the lay public is challenging the professional at both points. As lay men and women have become more knowledgable, they have become more critical of professional practice. Public disclosures of malpracticing physicians, incompetent lawyers, and misguided ministers have increased society's skepticism. Lawsuits have escalated dramatically, not only from clients, but also between professionals.

Lack of public confidence in professional competence has paralleled the charge of diminishing professional dedication. Historically, those practicing medicine, law, and religion were trusted because it was assumed their only interest was the welfare of those whom they served. Today people are not so sure if a professional practitioner can be trusted. "Reports abound of unnecessary surgery, unreliable dental practice, questionable legal advice, and poor-quality teaching."[40]

Since 1977 the Gallup poll has asked the public to rate the honesty and standards of the various professions and occupations. In the most recent poll (1989), 12 percent of the public said the clergy rated "very high" on ethical standards, and 43 percent gave a rating of "high." One person in three (35 percent) believes clergy are only average. In light of the many moral scandals among ministers in the eighties, the pollsters felt this was a positive result. The clergy have ranked first or second among the professions since testing began. Currently ministers have a 55 percent favorable rating and are second to pharmacists and druggists (62 percent), followed by physicians and dentists (52 percent). Lawyers ranked 22 percent, just below Senators (24 percent) and just above local politicians (21 percent). In 1985 the clergy had its highest positive rating of 67 percent.[41]

The point is obvious. Doctors, lawyers, teachers, and even ministers do not command the aura of respect and admiration they once did. Professionals themselves do not share common values, which has no doubt contributed to this question of competence and dedication.

Ministers in particular are confused about their own identity. James Glasse reported over two decades ago, what seems still to be true, that "the image of the ministry is cloudy, confused, and unattractive."[42] In particular, he noted three different images of ministry create an identity crisis for the clergy: the ministry as (1) a calling for a particular kind or person; (2) a calling from a particular kind of institution; (3) a calling to a particular kind of work.[43] In an analysis of the role of the minister, James Gustafson further pointed out:

> The problem the minister faces in any social context is that of determining *who he is* and *what he is doing* within the complexity of his functions. He frequently lacks, more than anything else, an awareness of what he is about, and therefore he has no central focus for the integration of his various activities.[44]

The crisis faced by ministers is similar to that of other professionals because both have been significantly affected by the shifts in cultural values in America this century. Perhaps the situation is best summed up by Martin Marty in a current text on clergy ethics in America. The highly respected historian contends the context for clergy ethics has changed to "a more privately contracted entrepreneurial understanding."[45] Five elements have intensified this centuries-long trend: (1) a secular view of the clergy; (2) the legal subordination of religion to the state; (3) modernity and modernization; (4) the moral specialization of the clergy; and (5) theological accommodation. Using a show business term, Marty explains that in days past the minister's identity was determined by being part of a church establishment or denomination, but now "you are only as good as your last act."[46]

As we have explored the factors that have contributed to this crisis in the professions, we have seen that Americans lack a shared moral tradition. This cultural change has created a social and personal crisis for professionals. An absence of shared values in our society has contributed to skepticism from without and an identity crisis from within. In a secularized, materialistic culture where moral values for so many are relative, what is a minister to be and to do?

This brings us then to the crux of the matter: Is the minister a true professional or not? If the minister does "profess" something, what is it he or she professes and in what way does this "profession" affect ministerial ethics?

The Minister as a Professional

To summarize then, we can now define a professional in this contemporary sense: a broadly educated person of highly developed skills and knowledge, who works autonomously under the discipline of an ethic developed and enforced by peers, who renders a social service that is essential and unique, and who makes complex judgments involving potentially dangerous consequences.[47] The professional is primarily concerned with communal interest rather then self, and more concerned with services rendered than with financial rewards.[48] The question we must now answer is this: Does the minister's vocation fit this general characterization of a profession?

The first thing we must admit is the concept of a professional does not neatly fit the clergy. On the one hand, there are several ways American ministers are *less than* professional. Many ordained ministers have something less than a higher education, and even more lack professional (theological) training. Although the clergy was the historical matrix from which the modern professions owe their origin, intellectual training among modern ministers varies greatly.[49]

Another sphere of difference is the social role of the minister, which today includes not only pastoral responsibilities, but also many other parish skills. The contemporary clergy, for example, must be adept in business administration and public relations. For these tasks most ministers are not grounded in any specific technical competence.[50] At the same time, theological education has moved away from the study of divinity to provide "a cafeterialike offering of studies in specialized disciplines and an accumulation of professional skills."[51] Too often this effort to prepare ministers for the multiplicity of vocational demands they face is incomplete and superficial.

Peter Jarvis has raised another question: Is the ministry an occupation, profession, or status? He noted two major difficulties: the concept of profession has undergone a transformation from status to occupation, and secondly, there are no universally accepted criteria for a profession. Jarvis concluded that the minister is something less than a professional because: (1) the ministry is so heterogeneous, it is impossible to argue it is either an occupation or profession; and (2) the ministry has become a status profession with no high social position and thus is anachronistic in a world emphasizing achievement and specialization.[52]

Although lack of autonomy and specialization may prevent ministers from consideration as professionals, Jarvis believed this "neither denies the possibility of individual ministers being professionals nor that they may develop expertise which makes them highly skilled practitioners."[53]

There is also an opposite sense in which the minister of a Christian church is something *more than*, or other than a professional. Similar to Kierkegaard's distinction between the apostle and the genius, there is a "nonprofessional" ingredient in the vocation of the religious calling. The minister's *vocatio* is not of this world.[54]

This distinction underscores the minister's unique authority, which is not ultimately grounded in technical competance, but in religious and moral tradition. This means the clerical office is legitimized by its charismatic witness, which does not maintain cultural tradition as much as reject self-sufficient culture, bringing it under the judgment of the One who transforms both church and culture.[55] Perhaps for this reason Jacques Ellul contrasted vocation and profession as a "total divorce between what society unceasingly asks of us and God's will. Service to God cannot be written into a profession."[56]

Two Duke University professors, Stanley Hauerwas and William Willimon, also believe the ministry is something more than one of the "helping professions." They resist placing the minister in this category because of the implied presumption that ministry is simply a matter of meeting the needs of people. This "sentimentality" makes a ministry of integrity impossible, for people "not trained to want the right things rightly" will determine ministry, rather than the gospel narrative. "Being a minister (like a pastor), is not a vocation merely to help people. We are called to help people 'in the name of Jesus.' "[57]

Having admitted these ways in which the modern minister of the gospel is unlike the traditional professional, let us also note some ways the ministerial vocation fits that designation.

Unlike the typical specialist today, the minister is usually concerned with the total person; he or she is a generalist with a broad educational background, traditionally a trait of the professional. As the status of professionals depends on technical competence in their field, the clergyperson depends on competence in certain theological disciplines, both theoretical and practical.[58] Church clerics, for example, must be able to explain the meaning of Christian marriage, as well as perform a wedding service.

As leaders in the colony which exists as God's redemptive community in the world, the service rendered by pastors and other ministers is both unique and essential. The message they preach and teach is "dangerous knowledge" (like that of other professions), for it reveals the real meaning and purpose of life, as well as knowledge of the One who is "the way and the truth and the life" (John 14:6).

As a professional, the minister of the gospel is dedicated to serving others. Financial reward and social status are not primary motivations; the minister puts the needs of others before his own, for this is what it means to be a "called" minister and a follower of Jesus.

Many ministerial bodies have developed "Codes of Ethics" for their clergy. As we explain in chapter 7, these codes are usually developed by peers for the purpose of guiding ministerial conduct, particularly in areas of unusual vulnerability. At the same time, there is a conspicuous absence of codes of ethics for large groups of ministers, particularly those of the "free church" tradition (which is a partial explanation).

The classic defense of the minister as a professional is set forth by James Glasse in *Profession: Minister*. Urging church leaders to reaffirm their vocational identity as professionals, Glasse suggested that a religious professional should embody five important characteristics. The Christian minister is:

- An *educated* person, the master of some body of knowledge. This knowledge is neither esoteric or mundane, but information essential to ministry and available through accredited educational institutions.
- An *expert* person, the master of a specific group of vocational skills. These abilities, while requiring some talent, can be learned and refined through practice and with supervision.
- An *institutional* person, relating to society and serving persons through a social institution, of which the minister is partly servant and partly master. Ministers are also part of an association of clergy, usually a denomination, to which they are uniquely responsible.
- A *responsible* person, one who "professes" to act competently in any situation that requires the minister's service, which includes the highest standards of ethical conduct.
- A *dedicated* person, who also "professes" to provide something of great value for society. The minister's dedication to the values of Christian ministry is the ultimate basis for evaluating ministerial service.[59]

Glasse builds his concept of "The Professional Perspective" on these five base points which all professions have in common. In order to identify the minister as a professional, the Vanderbilt University teacher traced the relationship of doctor, lawyer, teacher, and clergyman to these five factors.[60]

Adapting this model, Gaylord Noyce develops a grid that compares five professions (he adds business manager) in like manner. Though his list of elements are similar, the Yale professor adds several new characteristics. For him a professional (1) is educated in a body of knowledge; (2) makes a commitment of service; (3) is part of a peer group that sets standards of practice; (4) is in an institutional matrix that claims allegience; and (5) serves immediate goals in the name of certain ultimate values; which are (6) specific to that profession.[61] Noyce graphically illustrates how these aspects of obligations apply to the religious professional.

Reflecting on the grid, Noyce seemed to conclude that the minister belongs in the category of a professional.

> The ordained minister learns theology, and steps into service in relation not only to a denomination and through it to the whole church, but also to peers in the ordained ministry. Entry into the colleagueship is celebrated as the ordinand pledges churchly participation and loyalty. All of this is clearly designated for the mission of Christ and the extension of Christian faith, by means of the proximate goals of pastoral care and the building up of the church.[62]

In an article in *The Christian Century* titled "The Pastor Is (Also) a Professional," the ethics teacher adds, "Thus, rightly understood, the professional tag is not destructive. Quite the contrary. It can firm up our sense of purpose and our understanding of how to go about the work of ministry."[63]

What then can we honestly conclude? Should the minister today accept the title "professional," or should it be rejected? It is our conviction that there is more to be gained than lost by the minister assuming the designation of a professional.

That is not to say this title fits neatly or there are not some drawbacks to the proposal. Nevertheless, as Glasse and many others observe, there are two main reasons for concluding ministers are professionals: traditional identification and rational definition.[64] On the one hand, many clergy today do fit the traditional description in the historical sense: university educated, fulltime, resident, tenured, and salaried. On the other hand, even among denominations that allow less than these standards, expectations for ministers continue to rise toward professional standards in all categories. Most Protestant churches view their ministers as professional, whether they use the title or not.[65]

If we who are ministers call ourselves professionals, what significance does this have for ministerial ethics? Acknowledging the danger of being redundant, let us one more time affirm that if the Christian minister is a professional, he or she is committed to certain ideals. The standards of professional practice which apply to the Christian ministry include these ethical obligations:

1. *Education*. The minister will prepare for Christian service by experiencing a broad liberal arts education, followed by specialized training in theology and ministry. Ministers will also be committed to a lifelong process of study and growth which prepares them for continued service (2 Tim. 2:15).

2. *Competent*. The church shepherd will develop and refine pastoral gifts and vocational skills in order to act competently in any situation that requires the minister's services (Eph. 4:11-12; 1 Cor. 12:7f).

3. *Autonomy*. The minister is called to a life of responsible decision making involving potentially dangerous consequences. As a spiritual leader, the clergyperson will make decisions and exert pastoral authority in light of the servant-leader model exemplified by Christ (John 13:1-16).

4. *Service*. The minister's motivation for ministry will be neither social status nor financial reward, but rather out of *agape* love to serve others in Christ's name (1 Cor. 13).

5. *Dedication*. The minister "professes" to provide for society something of great value, the "good news" of God's salvation and the demonstration of God's love through Christian ministry. To these values the called of God is dedicated (Rom. 1:11-17).

6. *Ethics*. In relation to congregation, colleagues, and community, as well as in personal life, the ordained will live under the discipline of an ethic which upholds the highest standards of Christian morality (1 Tim. 3:1-7).

In conclusion, we have argued that vocation, in the specific sense of a calling by God, is the essential element that prevents the concept of a professional minister from degenerating into a private affair. We have not demanded the clergy exemplify the notion of the professional in every way. Yet we are convinced there are good historical and theological reasons for asserting the Christian minister is a professional. If we are right, then the recovery of the religious and social

The Minister's Vocation

meaning of the clergy vocation and profession can revitalize the church as well as build a foundation for an ethical ministry. Perhaps Paul Camenisch sums it up best:

> I would argue that the professional ethics model is useful and appropriate for the clergy as far as it goes. Seen positively as the standards that guide professionals in their relations to clients and the larger society in light of the special skills and knowledge they claim to have, the distinctive goal they pursue in their professional activity, and the atypical moral commitment they aspire to, professional ethics sets a floor below which the clergy ought not fall.[66]

The heart of this book will be an attempt to explain what this commitment to an ethical ministry means in these various arenas of the minister's life. Without being legalistic, we will attempt to apply and illustrate the ethical demands of the gospel upon the professional life of the Christian minister. It is our hope that by the time we reach the last chapter, the reader will be prepared to consider writing a personal code of ethics as a guide for his or her own ministry.

Our immediate task in the next chapter is to review the art of ethics, to assist the reader to think through her or his own method of doing ethics. In order to evaluate the ethical life of the minister, the clergyperson must first have a clear understanding of the role of character, conduct, and moral vision in the process of making good moral choices.

Suggested Readings

Campbell, Dennis. *Doctors, Lawyers, Ministers: Christian Ethics in Professional Practice*. Nashville: Abingdon, 1982.

Glasse, James D. *Profession: Minister*. Nashville: Abingdon, 1968.

Marty, Martin E. "The Clergy." In *The Professions in America*, ed. Nathan Hatch, Notre Dame: University of Notre Dame Press, 1988.

Noyce, Gaylord. *Pastoral Ethics: Professional Responsibilities of the Clergy*. Nashville: Abingdon, 1988, 197-209.

Reeck, Darrell. *Ethics for the Professions: A Christian Perspective*. Minneapolis: Augsburg, 1982, 15-41.

Wind, James P., Russell Burck, Paul R. Camenisch, & Dennis P. McCann, eds., *Clergy Ethics in a Changing Society* (Louisville: Westminster/John Knox Press, 1991), 11-133.

Notes

[1]Oliver Sacks, *The Man Who Mistook His Wife for a Hat* (New York: Summit Books, 1985).

Ministerial Ethics

[2]I am indebted to James F. Drane, *Becoming a Good Doctor* (Kansas City, MO: Sheed & Ward, 1988), 1, for the application of this story to ethics.

[3]James M. Gustafson, "The Clergy in the United States," in *The Professions in America*, ed. Kenneth Lynn (Boston: Beacon Press, 1967), 70.

[4]Ibid., 81.

[5]Janet F. Fishburn and Neill Q. Hamilton, "Seminary Education Tested by Praxis," *The Christian Century* 101 (1-8 February 1984), 108-112.

[6]Noyce, 11.

[7]Stanley Hauerwas and William H. Willimon, *Resident Aliens: Life in the Christian Colony* (Nashville: Abingdon, l989), 113.

[8]Ibid., 113-14.

[9]William F. May, "Vocation, Career, and Profession," a paper presented at "A Consultation on Evangelicals and American Public Life" sponsored by the Institute for the Study of American Evangelicals, 17-19 November 1988, 3,6.

[10]Barbara Zikmund, "Changing Understandings of Ordination" in *The Presbyterian Predicament*, ed. Milton Coalter, John Mulder and Louis Weeks (Louisville: John Knox Press, 1990), 154.

[11]Reeck, 33, from which the outline for this section and much of the content is gleaned.

[12]James Luther Adams, "The Social Import of the Professions," *American Association of Theological Schools Bulletin* 23 (June, 1958), 154.

[13]Reeck, 35.

[14]Anthony Russell, *The Clerical Profession* (London: SPCK, 1980), 6.

[15]Ibid.

[16]Kenneth S. Lynn, ed., *The Professions in America* (Boston: Beacon Press, 1967), xii.

[17]Robert N. Bellah and William M. Sullivan, "The Professions and the Common Good: Vocation/Profession/Career," *Religion & Intellectual Life* 4 (Spring, l987), 8.

[18]"Expectations for Baptist Clergy a Source of Stress," *The Baptist Messenger* (31 October 1991), 6.

[19]Campbell, 18-19.

[20]Ibid., 20-21. Martin Marty notes, however, that other models have shaped the American clergy, namely that of (1) public role in a congregational-territorial context (1492-1830s); (2) congregational-demonimational role; and (3) the emergent private-clientele expression. See "The Clergy" in *The Professions in America*, ed. Nathan O. Hatch (Notre Dame: University of Notre Dame Press, 1988), 76-77.

[21]Reeck, 38.

[22]Lisa Newton, "The Origin of Professionalism: Sociological Conclusions and Ethical Implications," *Business and Professional Ethics Journal* 1 (Summer, 1982), 33.

[23]Adams, 156.

[24]Edmund D. Pellegrino, "Professional Ethics: Moral Decline or Paradigm Shift?" *Religion & Intellectual Life* 4 (Spring, 1987), 27.

[25]Michael Bayles, *Professional Ethics: Second Edition* (Belmont, CA: Wadsworth Publishing Co., l989), 8-9.

[26]Wilensky describes four structural attributes: (1) a full-time occupation; (2) a training school which transmits knowledge and skills; (3) a professional association which sets standards; (4) the formation of a code of ethics. Hall describes five attitudinal attributes: (1) the use of the professional organization as a reference group; (2) a belief in service to the public; (3) a sense of calling to the field; (4) belief in self-regulation; (5) autonomy. See Thomas M. Gannon, "Priest/Minister: Profession or Non-Profession?" *Review of Religious Research* 12 (Winter, 1971), 67.

[27]Paul Carmenisch has noted, however, that even professional characteristics like "specialized skills" must be qualified for the clergy in that ministers must often be a jack-of-all-trades, standards of admission to the clergy profession are not uniform, and their skills are not consistently valued in the larger society. See "Clergy Ethics and the Professional Ethics Model" in Wind and others, 121-125.

[28]Ibid., 68.

[29]Ibid.

The Minister's Vocation

[30]A.M. Carr-Saunders and P.A. Wilson, *The Professions* (New York: Oxford University Press, 1933), 290.

[31]Adams, 153.

[32]See Dennis Campbell's chap. 2, titled "The Contemporary Crisis in the Professions," from which several themes in this section are developed.

[33]Bayles, ix.

[34]Max L. Stackhouse, *Public Theology and Political Economy* (Washington, D.C.: University Press of America, 1991), 172.

[35]Pellegrino, 21.

[36]Nathan O. Hatch, "The Perils of Being a Professional," *Christianity Today* 35 (11 November 1991), 27.

[37]Campbell, 31-36.

[38]Ann Landers, "Ann Landers," [New Orleans] *Times-Picayune* (12 July 1991), 3(E).

[39]Campbell, 36.

[40]Ibid., 38.

[41]"The Clergy Receives High Ethical Marks," *Emerging Trends* 12 (March, 1990), 1.

[42]Glasse, 13.

[43]Ibid., 14-16.

[44]James M. Gustafson, "An Analysis of the Problem of the Role of the Minister," *The Journal of Religion* 34 (July, 1954), 187.

[45]Martin E. Marty, "Clergy Ethics in America: The Ministers On Their Own," in Wind and others, 24.

[46]Ibid., 24-35.

[47]Reeck, 18.

[48]Campbell, 24-25.

[49]David L. Sills, ed. *International Encyclopedia of the Social Sciences* (New York: Macmillan and Free Press, 1968), s.v. "Professions," by Talcott Parsons.

[50]Ibid., 538.

[51]Noyce, 198.

[52]Peter Jarvis, "The Ministry: Occupation, Profession or Status?" *Expository Times* 86 (June, 1975), 264-266.

[53]Ibid., 267.

[54]Adams, 162.

[55]Adams, 162-163.

[56]Jacques Ellul, "Work and Calling," in *Callings*, by W.D. Campbell and J.Y. Halloway (New York: Paulist Press, 1974), 33.

[57]Hauerwas and Willimon, 121.

[58]Adams, 163.

[59]James D. Glasse, *Profession: Minister* (Nashville: Abingdon, 1968), 38.

[60]Ibid., 38-43, where the author discusses each in detail.

[61]Noyce, 21.

[62]Ibid., 23-24.

[63]Gaylord Noyce, "The Pastor Is (Also) a Professional," *The Christian Century* 105 (November 2, 1988), 976.

[64]Glasse, 47.

[65]Although the underlying assumption of this chapter seems to be that professionalism is a characteristic each minister develops, the reality of the matter is that social institutions, like the church and education, play a significant role in determining ministerial professionalism, even though ultimately each minister must decide to accept that vocational identity or not.

[66]Carmenisch, 131.

2

THE MINISTER'S MORAL CHOICES:

Endowed or Acquired?

On January 31, 1872, the renowned minister Henry Ward Beecher traveled to Yale to deliver the first of the Beecher Lectures on preaching. His biographer noted:

> He had a bad night, not feeling well. Went to his hotel, got his dinner, lay down to take a nap. About two o'clock he got up and began to shave without having been able to get at any plan of the lecture to be delivered within the hour. Just as he had his face lathered and was beginning to strop his razor, the whole thing came out of the clouds and dawned on him. He dropped his razor, seized his pencil, and dashed off the memoranda for it and afterwards cut himself badly, he said, thinking it out.[1]

A century later another renowned minister, Frederick Buechner, commented, "And well the old pulpiteer might have cut himself with his razor because part of the inner world his lecture came from . . . was the deep trouble that he was in or the deep trouble that was in him."[2] Rumors about Beecher's relationship with the wife of a parishioner had gone beyond the gossip stage. Embarrassing letters and tearful confessions had surfaced. A public trial for adultery was not far away.

So, as Beecher stood gazing into the hotel mirror, with soap on his face and a razor in his hand, what he saw was not himself. Everything he believed in and stood for and had come to Yale to talk about was not reflected in that mirror.

> Henry Ward Beecher cut himself with his razor and wrote out notes for that first Beecher Lecture in blood because, whatever else he was or aspired to be or was famous for being, he was a man of flesh and blood, and so were all the men over the years who traveled to New Haven after him to deliver the same lectures.[3]

Yes, as well as all ministers who stand behind pulpits less prominent than the one at Yale. They too can "cut themselves badly." How

42

do ministers keep their faces clean and their lives unscarred by ethical misconduct? Is there a single formula for learning to do the right thing? Are "good ministers" born that way, or do they learn how to make right moral decisions?

Already we are making moral choices. Some of them are fairly ordinary, such as choosing between recreation with the family or sermon preparation. Others are quite complex. A teenager reveals in counseling she is pregnant, but asks you not to tell her parents. What do you do? Every day ministers must make decisions that touch other people's lives, as well as their own. Yet, even as we decide, we often ask, "Did I do the right thing?" How do you know? Or more importantly, can you improve your ability to make the right choices?

A hotly debated topic in ethics today is whether or not ethics can be taught. In a *New York Times* article, Michael Levin asserted "ethics courses are an utterly pointless exercise . . . abstract knowledge of right and wrong no more contributes to character than knowledge of physics contributes to bicycling."[4] Teachers of ethics responded vigorously. Acknowledging Levin's contention that right living is mainly a matter of instilling good habits of the heart, they nevertheless asked, "Is there no place for reason?" A good ethics class, they claimed, accomplishes three things: it stimulates moral imagination, hones moral analysis, and elicits a sense of moral obligation.[5] These three goals spotlight the aims of this chapter.

In religious circles the argument against learning ethics takes a different form. There is a popular myth that ministers automatically know the right thing to do. As we noted in chapter 1, most ministers believe their vocation is a calling from God. In addition, the laity often assume that God only calls persons of good moral character..

As the minister develops moral sensitivity through education and experience, some think that by the time of ordination, an articulate ethical expert walks forth with credentials in one hand and resumes in the other. However, no one knows better than parsons that Solomonic wisdom is rare, even among the clergy. In order for a minister to develop skills in moral decision making, he must understand the role of virtues in character, the place of values in conduct, and the way to develop integrity through moral vision.[6]

In light of the recent moral failures of many prominent preachers, it is surprising that anyone believes ministers are innately endowed with moral character or discernment. Nevertheless, it is common in seminary classrooms to hear a young theologian say, "Why do I have to take ethics? I know what's right. I have the Bible. I am committed to do the will of God." Many experienced ministers also believe they need no special training in moral decision making. They believe that their enlightened conscience, the Scriptures, or common sense will carry them through.

This last statement raises a basic ethical question. Who, or what, determines right or wrong for the minister? This is the question of ethical authority. Is the answer found within the person? Has God given a trustworthy inner light to ministers—a moral gyroscope that always points northward toward God's perfect will? Thomas Aquinas thought so in his trust of reason as an infallible teacher. Joseph Butler elevated the conscience to the role of unerring guide. George Fox and the Quakers sought guidance from the "inner light" in deciding what was right or wrong.

Most Christian ministers look beyond themselves for some dependable ethical compass to navigate through moral storms. Evangelical clerics normally turn first to the Bible. Worshipers often hear their ministers proclaim, "Look to the Bible. It has the answer for every question." Certainly most Protestant clergy accept the authority of the Scriptures as the "main tangible, objective source for a knowledge of the will of God."[7] Yet, sometimes our understanding of the Scriptures is so limited, we simply view the Old Testament as a book of moral rules and the New Testament as an advanced ethic of principles.

Closer examination, however, reveals that the entire Bible includes diverse ways to do moral reasoning.[8] Two contemporary ethicists have appealed to their colleagues to reconsider the role of the Bible in Christian ethics. In *Bible & Ethics in the Christian Life*, Bruce Birch and Larry Rasmussen build a strong case for the Bible as the major "formative and normative" authority for Christian character development and moral decision making.[9]

Yet, simply saying, "Follow the Bible," does not solve all of our moral questions. Some ethical issues, like divorce and war, seem both to be condoned and condemned in the Scriptures. Also, a number of modern moral concerns, like artificial insemination and media morality, did not exist in biblical times. In order to properly apply the ethical teachings of the Scriptures to these and other issues requires skillful exegesis and sound hermeneutics.[10] The Bible has a rich vein of ethical gold to be mined by the minister "who correctly handles the word of truth" (2 Tim. 2:15).

The Bible, then, is our primary resource for ethical guidelines. "The Biblical writers do offer a helpful lead. They suggest what sort of ethical approach is appropriate for the Christian—even if a lot of the details remains to be filled in."[11] One way the "details are filled in" is through the work of the Holy Spirit, the subjective means of revelation. As Christ is the pattern for morality, the Holy Spirit is the power that makes living the resurrected life possible (Rom. 8:13-14). The apostle John wrote, "When he, the Spirit of truth, comes, he will guide you into all truth" (John 16:13). The word "truth" presumably includes moral truth, the Spirit's help and guidance in moral choices. The apostle Paul reminded early Christians that the *paraclete* of God is our abiding moral guide (Rom. 8:9-14; 1 Cor. 6:19-20).

Sometimes we limit the Spirit's work to sudden inspiration or direct prompting to a certain action. Without disputing the Spirit's guiding this way, we also believe He gives insight to Christians in the midst of serious reflection on moral decisions.

What about our Christian tradition, both the heritage of our Christian faith, and the present-day Christian community? Some of the best insights about Christian living are found in the writings of persons like Augustine, Luther, and Calvin, as well as modern thinkers like T. B. Maston, Lewis Smedes, and Stanley Hauerwas. Ethically serious ministers will read the great books that inform and inspire toward Christlikeness.

There are other resources. Moral reflection and the ability to analyze situations are extremely important aids in decision making. Prayer is a vital link to the mind of God and often the final way of confirming the Father's will; this was true in Jesus' life (Luke 6:12; Matt. 26:42; John 17). In sum, Christian ministers must use every means at their command in order to discover and to do the right thing.

These lists of resources bring to mind an important distinction. Is ethics a matter of character or conduct? Which is more important, virtues or values? Does what *I am* determine what I do, or does what *I do* shape who I am? The answer to both questions is, "Yes." Being affects doing and doing shapes being.

Although some ethicists believe that the key to morality is character development, an equal number argue that the secret to correct conduct is how you do ethics. Without diminishing the importance of either, our conviction is that both "being good" (character) and "doing good" (conduct) are necessary. The two elements are interdependent. Like the bow and the violin, they work together to produce the music that we call moral vision—a life-style of "living good." The deep belief in the mind of both authors of this text is that the best word to describe the minister's moral life is *integrity*—a term that is the theme of this book and the integratiing element that unifies character, conduct, and moral vision into a "life worthy of the calling you have received" (Eph. 4:1) as a minister of Jesus Christ.

Discovering the will of God and discerning the right thing to do is not always easy; doing the right thing is equally difficult. In Dante's

Inferno, the first group the poet meets in hell are those who could not make a moral decision. The process of learning what is moral for the Christian minister, as well as developing the fortitude to do the right thing is a lifelong challenge. To grow in the ability to analyze each situation correctly, to apply Christian principles and perspectives wisely, and to walk in the pathway that leads toward the ultimate will of God—this is the goal for the minister's moral choices.

As we begin the larger discussion of ministerial ethics, let us be sure that we understand the basics of Christian decision making. There are three major components in this task: character, conduct, and moral vision or integrity. Ethicists sometimes use the terms virtues, values, and vision to define these three dynamics in the moral life.[12]

"Being a Good Minister in a Not-So-Good World" is obviously a matter of being; however, it is also a matter of doing and a matter of living. Like a three-legged stool, each of these ethical supports is needed to keep us from falling and failing in our moral choices.

Being Good—The Ethics of Character

Henry Ward Beecher saw two images in his hotel mirror the night before the Yale lectures. He gazed both at the man he wanted to be and the person he had become. Although Reverend Beecher had an ideal image of himself mirrored in his mind, the face he viewed as he shaved troubled him. He was ashamed to look himself in the eye, for that meant facing his own failure and folly. Perhaps that is why he "cut himself badly."

Beecher is certainly not the only preacher who bleeds, "for all have sinned" (Rom. 3:23). In one way or another, every person of the cloth has felt the weight of his or her own humanity. We have all cut ourselves—if not in the flesh, then in the spirit. The question is not, "Have I ever failed?" Rather it is, "How do I live as a human being in the world and not be controlled by my human appetites?"

A large part of the answer is found in merging those two images in the mirror—synthesizing the ideal person we ought to be with the real person we are capable of becoming. It all begins with the development of the inner life—something we call *character*.

The Meaning of Character

Character is basic to all ethical decisions. Who you are determines what you do. Jesus stressed that truth in His teachings, especially in the Sermon on the Mount (Matt. 5—7). Scholars agree that this monumental message contains the essence of Christ's ethic; He emphasized again and again that character precedes conduct and morality is a matter of the heart (5:3-48). Jesus taught that it is futile to pray or give gifts to the poor in order "to be seen by others" (6:1-8, NRSV), for wrong motives nullify good deeds. He condemned the superficial righteousness of many scribes and Pharisees, not because their acts were wrong, but because they played the role of hypocrite (5:20; 6:5). Albert Knudson claimed that Jesus upheld two principles that all Christians accept: the principle of love and moral inwardness.[13] The first principle is the supreme Christian virtue (1 Cor. 13:13); the second is the key to Christian morality—character.

Though we all have an idea of what we mean by the term, *character* is not that easy to define. Theologian-ethicist Stanley Hauerwas describes character as "the qualification or determination of our self-agency, formed by our having certain intentions rather than others."[14] William Willimon calls it the

> basic moral orientation that gives unity, definition, and direction to our lives by forming our habits and intentions into meaningful and predictable patterns that have been determined by our dominant convictions.[15]

According to Willimon, character is formed consciously and unconsciously, in a community or a social setting.

A one-sentence definition or paragraph description cannot begin to do justice to the complexity of the concept of character. More important to the task at hand, however, is the need to understand how moral character is formed and how it functions in the Christian's ethical life.

In recent years the focus of decision making has shifted to the role of character and to the community, the place of its source. Perhaps no modern writer has emphasized the role of character in Christian ethics more than Stanley Hauerwas. In his view, what we *are* is the ultimate determinative of what we *do*. He says that individuals do not approach a moral choice objectively; "rather, each person brings the dispositions, experience, traditions, heritage, and virtues that he or she has cultivated."[16] These "habits of the heart" develop from the communities to which we belong: our family, our church, our schools, and our society.

If character is that inner "moral orientation" that shapes our lives into "meaningful and predictable patterns," then the Christian minister must internalize "both the demands and limits of professional life to the point of behaving ethically most of the time as though by instinct."[17] This reality, that being shapes doing, forces us to rethink our whole approach to personal and social ethics. "The first task of Christian social ethics, therefore, is not to make the 'world' better or more just, but to help Christian people form their community consistent with their conviction."[18]

Like Beecher, we look into the mirror each morning, gazing at two images. One is clear and distinct; it is the real person that we are. The other is a hazy projection from our inner being; it is the person we hope to be. Rather than always asking, "What should I do?", the primary question is, "What should I be?"

The Creation of Character

Darrell Reeck has described character ethics as "expressive ethics." The question posed is, "What moral values do you wish to manifest through your life and practice?"[19]

Character consists of those personality traits that are moral and which traditionally have been called *virtues*.[20] Throughout history, character ethics has encouraged the cultivation of moral excellences considered essential to the "good" life. Ancient Greek philosophers listed four traits as cardinal virtues: prudence or wisdom, justice, temperance or moderation, and courage. Christian theologians like Augustine and Aquinas accepted these ideal traits as the very best virtues that humanity could discover through reason. To these cardinal virtues, they added the three theological virtues of faith, hope, and love, virtues received from God's revelation.

> For the Greeks, as well as the Christians, virtue was the central concept for moral reflection. Although there was no complete consensus about what constitutes virtue or which virtues should be considered primary, it was accepted that consideration of morality began with descriptions of the virtuous life.[21]

For many centuries the Christian moral life was considered largely a matter of pursuing the right virtues. Once the virtuous life was achieved, one was believed to have become became a "good person."

While virtue has had an important place in Christian ethics from the beginning, there has also been some suspicion of it. Reformers like Luther saw the inherent danger in such a quest. Much evil comes from the corruption of good, and much vice develops from the perversion of virtue. Luther believed that the very pursuit of morality inevitably led to self-righteousness. Rejecting the Aristotelian idea that ethics was a movement from vice to virtue, the German Reformer said that, if there be a "movement," it is from vice *and* virtue to grace.[22]

A modern theologian, Reinhold Niebuhr, has reminded us that human nature has a tremendous capacity for self-deception, accepting evil in the guise of good.[23] In our zeal to defend orthodoxy and uphold righteousness, we may sometimes manipulate the truth to suit our own purposes, read data with a bias, or use people to achieve our grand goals.

In spite of these built-in dangers, character remains the single most important factor in ethical decision making. Persons must *be* something before they can *do* anything. Persons of integrity not only tell the truth—they are truthful.

Writing to ministers, Karen Lebacqz pleads for two basic character traits: trustworthiness and prudence. Ministerial character absolutely requires trustworthiness. A minister must be "a person of integrity who not only does the 'right' thing, but is an *honorable person*."[24] Trustworthiness, wrote Lebacqz, means that a minister is a "trustworthy trustee," one who can be trusted to be honest, fair, helpful, and not hurtful. The Christian minister must be not like Judas, but like Jesus.[25]

No real Christian ministry can exist without the ability to discern the truth—prudence is Lebacqz's word for it. This virtue helps ministers perceive what is required them in any situation. Prudence, or discernment, is the ability to make right decisions and thus is central to ethical decision making.[26]

Lewis Smedes agrees. A key element in Christian decision making, declares the Fuller Seminary professor, is "the ability to see what is really going on, the small things . . . the difference between things . . . what is new and what is bizarre . . . what is excellent and what is only good."[27]

Yale professor Gaylord Noyce has recently addressed the professional responsibilities of the clergy in his book *Pastoral Ethics*. The basic character trait necessary in ministers, Noyce wrote, is "faithful integrity." A responsible shepherd of God strives to be "a person of religious integrity, a person of faith and spiritual wisdom."[28]

Seminary professors Walter Wiest and Elwyn Smith have written a basic ministerial ethics text in which they center ethical ministry around the nucleus of truth, "which includes both truthfulness and being true."[29] The Presbyterian ministers believe that a primary requirement of clerical ministry is being honest about one's self, the gospel preached and taught, and pastoral service.[30]

In the recent text produced by the Chicago Area Clergy Ethics Study Group, Dennis McCann has proposed a unique character trait as the distinctive of clergy ethics.

> I will argue that a capacity for self-sacrifice is and ought to be the indispensable first principle for clergy ethics, regardless of specific

denominational traditions, precisely because the role of the clergy in any society is to be the institutional bearers of whatever learning and teaching about sacrifice inevitably goes on in that society.[31]

Though he is addressing the social function of ministry, the DePaul University professor argues that this "capacity for self-sacrifice" should be the hallmark of clergy ethics.

Although these various writers differ on what is the most important clergy virtue, they unanimously agree that ministerial morality always begins with character. The minister's moral life must reveal a cluster of significant virtues.

Lewis Smedes' book, *A Pretty Good Person*, takes an incisive look at character. In order to live the "good life" and become a "pretty good person" requires living with common qualities like "gratitude, guts, simple integrity, self-control, discernment, and fair love."[32] Not only do individual virtues help us to be better persons, but taken together in relationship to each other they produce a whole person. In order to achieve good character, wholeness is important. In this recent book about character, Smedes concluded that character is a living network that links all virtues, each depending on the other.

> Without gratitude there can be no integrity; ingratitude falsifies life at the start. But integrity needs courage when honesty runs the risk of trouble. And courage needs discernment so that we can see what is going on and know when bravery calls us to act and when it calls us to stay where we are. But discernment needs self-control because when we fly off the handle we cannot see what is going on; and when we cannot see what is going on we usually end up making a mess of things.[33]

The Centrality of Character

Character ethics, then, is basic to ministerial ethics. The clerical collar does not guarantee ethical conduct; what exists under that collar does significantly affect every moral choice. In fact, character is the link between a person's past and future. A minister who has proved to be trustworthy in previous church relationships usually can be counted on to continue that pattern in the future. There is an overwhelming consensus that character is central to the clergy role. Nolan Harmon put it succinctly years ago, "The Christian minister must *be* something before he can *do* anything. . . . His work depends on his personal character."[34]

Numerous writers across the years have sounded that same note of conviction: "What the minister *is* will be his greatest sermon:";[35] "What he does is sometimes not nearly so important as what he is";[36] "I do not just *perform* a ministry, I *am* a minister."[37] Although ministry has changed over the years, this theme of *being*, not merely *doing*, has remained at the forefront of ministerial ethics.

A three-year study by the Association of Theological Schools identified qualities church people look for in young ministers. Four of the five leading characteristics focus on the minister as a person. Similarly, the three images ranked least desirable also dealt with issues of character. All forty-eight denominations agreed that "service in humility" is most important. Lebacqz believes the phrase stresses humility rather than service and thereby affirms that character, not just function, is central to the clergy role.[38]

As Reeck has pointed out, character ethics enables ministers and other professionals to fulfill their role in two ways: first, "a certain sense of calmness in doing the right thing and courage in resisting the wrong," and second, "a measure of discretion" leaving "final judgment up to the individual."[39]

Reeck also admits that in this individuality lies one of the weaknesses of character ethics. Social and institutional moral values are often not based on personal ethics; they are usually based on social survival goals like economic profit. Wise ministers, while retaining their inner convictions, must learn how to deal with social structures inside and outside the church. The correct way to express ministerial virtues in real life dilemmas is not always clear. For example, confidentiality may be a trait to which you are committed in ministry, but if a counselee threatens suicide, withholding that information is more a vice than a virtue.

Acting ethically always involves more than just having a sterling moral character. That is certainly basic, but the moral life is more than simply being a good person. Along with a healthy, wholeness of *being*, a consistent method of *doing* is needed. To character and its virtues must be added conduct and its values—the perspectives, obligations, and aspirations that guide the Christian minister in making right choices.

Doing Good—The Ethics of Conduct

Henry Ward Beecher's mirror may not have been cracked, but a close examination would surely have revealed several fractures. As he stared into the looking glass that night in New Haven, he saw some lines in the hotel mirror. These imperfections distorted the image he saw, reminding him perhaps that his own life was about to crack open like a shifting geological fault, triggering a Richter scale earthquake.

Ministerial mirrors have many weak points that often break under pressure. Traditionally, books addressed to pastors have focused on certain areas of conduct that seem to tempt ministers more than others. Due to the nature of the profession and the unique vulnerability of the minister, clergy ethical misconduct seems to major on sex, money, and power. These topics will be discussed fully in chapter 3.

Quaker theologian Richard Foster has called attention to these three temptations. Asking Christians to reconsider the monastic quest for spirituality, his book reviews the early struggle of the religious hermit with "worldliness." In order to renounce the material values of society, the monk took a vow of poverty; to flee the follies of the flesh, the celibate pledged chastity; to conquer the inner will, the recluse pledged obedience to ecclesiastical authority.

Warning our generation not to misjudge the monastics, Foster calls us to reexamine the monastic dilemma. Rather than accept the monastic ideal uncritically, Foster develops his concept of the disciplined Christian life on this monastic pursuit and made it relevant for our day. "We are faced with the necessity for framing a contemporary response to the issues of money, sex and power."[40]

Modern ministers are especially vulnerable to this trilogy of temptation; the three are uniquely related. "Money manifests itself as power. Sex is used to acquire both money and power. And power is often called 'the best aphrodisiac.' "[41] The minister's world often seems like an ancient Roman coliseum with three voracious lions—greed, lust, and power.

J. Clark Hensley has written a practical handbook for young ministers entitled *Preacher Behave!* One entire chapter is given to integrity, in which the denominational leader identifies several issues as particularly crucial for the clergy: confidentiality, financial honesty, competency, time-management, speech, plagiarism, sexual temptation, and devotion.[42]

Earlier we noted that Wiest and Smith identified truthfulness as the central issue of ethics in ministry. For these seminary professors, the principle of truthfulness applies to today's ordained in five areas of ministry: letters of recommendation, plagiarism, theological differences with the laity, theological growth, and confidentiality.[43]

The point made by all of these authors is this. Ministerial behavior is a crucial ingredient in the performance of ministry. To act in ways both unethical and indiscreet can seriously jeopardize a person's ability to serve the church of Jesus Christ.

A few years ago a prominent televangelist was photographed leaving a motel with a prostitute. After a tearful confession on television, he continued his ministry. A few months later a newspaper reported a new incident. A woman who was riding with this evangelist when he received three traffic tickets said she was a prostitute whom the preacher had picked up for sex. A week later he defended his return to his pulpit by saying, "God told me to!" How can this man maintain any credibility as a minister?

The Meaning of Values

As *being* centers on virtues, *doing* revolves around values. What do we mean by values? Values are "moral goods to be realized in society."[44] They are the ideals and concepts that any group considers to be of great worth. In the United States, for example, freedom and justice are important values. One function of a value is to highlight the consequences of behavior in society. When someone violates an accepted value, he or she threatens the unifying beliefs of that community.

The people of faith, the Christian church, have been called forth to be an alternate community, "a society shaped and informed by the truthful character of the God we find revealed in the stories of Israel and Jesus."[45] The biblical writers often use the word *good*, to identify moral and spiritual values.

> He has told you, O mortal, what is good;
> and what does the Lord require of you
> but to do justice, and to love kindness,
> and to walk humbly with your God?
> (Mic. 6:8, NRSV)

Over the centuries certain values kept appearing as reminders to God's people that they were "resident aliens . . . a colony, an island of one culture in the middle of another."[46] These essential "goods" revealed the nature and character of God, especially in the story of Jesus in the Gospels. From these values come the theological perspectives that ground us, the obligations that bind us, the norms that guide us, and the goals that motivate us.

The Theological Question

Just as virtue emphasizes moral character within, values stress moral ideals realized without. As the minister considers the role of values in ethical life, the first question raised is theological: "What moral values stabilize the clergy?"

Basic to Christian ethics is our understanding of the moral nature of God. Leviticus 19:2 is the *shema* of our ethical belief: "Be holy because I, the Lord your God, am holy." Biblical faith is an ethical religion because the one and only true God is holy, righteous, and just. God's moral character is revealed throughout the canon, both in the way God relates to His creation and the conduct expected from those created in God's image (Gen. 1:27).

The climax of God's revelation was the incarnation—the life, death, and resurrection of Jesus Christ of Nazareth. "The Word became flesh and made his dwelling among us. We have seen his glory, the glory of the One and Only, who came from the Father, full of grace and truth" (John 1:14). Jesus' entire life was in perfect harmony with the ethical ideals He taught. There is no other religion where the historic founder is himself the norm and the illustration of the values he professes.

One statement captures the essence of Jesus' ethics. This is His answer to the lawyer's question, "Teacher, which is the greatest commandment in the Law?" (Matt. 22:36). The reply of the Rabbi from Nazareth was based on two key Old Testament passages, Deuteronomy 6:5 and Leviticus 19:18:

> " 'Love the Lord your God with all your heart and with all your soul and with all your mind.' This is the first and greatest commandment. And the second is like it: 'Love your neighbor as yourself' "
> (Matt. 22:37-39).

These two commandments of love, one vertical and one horizontal, are the fulfillment of the entire Old Testament revelation (v. 40). In other words, Christianity is an ethical faith because Yahweh, the God whose nature is "steadfast love" (Hos. 11:1-4), expects His covenant people to love as He loved.

Reinhold Niebuhr, however, has reminded contemporary believers that self-sacrificial love generally does not work in society, due to a different set of values in social groups. As Niebuhr put it, individuals and groups have different moral possibilities (as the title of his book, *Moral Man and Immoral Society* suggests).[47] Although love is the ideal for personal relationships, in social organizations justice is often the best humans can achieve.[48] For ministers of the church, this is a reminder that social groups (committees, the churches, denominations) usually operate by a different set of values. Christian love may seem to be absent from decisions like who pays for medical benefits for the minister; fairness is probably a more realistic goal.

Moral values, like love and justice, are a major guide for ethical conduct. One of the ways we discern the "good" is through our understanding of the nature and will of Yahweh for humankind. This is foundational. Our new relationship to God and to the Creator's redeemed community, "where people faithfully carry out the task of being a witness to the reality of God's Kingdom,"[49] is the basis for our ethical way of life.

The Question of Obligations

After determining the theological perspectives that ground us, there is a second matter. Are there obligations that bind the minister? Are there moral imperatives the clergyperson must always follow? The deontological question is, "What duties are necessary for the minister?" Sometimes labeled the ethics of obligation (Greek *deontos*), this approach seeks to define the moral principles or laws that must of necessity be obeyed. Darrell Reeck pointed out that "if one of the weaknesses of character ethics is to specify with clarity what a person ought to do," then "that deficiency is satisfied to some extent by. . . the ethics of obligation."[50]

The Bible gives various examples of deontological duties. The two tables of the law were neither ten suggestions nor multiple choice options. The Ten Commandments were moral absolutes (Ex. 20:1-17). New Testament moral imperatives, such as the Golden Rule (Matt. 7:12) and the call for nonretaliation (Matt. 5:38-39), are "ethical ideals and principles which are implicit in that new relationship to God into which a man enters when the Kingdom is established within him."[51]

The Christian philosopher Immanuel Kant is sometimes called the "dean of the deontologists." Kant concluded that there are universal moral absolutes. He called them "categorical imperatives"; they must be followed without exception. One was the maxim to always treat persons as an end, never as a means.[52]

A more recent ethicist, W. D. Ross, developed his own list of absolutes, which he called *prima facie* duties. The two Latin words mean "on first appearance" and suggest for Ross duties to be followed. Examples of *prima facie* duties are fidelity, gratitude. justice, duties of beneficence (helping those who cannot help themselves), and nonmaleficence (no injury to others).[53]

Applying this to ministers, Karen Lebacqz wrote that "certain acts tend to be right because of the nature of the act that they are;"[54] The ethics professor listed the following responsibilities as compulsory for the clergy, all other things being equal: promise keeping, truth telling, beneficence, nonmaleficence, and justice.[55]

Obligations also include rules. Just how should biblical norms, church codes, and governmental edicts be understood by the minister? Laws are written to be obeyed. The Bible gives specific guidance on many subjects. "Fear God and keep his commandments, for this is the whole duty of man" (Eccl. 12:13). Both Testaments define in detail behavior that is considered moral and immoral. Can a prophet of God take these commandments seriously without becoming a legalistic Pharisee?

First let us affirm that rules do have value. Biblical norms give guidance for ordinary, everyday decisions. This is especially true for new Christians who are moral and spiritual infants as they begin this new life in Christ (1 Cor. 3:1-2). Several lists of vices and virtues appear in the Pauline Letters; new Gentile converts in a pagan, immoral Roman world needed immediate guidance for their daily lives.

Rules also describe the kind of person Christians ought to be. They spell out how those who have been captured by Jesus Christ act in certain situations. Biblical norms also inform the unbelieving world what to expect from the disciples of Jesus. Rules do have positive value.

What about a code of ethics for the church professional? Many professional roles carry obligations specific to them, often expressed in an ethical code. Doctors, lawyers, and scientists practice within self-imposed limits, usually expressed in a code of ethics sanctioned by some oversight committee.[56] The professional nature of the minister's work would seem to suggest a similar set of mutually accepted rules of conduct. Chapter 7 will address that need and pose the possibility of a code of ethics for ministers.

At this point, however, the question of ministerial codes relates to the value of rules and the dangers of prescriptive ethics. Legalism has always been a virus of religion. In Jesus' day, Sabbath laws had become burdensome restrictions. In their zeal to keep the letter of the Torah, orthodox rabbis missed the spirit of the law, even accusing Jesus of breaking the law of Moses (Mark 2:23-24). Jewish casuistry, with its meticulous regulations, continues to reduce the faith of Abraham to a set of rules.

Christians are also drawn toward legalism. Most evangelicals resist papal pronouncements, church dogmas, and authoritative creeds of conduct that eliminate the priesthood of every believer. Yet, it is easy for ministers to turn the Bible into a rule book, to rely on the judgments of a religious hero, or to allow some church tradition to become the rule of faith. Ministers ought to know better, yet many of us are guilty on occasion of regressing to some ancient list of "dos and don'ts," rather than seeking the will of God.

Legalism is an inadequate approach to decision making for several reasons. First, any list of laws is never long enough. A code can never cover every possible circumstance. Also, to keep some laws requires breaking others. To save a life, some have felt it necessary to tell a lie (Ex. 1:19). Finally, and this is perhaps the greatest weakness, legalism almost always hinders moral maturity and stimulates egoistic pride. Ethical bed-babies and the self-righteous are undocumented aliens in God's kingdom.

To guard against even subconscious legalism, the church minister must understand the relation between norms and values. Every biblical rule expressed a value; this value is the reason behind the rule. For example, the Seventh Commandment, "You shall not commit adultery" (Ex. 20:14), does not condemn sexual desire. The purpose of this word from God was to protect marriage and family life. Stated as a principle, the seventh word in the Decalogue declared, "Marriage is an intimate sexual union excluding all sexual partners other than husband and wife." The ethical emphasis of the Bible, as T. B. Maston often said to his students, is on principles rather than rules.[57]

The Question of Consequences

Values also have to do with teleology, the ethics of aspiration which asks, "What is the purpose or end result of my action?" *Telos* is the Greek word for *end* or *goal*. This focus on consequences has raised another ethical issue, how to act in such a way as to bring a better state of affairs.

The nineteeth-century social philosopher and reformer, John Stuart Mill, articulated a policy called utilitarianism. In short, his goal was to bring the greatest good to the greatest number of people. The value of utilitarianism is that it forces a person to consider all of the relevant factors in a decision and its consequences. Its weakness, of course, is that you never know for sure what the consequence may be. A minister may believe that a family will respond positively when informed of a teenager's drug problem; however; the opposite may occur.

Consequentialism is present in both the Old and New Testaments.[58] Wisdom literature seldom takes the imperative form, but usually gives practical advice about how to achieve the good life (Prov. 9:10). Hebrew midwives who "feared God" made their decision to deceive Pharoah on the basis of consequences: to save the male babies. God apparently approved of their decision (Ex. 1:15-20).

Jesus had numerous conflicts with religious leaders over the observance of Sabbath laws. The Lord of the Sabbath was concerned that the purpose of the day of rest was not lost in Jewish casuistry, "for the Sabbath was made for man, not man for the Sabbath" (Mark 2:27). In the Sermon on the Mount, Christ stressed motives, noting that good deeds may be corrupted by wrong reasons. The apostle Paul often evaluated consequences before making a final decision. He once took a vow and shaved his head, not because of religious obligation, but probably in order to conciliate Jewish Christian leaders (Acts 18:18), a practice he followed on other occasions (Acts 15:29; 16:3). The end result of any moral choice must be taken into account as part of the total decision.

The teleological question is usually raised when two values seem to be in conflict. When Nazis came knocking on Corrie ten Boom's door during World War II, the heroine of the historical story *The Hiding Place* faced a dilemma. Would she reveal that Jews were hiding in her house, or would she lie to the Gestapo? Her decision involved consequences; to tell the truth meant Auschwitz and the "final solution." With much courage and some anguish she chose a "lesser evil" in order to achieve a higher good; she sent the soldiers away. Her decision was like Rahab's misleading of the king of Jericho (Josh. 2) or Elisha's deception of the Syrian soldiers (2 Kings 6).

Sometimes a minister must decide if revealing the whole truth would do more harm than good. A wife asks her pastor, who is counseling her husband, if her spouse is having an affair. Is the minister guilty of breaking the Eighth Commandment if he conceals what he knows?

Though it may appear to be the best you can do in some unique circumstances, let us never forget that the "lesser evil" is an evil and not a good. A repentant spirit is in order. The Christian minister should always regret the necessity of such a choice and should work toward the day when such conflicts are eliminated, or at least minimized.

Lewis Smedes reminds us that in the "crooked ways of the world," we can deceive ourselves into believing our loving lies are gallant, when they may only be a way to save us from trouble.

> Telling one loving lie does not turn a person of integrity into a liar any more than one wrong note turns a concert violinist into a barn dance fiddler. But if you get used to getting away with a wrong note, you may get careless with yourself, and become just another fiddler when you could have been an artist.[59]

For the minister to be a good minister is a matter of learning how to *do good*. Doing good is very much a matter of values, deciding what moral goods in society are worth preserving and what rules, principles, and ideals apply to each moral question. Theological perspectives are basic; what we believe about God as Creator, Redeemer, and Governor influences our ability to make good moral choices. For the minister there are moral duties that must be followed, relevant norms that must be heeded, and social consequences that must be considered.

Yet, once more we must say that making good moral choices is more than being a good person (character) and doing the right thing (conduct). There is also a third component called *moral vision*, or *integrity*, which is the most unique one of the three, for this approach to decision making creates a new way to perceive ourselves and others.[60] This new moral vision not only completes the trilogy of major components in ethical decision making, but it also unifies both character and conduct into a wholeness of life that is best described by the moral ideal of integrity.

Living Good—The Ethics of Integrity

In his hotel room the night before he delivered the Yale lectures, Henry Ward Beecher wiped blood from his cleanly shaven face. He cut himself, for in the mirror he faced a contradiction between the person he saw and the message he preached.

In vivid contrast is the story of another pastor, Frederick W. Robertson, a well-known and highly esteemed preacher in nineteenth-century England. Robertson's pulpit ability was rivaled only by his character and Christlike conduct. One shopkeeper showed a customer a photograph of Robertson which he had placed on a back wall. Whenever the merchant was tempted to shortchange or dupe customers with inferior goods, he went into the back room to look at the face of the preacher.[61]

Integrity is the word for it. It is a moral ideal, a Mount Everest on which every minister hopes to stand. George Wharton Pepper, one of the few laypersons to deliver the Yale Lectures on Preaching, spoke for the laity when he said, "It is impossible to exaggerate the weight which the man in the pew attaches to the integrity of the preacher."[62]

No other professional is expected to model integrity as is a church minister. "Misconduct is inexcusable among professionals, but glaringly so among preachers."[63] After challenging the notion that ministers are superhuman and not subject to normal human faults and foibles, Karen Lebacqz nevertheless retorts:

> The minister is expected to embody trustworthiness in such an integral way (i.e., to have such integrity) that even the slightest failure becomes a sign of lack of integrity. This does not mean the minister is permitted no faults. It means that the minister is permitted no faults *that have to do with trustworthiness.*[64]

We have chosen the term "integrity" as the best word to describe the ethical wholeness of life demanded of the Christian minister. Our contention is that the morally mature minister experiences concommitant growth in three vital areas: character, conduct, and moral vision. Like a trio of overlapping concentric circles, these three elements interface to produce a morally complete person. Each is necessary, and none is complete without the other two.

The virtuous life, without the ability to discern values, usually fails to touch the world around us. Restricting the ethical life to the exclusive task of discerning right and wrong values often causes us to lose touch with the world above us. The absence of responsible "being" and "doing" in a pastor prevents the development of moral vision, the world within us. As Birch and Rasmussen concur,

> moral vision establishes the reference point for the other elements in the moral life. It sets the terms for that which will be included and excluded. It confers status upon that which is of greater importance, lesser, and, indeed, of no importance at all. Formation of moral character, together with decision making and action, are pervaded by the reigning moral vision.[65]

As three concentric circles form a new shape at the center where the trio overlap, so in the minister's moral life a dynamic center is formed that integrates character, conduct, and moral vision into one complete life of integrity.

The Meaning of Integrity

The term "integrity" appears sixteen times in Scripture. The Hebrew word for it is *tom* or *tummah* and means "whole, sound, unimpaired, perfection." It is used to describe biblical characters like David (Ps. 7:8), Solomon (1 Kings 9:4), and Job (Job 2:9). None of these men were morally perfect, but they each modeled a life of wholeness and maturity.

In the New Testament Paul reminded Timothy that in personal character, family relationships, and spiritual commitments, the one called to shepherd God's flock must be above reproach (1 Tim. 3:1-7).

Modern dictionary definitions of *integrity* explain the word to mean "soundness, adherence to a code of values, the quality or state of being complete or undivided." Charles Swindoll adds, "When one has integrity there is an absence of hypocrisy. He or she is personally reliable, financially accountable, and privately clean . . . innocent of impure motives."[66]

Integrity includes both who you are and what you do. It is the way you think as well as how you act. It is also

> ethical soundness, intellectual veracity, and moral excellence. It keeps us from fearing the white light of close examination and from resisting the scrutiny of accountability. It is honesty at all cost . . . rocklike character that won't crack when standing alone or crumble when pressure mounts.[67]

The Creation of Integrity

How does the minister develop these three elements of the moral life into one organic whole called integrity? Theology and ethics have emphasized recently the role of narrative, or story, in the Bible and in the Christian life. Narrative ethics asserts that we create ourselves and write our own story according to moral convictions we receive from the communities to which we belong. Hauerwas contends that this claim about the significance of narrative and community for theological understanding is not

> just to make a point about the form of biblical sources, but involves claims about the nature of God, the self, and the nature of the world. We are "storied people" because the God that sustains us is a "storied God," whom we came to know only by having our character formed appropriate to God's character.[68]

As believers identify with this story and make it their story, they become a part of the Christian community, which nurtures and reinforces in them the virtues and values of the kingdom of God.

This is narrative ethics. A new way of life calls believers to make this story their own; if they do, they will receive moral guidance and hear the moral demands of the gospel. Sometimes called the ethic of discipleship, narrative ethics focuses on the life and teachings of Jesus as a call to radical obedience. "Rather than reducing Jesus' teachings to principles or values, costly witness is called for. It is to live in the liberty that the new age has dawned in Christ."[69]

In short, these approaches called "narrative," "community," and "discipleship" ethics all point to the importance of integrating all elements in decision making. The virtues and values revealed in the Scriptures are not isolated from the biblical story, which is the story of the people of God who share a new vision.

The ultimate test of any story is the sort of person it shapes. As ministers of Jesus Christ and proclaimers of "The Story," we are compelled to ask, "Does my story fit God's story?"

Before the turn of the century, Charles M. Sheldon wrote the devotional classic *In His Steps*, which posed the ethical question, "What would Jesus do?"[70] Though idealistic in its application, the novel was accurate in its basic theme. The example of Jesus is our guiding story.

How do we follow the example of Jesus? Is it possible in this modern world for a minister to live like Jesus lived and love the way Jesus loved? To be accepted as a disciple means learning to imitate a master. It is not a matter of doing our duty, but living His story. "The problem lies not in knowing *what* we must do, but *how* we are to do it. And the how is learned only by watching and following."[71]

Whether you call it discipleship or moral vision or integrity, the challenge is the same, we are to "walk as Jesus did" (1 John 2:6). T. B. Maston's last book, *To Walk as He Walked*, was based on this his favorite Scripture. The renowned ethicist called for Christians to reexamine the historic Jesus and the life He lived. "The major recurring question for us is, How much do we walk as He walked?"[72] What gives a minister integrity is the way the events of his or her life embody the gospel story, the life and teachings of Jesus the Messiah.

For example, the stories told by Christ, such as the parable of the good Samaritan, teach us how to perceive people. Lebacqz reminds us that we often miss the point Jesus makes here. The question introducing the story, "Who is my neighbor?", was addressed to Jews. The parable tells the injured Jew lying on the roadside that his neighbor is his enemy! The Samaritan you hate and the race your friends despise is the compassionate one who stopped and gave you aid. "The meaning of the story goes far beyond simple rules about helping others, . . . It has to do with vision."[73]

Do you want to be a minister of integrity? Then model your life and ministry after the life and teachings of Jesus Christ. The incarnate Son of God perfectly exampled in His humanity the life of integrity we are to follow.

The Practical Question

At this point you may be saying, "All of this sounds well and good, but specifically, how does a minister put it into practice in everyday life?" Good question. First, let us agree that every person called to the ministry wants to achieve that wholeness of life and soundness of character that marks a Christian leader who makes good moral choices.

Second, let us reaffirm the inadequacy of singular approaches. Any list of moral rules fails at several points, even if the rules are from the Bible or orthodox church teachings. Likewise, great ethical principles like love and justice, though important values, do not by themselves give complete guidance. Listening for some inner voice alone is also inadequate, for it is too subjective. Even looking for the lesser evil or the greater good does not resolve all moral conflicts.

What then can the church's moral leader do? There is no single method of ethics that covers the entire range of moral experience. Different styles of moral reasoning fit various moral questions. In a book written to help professionals, Darrell Reeck concluded:

> astute people in actual practice use a mix of types of ethics. In day-to-day situations they may operate with reference to a set of principles that are perhaps even only somewhat dimly perceived. When they face unique, nonrepetitive decisions, they may bring calculations of conse-

quences into operation. If really pushed to the wall in a situation in which they cannot compromise, they may act according to principle without any regard to consequences. As people mature in decision making they achieve an artful ability to make appropriate ethical responses by drawing selectively from their repertoire of ethical knowledge.[74]

By "artful ability" it seems Reeck is alluding to the quality that we have called moral vision.

Perhaps the most important characteristic that we have not mentioned until now is the attempt to be consistent. For the minister to be inconsistent in moral thinking and actions is not only irrational, but it also raises serious questions about personal integrity. The vice Jesus condemned with His harshest words and most scathing denunciation was hypocrisy (Matt. 23).

> Hypocrisy can mean a failure to practice what one preaches; it can also entail an attitude of rigorous moral scrupulosity in one area co-existing with an attitude of libertarian indifference in a comparable area. Hypocrisy may consist in a failure to carry through the implications of one's moral stances consistently.[75]

For example, if a minister denounces explicit sexual scenes on television, does he also condemn excessive violence? Do his views about war and peace tie in with His attitude about life-taking in euthanasia and abortion? Would you be honest if you knew that you could get away with being dishonest? Plato highlighted this in the myth of the ring of Gyges about a shepherd who found an unusual gold ring. By turning the jewel to the inside of his hand he could make himself invisible. The result? A good man became a thief.[76]

Our contention has been that of all the different methods used to make good moral decisions, three are basic: *character*, *conduct*, and *moral vision*. The character of the Christian minister is basic; being precedes doing. Developing the right virtues is essential to effective ministry.

The ability to discern and apply social values is also crucial. The well-grounded pastor will recognize which duties are obligatory and which goals serve as guidelines for achieving the will of God.

Finally, through personal identification with Jesus the Christ and full participation in the gospel story, the ethical leader of the church will gain a moral vision that synthesizes and harmonizes being, doing, and living into a life of moral integrity.

We return to the initial question of this chapter: Are the minister's moral choices endowed or acquired? By now, the answer should be clear. Ethical integrity is not genetically inbred at birth or miraculously infused at baptism or ordination. The prophet of God must grow in faith and morals as do all believers. Learning how to make good moral choices is a lifelong process called Christian discipleship.

In the closing lines of his excellent book *Choices*, Lewis Smedes wrote, "After all is said and done, being right is not the most important thing in the world. Being forgiven is."[77]

Thus far we have attempted two tasks. First, we have explored the meaning of the minister's vocation, suggesting that the traditional professional role of the clergy has significant ethical implications. Second, we have sought to establish a method for making good moral choices by properly relating character, conduct, and moral vision into a life of ethical integrity.

Now it is time to move into the more practical aspects of ministerial ethics, as we ask what it means to be an ethical minister in relation to one's personal life (ch. 3), congregational life (ch. 4), life with colleagues (ch. 5), and life in community (ch. 6).

Suggested Readings

Birch, Bruce C. and Larry L. Rasmussen. *Bible & Ethics in the Christian Life: Revised*. Minneapolis: Augsburg, 1989. Chapters 3,4,5,6.

Hauerwas, Stanley. *A Community of Character*. Notre Dame: University of Notre Dame Press, 1981. Chapters 2,3,5,6,7.

Higgenson, Richard. *Dilemmas: A Christian Approach to Moral Decision Making*. Louisville: Westminster/John Knox Press, 1988.

Lebacqz, Karen. *Professional Ethics: Power and Paradox*. Nashville: Abingdon, 1985.

Maston, T. B. *To Walk as He Walked*. Nashville: Broadman, 1985.

Smedes, Lewis B. *A Pretty Good Person*. San Francisco: Harper & Row, 1990.

Tillman, William M., Jr., ed. *Understanding Christian Ethics*. Nashville: Broadman, 1988. Chapters 2,3,4.

Notes

[1]Lyman Abbott, *Henry Ward Beecher* (Hartford: American Publishing Co., 1887), 210.

[2]Frederick Buechner, *Telling the Truth* (New York: Harper & Row, 1977), 2.

[3]Ibid.

[4]Michael Levin's article of Nov. 15, 1989 was titled "Ethics Courses: Useless" and was published in *Update* 6 (November, 1990): 3, along with three typical responses from ethicists.

[5]Ibid., 4-6.

[6]See Bruce Birch and Larry Rasmussen, *Bible & Ethics in the Christian Life: Revised* (Minneapolis: Augsburg, 1989), 43-62, for an excellent discussion of these elements.

[7]T. B. Maston, *Why Live the Christian Life?* (Nashville: Broadman, 1974), 98.

[8]See Richard Higgenson, *Dilemmas* (Louisville: Westminster/John Knox Press, 1988), 55-77, where he details the use of deontological rules and consequentialist principles for moral reasoning in both Testaments, as well as the use of story, imitation, key themes, and scales of values.

The Minister's Moral Choices

[9]Birch and Rasmussen, 14-16.

[10]In addition to Birch and Rasmussen, see also Thomas Ogeltree, *The Use of the Bible in Christian Ethics* (Philadelphia: Fortress, 1983); H. Edward Everding, Jr. and Dana Wilbanks, *Decision Making and the Bible* (Valley Forge: Judson, 1975); and T. B. Maston, *Biblical Ethics* (Macon, GA: Mercer University Press, 1982).

[11]Higgenson, 76.

[12]Birch and Rasmussen, 42-65.

[13]Albert Knudson, *The Principles of Christian Ethics* (New York: Abingdon, 1942), 39.

[14]Stanley Hauerwas, *Character and the Christian Life* (San Antonio: Trinity University Press, 1975), 115.

[15]William Willimon, *The Service of God* (Nashville: Abingdon, 1983), 28-29.

[16]D. Glenn Saul, "The Ethics of Decision Making," in *Understanding Christian Ethics*, ed. William Tillman, Jr. (Nashville: Broadman, 1988), 90.

[17]Walter E. Wiest and Elwyn A. Smith, *Ethics in Ministry: A Guide for the Professional* (Minneapolis: Fortress Press, 1990), 182.

[18]Stanley Hauerwas, *A Community of Character* (Notre Dame: University of Notre Dame Press, 1981), 10.

[19]Darrell Reeck, *Ethics for the Professions: A Christian Perspective* (Minneapolis: Augsburg, 1982), 43.

[20]Ibid., 101.

[21]Hauerwas, *A Community...*, 111. For a thorough explanation of the origin and function of virtue in human nature, see chapter 6.

[22]Birch and Rasmussen, 46.

[23]Reinhold Niebuhr, *The Nature and Destiny of Man* (New York: Chas. Scribner's Sons, 1943).

[24]Karen Lebacqz, *Professional Ethics: Power and Paradox* (Nashville: Abingdon, 1985), 76.

[25]Ibid., 77-91.

[26]Ibid., 114.

[27]From a lecture delivered by Lewis Smedes at New Orleans Baptist Theological Seminary (7 March 1991), on "How the Bible Is Used in Moral Decision Making."

[28]Gaylord Noyce, *Pastoral Ethics: Professional Responsibilities for the Clergy* (Nashville: Abingdon, 1988), 30-31

[29]Wiest and Smith, 21.

[30]Ibid., 23.

[31]Dennis P. McCann, "Costing Discipleship: Clergy Ethics in a Commercial Civilization," in James P. Wind, Russell Burck, Paul R. Carmenisch, and Dennis P. McCann, eds., *Clergy Ethics in a Changing Society* (Louisville: Westminister/ John Knox Press, 1991), 157.

[32]Lewis B. Smedes, *A Pretty Good Person* (San Francisco: Harper & Row, 1990), 3.

[33]Smedes, 172.

[34]Nolan Harmon, *Ministerial Ethics & Etiquette: Revised Edition* (Nashville: Abingdon, 1978), 34.

[35]Dudley Strain, *The Measure of a Minister* (St. Louis: The Bethany Press, 1964), 21.

[36]John B. Coburn, *Minister: Man-in-the-Middle* (New York: McMillan, 1963), 159.

[37]David K. Switzer, *Pastor, Preacher, Person: Developing a Pastoral Ministry in Depth* (Nashville: Abingdon, 1979), 16.

[38]Lebacqz, 64. See also Henlee Barnette, "The Minister as a Moral Role-Model," *Review & Expositor* 86 (Fall, 1989): 513.

[39]Reeck, 47.

[40]Richard Foster, *Money, Sex & Power: The Challenge of the Disciplined Life* (San Francisco: Harper & Row, l985), 15.

[41]Ibid.

[42]J. Clark Hensley, *Preacher Behave!* (Jackson, MS: Dallas Printing Co., 1985).

[43]Wiest and Smith, 37-54.

[44]Birch and Rasmussen, 50.

[45]Hauerwas, *A Community...*, 92.

Ministerial Ethics

[46]Stanley Hauerwas and William H. Willimon, *Resident Aliens* (Nashville: Abingdon, 1989), 12.

[47]Higgenson, 107, who also notes that Niebuhr agreed a more accurate title would probably be, *The Not So Moral Man in His Less Moral Communities.*

[48]Niebuhr, 248.

[49]Hauerwas, *A Community . . .* , 109.

[50]Reeck, 47.

[51]L. H. Marshall, *The Challenge of New Testament Ethics* (London: MacMillan, 1960), 100.

[52]John Macquarrie, ed., *Dictionary of Christian Ethics* (Philadelphia: Westminster Press, 1967), s.v. "Kant and Kantian Ethics," by A.C. Ewing.

[53]W. D. Ross, *The Right and the Good* (Oxford, Great Britain: Oxford University Press, 1946), 19-21.

[54]Lebacqz, 24.

[55]Ibid., 75.

[56]Birch and Rasmussen, 56.

[57]Maston, *Biblical Ethics*, viii; 168.

[58]Higgenson, 55-69.

[59]Smedes, 85.

[60]Birch and Rasmussen, 59.

[61]Barnette, 514-515.

[62]George Wharton Pepper, *A Voice from the Crowd* (New Haven: Yale University Press, 1915), 23.

[63]Strain, 50.

[64]Lebacqz, 89.

[65]Birch and Rasmussen, 62.

[66]Charles R. Swindoll, *Rise & Shine: A Wake-Up Call* (Portland, OR: Multnomah Press, 1989), 190.

[67]Ibid., 191.

[68]Hauerwas, *A Community . . .* , 91.

[69]Saul, 94. For a recent example of narrative ethics written in a "baptist" theology, see James McClendon's *Systematic Theology: Ethics* (Nashville: Abingdon, 1986).

[70]Charles M. Sheldon, *In His Steps* (Chicago: Moody Press, 1956).

[71]Hauerwas, *A Community . . .* , 131.

[72]T. B. Maston, *To Walk as He Walked* (Nashville: Broadman, 1985), 9-11.

[73]Lebacqz, 103.

[74]Reeck, 55.

[75]Higgenson, 230.

[76]Barnette, 514.

[77]Lewis Smedes, *Choices: Making Right Decisions in a Complex World* (San Francisco: Harper & Row, 1986), 81.

3

THE MINISTER'S PERSONAL LIFE:
Incidental or Intentional?

Political writer and analyst Theodore H. White concluded his study of former President Richard M. Nixon and the Watergate scandal with these words:

> The true crime of Richard Nixon was simple: he destroyed the myth that binds America together. And for this he was driven from power.
>
> The myth he broke was critical—that somewhere in American life there is at least one man who stands for law, the President. That faith surmounts all daily cynicism, all evidence of suspicion of wrong-doing by lesser leaders, all corruptions, all vulgarities, all the ugly compromises of daily striving and ambition. That faith holds that all men are equal before the law and protected by it; and that no matter how the faith may be betrayed elsewhere, at one particular point—the Presidency—justice will be done beyond prejudice, beyond rancor, beyond the possibility of a fix.[1]

If White's analysis that the nation needs the assurance that at least one person acts with personal integrity is true, it is even more true for Christians. Christians and the church need to be assured that the Christian minister is at least one person with integrity. Ministers must build integrity into their personal life and ministry. The ministry is built on the trust that people have in the minister's spiritual and ethical wholeness. If integrity is missing, the ministry is in danger.

Integrity appears in the minister's personal life and conduct. Instructive insight can be seen in the incident of Jesus with the Samaritan woman at the well recorded in John 4. The disciples had gone into Sychar to buy lunch. At noon Jesus was seated at the well when the unnamed Samaritan woman came for water. Jesus engaged her in conversation. "Just then his disciples returned and were surprised to find him talking with a woman. But no one asked, 'What do you want?' or 'Why are you talking with her?' " (John 4:27). The disciples had such trust in Jesus, such confidence in His personal integrity that no one questioned His relationship with the woman.

Integrity in the minister's personal life is intentional. Integrity does not just happen with the individual's commitment to ministry. The minister must work at being a person of integrity in his personal life.

What are the major problem areas in the minister's personal life? R. H. Whittington, longtime religion professor at Louisiana College, repeatedly warned his students: "Boys, pay your bills and keep your zippers up." He identified sex and finances as major areas of potential problems. Richard Foster identified a triple ethical threat to Christian discipleship: money, sex, and power, adding one more element to the two mentioned by the professor. Foster wrote: "The issues of money, sex, and power catapult us into the arena of moral choice."[2] In a *Time* magazine article, Billy Graham said that Satan attacks God's servants in the three areas of sex, money, and pride.[3] Taking these understandings of the major problem areas for ministers into consideration, in this chapter we will also address the minister's conduct in relation to self, family, finances, and sex. In chapter 4 we will consider the problem of power. Being a good minister in a not-so-good world involves the minister's personal life in these four key areas.

In Relation to Self

Self-esteem

Ministers are people before they are ministers. A positive self-concept and appropriate self-esteem are essential for a healthy, effective minister. Walter E. Wiest and Elwyn A. Smith remind us that "persons called to the clergy profession live always in tension between two realities: their humanity—who they are and what they are, their best and their worst, their gifts and their limits—and the special demands of their calling."[4] That tension can work on one's self esteem if a minister does not handle it properly. Two areas particularly demand attention: ego and role.

An inflated ego is a problem for many ministers. Their self commands attention from others and demands authority over others. The ability to serve humbly and to live gently and kindly are difficult for those who struggle with massive egos. This results in their unwillingness to share credit or attention with fellow members or staff, in an assertiveness that leaves little place for initiative from others, and in an insistence on their own views.

Some ministers, however, suffer from underassertiveness. Their ego is so small that humility becomes a vice. These people have difficulty leading a congregation and confronting persons with either the demands of the gospel or the specifications for a job.

The problem of role identity plagues those who cannot find identity outside their ministry. They define their lives entirely in terms of their ministerial vocation. These individuals face difficulty when anything jeopardizes their ministry or when they face retirement.

Ministers with healthy self-esteem recognize that they have worth, value, and dignity apart from the ministry to which God has called them. Their identity rests in who they are as persons more than in what they do as ministers.

Health

In addition to a healthy self-esteem, ministers must also pay attention to physical health. Working to the point of exhaustion, without days off or vacations, seems like commendable dedication, but actually, it may be a foolish expenditure of strength. To lose your health means to lose ministry. If dedicated ministers were to pace themselves, care for their bodies, and guard their health, they would then expand their ministries rather than cut them short by an early death or failing health.

Catherine Marshall memorialized her husband, Peter Marshall, in *A Man Called Peter*. Immediately after recovering from a heart attack, he plunged back into his duties as pastor of the New York Avenue Presbyterian Church in Washington, D.C., and as chaplain of the U.S. Senate. Shortly thereafter he suffered another heart attack and died as a relatively young man. Through his biography we learn of the significant ministry of Peter Marshall. Yet how much longer could that ministry have been extended and how many more lives could Marshall have touched had he properly regarded his health?

Kenneth Cooper, the physician who pioneered aerobics, spoke to all of us when he emphasized total well-being through aerobic exercise, a positive eating plan, and emotional equilibrium. He asserted that

> total well-being *can* provide the physical and emotional base for finding and savoring . . . goals. For example, it will undoubtedly enrich a career or a deep spiritual commitment, especially as you get more involved in these endeavors and as the time and energy demands they place on you become greater.[5]

Cooper emphasized the importance of health for both achieving and enjoying the goals you have in life. That same principle applies to ministry. A healthy person can minister better and enjoy it more over a lifetime. This is a matter of Christian stewardship. Stewardship involves how you use your money, but it also involves how you use the body God has entrusted to you.

Nutrition, rest, exercise, and recreation combine to enrich your health. These may seem secondary to high-energy, high-achieving, hard-driving persons. However, to extend life and to enrich ministry, good health habits are important components of a minister's life. A day off each week and a vacation each year contribute to the overall health of the minister. Recreation or a hobby that both provides enjoyment and diverts the mind from ministering tasks are important for a balanced life.

Life-style

The life-style of ministers is another important element in their total witness. Their life-style should confirm rather than contradict the gospel they proclaim.

In the span of several months in 1987 and 1988, the life-styles of several well-known American ministers revealed serious differences between what they practiced and what they preached. One televangelist announced that God would take his life unless his listeners responded with a large contribution before a deadline. Another lost his television network with the revelations of an extravagant, opulent life-style combined with sexual immorality. Ironically, one well-known televangelist who made public another televangelist's moral failures was himself disciplined by his denomination and deprived of his ministerial credentials due to his own moral failure. The life-styles of these ministers simply did not square with their proclamations.

For a minister to preach restraint and personal discipline while practicing conspicuous consumerism is not consistent. Asking for sacrificial giving and personal commitment from church people, while refusing to give sacrificially or to alter personal plans to meet another's needs, will not be a convincing testimony of Christlikeness. One of us regularly parked in the minister's parking area of a denominational hospital in a major Texas city where a white Cadillac with a red leather interior was also often parked. That luxury car sported a personalized license plate with the Greek word *doulos*, the Greek word for "servant." In a metropolitan area with many pressing human needs, *doulos* just did not seem an appropriate insignia for a white Cadillac with a red leather interior.

Spiritual Growth

The cleric is a ministering person, as well as a pilgrim of faith. Continued spiritual growth is as important for the minister as it is for the parishioner. The apostle Paul advised: "Run in such a way as to get the prize. . . . I beat my body and make it my slave so that after I have preached to others, I myself will not be disqualified for the prize" (1 Cor. 9:24-27). The minister also needs spiritual discipline and growth.

"Familiarity breeds contempt," states the proverb. Few ministers will treat the Bible or spiritual disciplines with contempt, but some ministers may treat both the Bible and spiritual disciplines with such familiarity that these religious matters lose some of their mystery and wonder.

When David consolidated his kingship and established the capital at Jerusalem, he moved the ark of the covenant to Jerusalem. The narrative in 2 Samuel 6:6-7 records: "When they came to the threshing floor of Nacon, Uzzah reached out and took hold of the ark of God, because the oxen stumbled. The Lord's anger burned against Uzzah because of his irreverent act; therefore God struck him down and he died there beside the ark of God." One obvious element in Uzzah's death was that he showed too much familiarity with the holy.

In handling spiritual things regularly, ministers can easily become too familiar with the holy. What they teach to others by way of spiritual disciplines and exercises become perfunctory to them. A serious ethical issue arises when ministers require of others what they do not practice themselves, or practice so routinely that the spiritual discipline loses all real meaning.

Education does not end with seminary. Learning about the Bible, about God, and about the relationship between God and humankind is a lifelong activity. As your life unfolds and new life experiences occur, your understanding of God and of spiritual matters as well as your theology should grow. These spiritual matters always have a challenge to them and an element of mystery about them. No matter how often you have performed a wedding or baptism, conducted a funeral, preached a sermon, or offered a prayer, the event must never simply become a repetitious act with no heart in it.

God commanded Moses to say to the people of Israel: "Be holy, for I the Lord your God am holy" (Lev. 19:2). Jesus commanded His disciples to "Be perfect, therefore, as your heavenly Father is perfect" (Matt. 5:48). The word that is translated "perfect" can mean whole or complete or perfect for its purpose. Whatever meaning is assigned to the word, the basis of comparison is God, God as made known in Jesus Christ. The apostle Peter admonished us to "grow in the grace and knowledge of our Lord and Savior Jesus Christ" (2 Pet. 3:18). To follow the directive of Moses, the command of Christ, and the admonition of Peter, the minister must continue to be a true disciple of

Jesus Christ, a student of the Word of God, and a practitioner of the disciplines of the Christian life.

For the preacher the Bible should not become simply the source of sermons and the texts for teaching. Seminary professor Charles Bugg asked, "What about approaching the Bible in a *formational* way instead of just as information to be explored? By this I mean, what about allowing the power of the Bible to speak to my own life and to continue to form and reform me."[6] The cleric should read the Bible devotionally. Other devotional reading such as the classic Christian devotional works, sermons by pulpit masters, or contemporary devotional materials should also be included. The growing minister needs to read the more difficult theological, biblical, historical, and ethical materials, as well as more general reading.

The common spiritual disciplines that ministers recommend to others must become the their practice also if their lives are to ring true. You do not have to look for esoteric methods or hidden keys to spiritual growth. For the ministers as for other church members, spiritual growth comes from the regular practice of prayer, Bible study, worship, and Christian service.

The secret of a long ministry in one location is the continued growth of the minister. As long as you are growing spiritually and as long as you are relating personally to the people with whom you serve, effective ministry can continue.

In Relation to Family

The Minister's Family Life

For many years a billboard on Louisiana Highway 6 just north of the city of Natchitoches, Louisiana, contained a message from the Church of Jesus Christ of Latter-day Saints, the Mormons. The message on the billboard proclaimed, "No other success compensates for failure in the home." This quotation should be prominently displayed on every minister's study desk. The family is a very important ingredient in the pastor's life; why then does it often rank second place, or even lower, in that pastor's list of priorities?

In American non-Catholic churches the general assumption is that the minister will be a married person with a family. That assumption is reinforced with the ministerial qualifications for both pastors and deacons given in the Pastoral Epistles (1 Tim. 3:1-11 and Titus 1:6-9). Some church groups even require that clergy be married and have children before they are eligible for ministerial leadership positions.

For many years, divorce in the minister's family was unthinkable. Troubled clergy marriages continued in quiet desperation or armed truce. Today some of these marriages are being terminated. The incidence of divorce among clergy couples is much higher now, but it is still not well accepted. Dean Merrill observed in *Clergy Couples in Crisis*:

> Some denominations still automatically defrock a divorcing pastor; others require an unpaid sabbatical of varying lengths. In still others, leadership may be willing to aid, counsel, and eventually guide the divorced minister toward another parish, but local congregations remain wary. If a church does vote to accept such a pastor, the official act is only part of the battle; the trust and respect of individuals must still be won, often over a long time and at great cost.[7]

The failure of a clergy marriage is considered a tragedy, in many cases a fatal tragedy, as far as continuation in the ministry is concerned.

Divorce is not the only problem in the minister's family. The quality of the marital relationship between the minister and the spouse must also be considered. For his doctoral dissertation a Mississippi Southern Baptist pastor did a research project on marital satisfaction among pastors' wives. He discovered four factors that caused less satisfaction in their marriages: the disruption of time together, the state of anxiety brought on by church expectations, loneliness, and the fewer days of dual devotions.[8] These were not ministers who had terminated their marriages, but people who experienced less satisfaction in their marriage than they desired. The primary relationship in the clergy family is the relationship between the minister and spouse. That husband-wife bond must be stable and strong before the family can be stable and strong.

Add to that need the problems that ministers often have with their children, and the significance of the minister's home life increases. Ministers' children are really not a great deal different from other children. They face the same stresses and temptations as others; and they experience the same disappointments and failures as others. The incidence of ministerial problem children is not likely any higher than other groups, but may be more apparent due to the high visibility of minister's families. Such high achievers as Orville and Wilbur Wright, Martin Luther King, Jr., Harriet Beecher Stowe, John Tower, Walter Mondale, Albert Schweitzer, and Paul Tillich were all ministers' children.[9] Minister's children are not all problem children; some of them have obviously done quite well. J. Clark Hensley suggested, "Look at *Who's Who* and you will discover more sons and daughters of clergymen than any other profession."[10]

Another factor that must be considered is the effectiveness of ministry. When the minister has a satisfying relationship with spouse and children then that person will be more effective in ministry and more fulfilled as a person. Ministers find it difficult to fight the devil, the deacons, and the darling at home at the same time. Marital satisfaction adds to the personal peace and satisfaction of the minister.

A Model for Others

Part of the challenge for the minister in his home life is that his marriage is considered a model for church families. That can be a positive role which models to others how a couple can stay in love, stay married, and function as a Christian family even with stress, long work hours, inadequate income, and the demands of children.

The minister's marriage can be a problem when the model is negative rather than positive. As David and Vera Mace observed:

> A Christian minister's task is to proclaim the message of divine love and to help those who respond to it to grow in love for one another. A married minister can therefore be reasonably expected to provide in his own marriage relationship an image and example of how other people, through their united love for God, can grow in the quality of their love for each other. When a minister's marriage does not demonstrate the warmth and tenderness of human love at its best, an observer could justifiably say, "If his religion doesn't work in this closest of all human relationships, how can we be sure that it is really true?"[11]

The Key Ingredient

Time together is the key ingredient for a happy home life for the ministerial family. And time together is a most difficult feat for a ministerial family.

When the authors were both in seminary, a chapel speaker once said if a minister parent were away from home every evening, it did not make any difference to his children whether he was at the church or at a bar. He was not home with them. Perhaps it is an overstatement, but it makes a valid point. Time with the family is necessary for a strong and fulfilling home life. Each preacher has probably sermonized about affluent parents who gave their children everything they wanted but themselves. That same principle applies to the minister's family.

How can time be reserved for the family? By scheduling it and protecting those times. Time with family members is as important an appointment as you have. Many ministers set aside specific times each week or each month so that a child could have some time alone with her ministering parent. Some ministers will block out an evening for a date with the spouse periodically, weekly or monthly. They will eat out, take in a movie, or just visit with one another. Occasional evenings out of town without the children are helpful, if child care can be arranged and the budget can be stretched to allow it. In the

Maces' study of clergy couples, 68 percent of the wives surveyed listed "the need for time alone together" as their greatest difficulty in adjusting to being married to ministers.[12]

A popular religious writer told how he handled trying to get into the bloodstream of his family's life. One of the mechanical things that he would do was to take a new appointment calendar early each year and mark each family member's birthday, their wedding anniversary, and some family vacation time with the notation "Commitment to Family." Later in the year if someone would call about a project or a meeting, he would reply by saying that he already had a commitment on that date. After he started that practice, the first time an invitation came to participate in a big meeting on a child's birthday, he said "no." The caller sensed his hesitation and asked why he could not come since it was a big convention and his witness might reach a lot of people. He was a little embarrassed to tell his friend that it was his daughter's birthday, but he added that the caller could get a half-dozen speakers for the meeting, but that he was the only daddy his daughter had. The man was quiet on the other end of the line for a few seconds, then he replied: "I wish I could do that." The writer concluded: "I may not make as many speeches, attend as many meetings, or write as many books for Christ. But I hope I will at least have lived for Him in my own home."[13] The writer's caller could have achieved that goal the same way that the writer did. You also will have to do it that way to have time with your family. Plan to spend quality time with your children and your mate. Protect that time. Effective time management techniques and specific agreements with the congregation will help you achieve that worthy goal.

The Major Factor

The major factor in successful family life is commitment. The commitment to one another is essential for any marriage, especially a clergy marriage. For each partner, no question should exist about the personal commitment in love that each one has made to the other.

By the very nature of ministry, ministers are often placed with people of the opposite sex other than their mate. This calls for a high degree of trust by the spouse. The minister must first be a person of absolute integrity; but she must also be a person that her spouse can trust because he is sure of her commitment to him.

That commitment is one way of building family solidarity. When children see by their parents' actions and attitudes that they love and trust one another, children grow up with a model of commitment in Christian marriage. The children understand that commitment is at the heart of marriage. However marital love is defined, exclusive commitment to one another must be at the center of it.

Commitment to one another is both undergirded and strengthened by commitment to Christ. In the Maces' study, 63 percent of the husbands and 65 percent of the wives cited "Shared Christian Commitment and Spiritual Resources" as the leading advantage of clergy marriage.[14]

The Single Minister

Ideally, no difference should exist between the single minister and the married minister in church service. But, as in other areas, we do not live with the ideal but with the actual. In many cases churches consider calling the single minister with some hesitation. People may question why they are still single. Married persons may be suspicious of an unmarried minister being with their spouse. Parents may be hesitant to trust their children with single clergy.

More people today are waiting longer to marry or are consciously choosing singleness. Jesus never married. It is doubtful whether Paul was married during his time of missionary activity. A person is no less a person nor no less a minister because he is single, whether by choice or by circumstance. The single minister is still a part of a family, her family of origin if no other. And all are a part of the family of God.

The church should not expect the single minister to spend more time in ministry, just because he or she does not have a marriage mate and a family. The church should call a person to ministry on the basis of that person's dedication to Christ and ability to perform the ministering task required. Neither should a church attempt to pay that individual less money for the same or similar ministry just because they do not have a family to support. The position should be paid according to the job description, not according to marital status.

The same principles of ethical behavior and personal integrity apply to the single minister as to the married minister. In some cases and in some places, the single minister will have to be doubly certain that he has conducted himself ethically and above suspicion for his ministry to be effective.

In Relation to Finances

Managing Money

"Boys, pay your bills," the professor warned in earlier days. The warning was well deserved for many ministers have not developed the ability to manage money. So notorious have clergy often been in financial mismanagement that in some financial circles people are warned against lending money to the professions that begin with "P": plumbers, painters, prostitutes, and preachers.

When all the evidence is in, actually ministers have not done so badly in money management on their limited incomes. Their groceries cost the same as anyone else's; college tuition for their children is as high as it is for others; the utility companies do not give professional discounts. Even though clergy salaries have risen, the Executive Director of the Minister's Financial Services Association in Lubbock, Texas, made an important observation. When the minister's salary is compared with the median income of people across the nation with graduate education equivalent to seminary many ministers "could possibly be significantly underpaid".[15] According to the 1992 Church Compensation Report compiled by *Christianity Today*, Inc., Christian clergy salaries rose an average of only 7.4 percent from 1988 to 1991, less than half the inflation rate. Even when the total compensation, which rose 12.6 percent in the same period, is considered, pastor's salaries still lagged behind inflation which was 16 percent for the period of 1988-1991.[16] Among the ministers in the *Christianity Today* survey only 1 percent felt that they were overpaid. Those feeling that they were "fairly paid" were 66 percent of the senior pastors and 59 percent of the solo pastors surveyed. That means that 34 percent of the senior pastors and 41 percent of the solo pastors felt that they were to some degree underpaid.[17] Understanding that the minister's salary is below average and that his or her family has the same needs as similar families in the community, many ministers have performed little short of the financially miraculous in adequately feeding, clothing, and educating their families on salaries that are not comparable to other professionals.

However, there are enough examples of ministers who have owed money to many merchants in their town, who have been late in paying their bills, or who have expected discounts, gifts, or special favors that the belief that ministers cannot manage money persists.

People are very sensitive about money. Church leaders do not appreciate being embarrassed by their minister's financial irresponsibility. One large church in a metropolitan southwestern city actually garnisheed one of their minister's paychecks for a year in order to rescue him from indebtedness.

The discipline to plan a budget, the ability to live within that budget, and the art of balancing a checkbook, are all essential skills for Christian ministers. To handle finances responsibly may be more of a spiritual discipline than many clergy have thought. The failure to handle finances properly has diminished the witness of too many church overseers.

John Wesley's rule of life was to *save* all he could and *give* all he could. When he was at Oxford, Wesley had an income of thirty pounds a year. He lived on twenty-eight pounds and gave away two pounds. As Wesley's income increased to sixty pounds a year, ninety pounds and one hundred twenty pounds annually, he still lived on twenty-eight pounds and gave the balance away.[18] The founder of Methodism managed his money well.

The minister should certainly practice the basic principles of Christian money management, beginning with Christian stewardship. For many clergy the tithe (Mal.3:10) is considered a biblical standard and a minimum starting point for Christian stewardship. The Christian minister should also practice the responsible handling of debt. Taking their cue from Romans 13:8, some think that a Christian should have no debt. A disciplined savings plan, conservative spending, and the avoidance of conspicuous consumerism are all important factors in Christian money management.

Money Matters

Richard J. Foster referred to the "dark side of money" and the "light side of money." By the "dark side of money" he meant the way that money could be a threat to our relationship with God and the radical criticism of wealth found in many of Jesus' words. The "light side of money" referred to the way in which money can be used to enhance our relationship with God and bless humankind.[19]

The misuse of credit looms as an expression of the dark side of money. Many ministerial families have drowned in an ocean of credit. The responsible use of credit is a challenge for the minister. Well-meaning, good-intentioned people have often prompted the minister into more credit than he can handle on his ministerial salary. Businesses may think they are helping by extending easy credit to the minister. That may be their way to show appreciation of the minister. But before the church leader realizes what he has done, the total amount of money that is owed on credit has become more than he can handle. Some payments are skipped, other payments are delayed, and he falls farther behind in the repayment of his accounts. The word will then often circulate around the community that the preacher does not pay his bills. The pastor's credit rating will show him to be a bad credit risk. If he is called to a new ministerial responsibility, the cleric leaves the community for the new field while still having outstanding balances on his accounts. The report circulates through the community that "Pastor Jones left owing everybody in town." Whatever scenario takes place, the result is not positive either for the ministry in general or that minister in particular.

In some communities ministers are given professional discounts by some health professionals and ministerial discounts by some businesses. While that practice may not be as widespread as it once was, it is still prevalent in many communities. It probably began as an attempt to help the minister. The merchant was favorable toward the church and friendly toward the minister. Knowing that her salary was low, he tried to help her by giving a discount. The health professional recognized the minister as a fellow professional in a caring profession and responded by giving a professional discount. The church was considered a nonprofit organization which functioned for the general well-being of the community. A discount was considered a form of donation to the church. The church was aided by the discount. The minister's insistence on a discount, however, or inquiry about a discount before making a purchase, only adds to the perception of the minister as a moneygrubber.

Some people think that ministers always have their hand out for a special favor or a discount. Unfortunately, enough ministers have followed that practice for that perception to persist. Some ministers have perfected the art of begging or of making subtle suggestions to the extent that people feel an obligation to do them special favors. The situation would be healthier if the minister were paid an adequate salary and given the freedom to choose his goods and services at the place he desires with no expectation of a discount.

If a person knows that an individual is a minister and voluntarily offers a discount to him, that is a different situation. Then the minister may feel free to accept it as a gift and respond accordingly, including a "thank-you" note for the kindness. That is different than placing the clergy sign next to the gas tank of the car or of making an issue out of being a minister when the introductions are made. Some people will give gifts to their minister as acts of love, not in response to hints or requests or in an attempt to curry favor. These gifts are accepted graciously for what they are.

One of us saw a bank slogan that proclaimed: "Where money matters but people count." In the minister's relationship to money, people always count and money matters should be handled responsibly and with care.

Practicing What You Preach

The preaching and teaching of Christian stewardship is practiced by most churches. For many of these congregations, tithing is both taught and promoted as the biblical standard for Christian stewardship. As a basic practice, the minister should consistently practice what he preaches concerning Christian stewardship. Landrum

Leavell, II, the president of the New Orleans Baptist Theological Seminary, in a commencement address to the students of that seminary urged them to adhere to their monetary vow of tithing. "God has called you to be a leader and if you don't have enough faith to trust God with your material possessions and be a storehouse tither, you don't have enough integrity to make it in the ministry."[20]

By definition, a steward is one who manages the affairs of another. Christian stewardship speaks to the Christian's, in this case the minister's, management of what God has entrusted to him. Christian stewardship is the total response of the individual to the grace of God. Stewardship involves money. In fact, it is usually narrowly defined only in terms of money. But stewardship is more than money; it is the self. All that the minister is, as well as all that the minister has, has been entrusted to her by God. How that trust is managed is Christian stewardship. When it comes to money, the practice of Christian stewardship by the parson as well as by the parishioner is essential. The minister's message on stewardship will hardly ring true if she has not practiced it as well as taught it.

In Relation to Sexuality

At the time this chapter is being written jury selection is underway in New Orleans, Louisiana, for a trial that could be spectacular. One well-known Christian evangelist sued another nationally known televangelist for $90 million for defamation of character. Marvin Gorman helped to topple the evangelistic empire of Jimmy Swaggart by releasing compromising photographs of that preacher. In the lawsuit Gorman accused Swaggart of conspiring to destroy his television ministry through false accusations of immorality, while Swaggart himself was dallying with prostitutes. Gorman admitted a single "immoral act" with a woman. Swaggart made a tearful confession on his television show that he had sinned. While he did not specify his sin, the confession came after Gorman had provided church officials with photographs of Swaggart outside a motel with a prostitute.[21]

Obviously, the personal and professional lives of these ministers were deeply affected by sexual indiscretions, to say the least. But how much of a problem is sexual temptation to modern ministers?

Incidence

Most Christian ministers are persons of integrity who behave ethically with regard to sexual matters. National statistics on sexual misconduct by ministers are not available. One three-year survey of religious and secular counselors conducted by the Wisconsin Coalition on Sexual Misconduct found that 11 percent of the perpetrators were ministers and that 89 percent of the victims were women.[22]

Leadership, a journal for church leaders, published a survey of three hundred pastors. 12 percent of the ministers polled admitted having had sexual intercourse with someone other than their spouse since they had been in ministry. 33 percent of those polled acknowledged "sexually inappropriate" behavior with someone other than their spouse without any definition of that conduct. Another 18 percent confessed to other forms of sexual contact with someone other than their spouse.

Interestingly enough, at the same time *Christianity Today* (the parent magazine of *Leadership*) conducted the same survey with nearly one thousand subscribers who were *not* pastors. In this survey they discovered that 45 percent indicated that they had done something sexually inappropriate, 23 percent had engaged in extramarital intercourse, and 28 percent acknowledged they had engaged in other forms of extramarital sexual conduct. These incidences of immorality were nearly twice that of the pastors surveyed.[23]

A 1984 study that included questions about the minister's sexuality revealed startling statistics. Among four major denominational groups, 37.15 percent of the respondents acknowledged that they had engaged in "inappropriate sexual behavior for a minister." In addition to this, 12 percent admitted to having sexual intercourse with a member of their congregation other than their spouse. This last figure of sexual relations with parishioners exceeded the client-professional rate for both physicians and psychologists. These were the same statistics found by the *Leadership* survey previously cited which was conducted three years later.[24]

The research of pastoral counselor G. Lloyd Rediger led him to assert that 10 percent of clergy are guilty of sexual malfeasance. He believes that another 15 percent are approaching the line of misconduct.[25]

What would be considered sexual misconduct by a minister? Rediger identified six specifics of what he called sexual malfeasance. These are:

- Sexual intercourse with persons outside of a marriage covenant. This includes rape, "consenting adult," children, and incapacitated persons.
- Oral sex with persons outside of a marriage covenant.
- Unwanted or inappropriate physical touch outside of a marriage covenant. This includes genital fondling, foreplay and any physical contact not appropriate to pastoral ministry or normal friendship.

- Physical-sensual displays of the body or titillation of senses in ways suggestive of inappropriate sex.
- The use of pornography, individually or with others, in ways intended to stimulate erotic fantasies of inappropriate sexual behavior.
- Verbal and visual contact with another person which implies or demands inappropriate sexual response.[26]

These six areas of sexual activity challenge ministers to the highest level of ethical conduct.

In addition to the number of ministers involved in sexual misconduct, attention must also be given to the number of persons victimized by them. Marie M. Fortune told the story of Peter Donovan, pastor of First Church, Newburg (all names of persons and places were fictitious) in *Is Nothing Sacred? When Sex Invades the Pastoral Relationship*. Formal charges were lodged against the pastor by six women. The charges included sexual contact with counselees and employees, misuse of Donovan's pastoral office to coerce or manipulate parishioners, verbal threats to intimidate those who might report his activities, and the use of physical force to engage in sexual intercourse. Three others signed complaints and four other verbal allegations were given by women not willing to come forward. As many as forty-five church members may have been that pastor's victims.[27]

In many instances, the clergy sexual offenders have had multiple offenses. In one case reported by *Newsweek*, while attempting to seduce one woman her minister boasted of having slept with thirty other women.[28]

Causes

Any number of factors can cause a minister to practice sexual indiscretion. Some, like Peter Donovan, would be sexual predators who prey on women in the church. Many of these would be considered sexual addicts, who probably have a deep-seated emotional illness as well as a moral problem. Some would point out that it is precisely because clergy are "generally compassionate, people-oriented professionals that some may yield to inappropriate intimacy."[29]

Peter Rutter, a San Francisco, California, psychiatrist emphasized the vulnerability of any professional to sexual misconduct.

> What I have come to call sex in the forbidden zone—sexual behavior between a man and a woman under his care or mentorship in a professional relationship—can occur any time a woman entrusts important aspects of her physical, spiritual, psychological, or material welfare to a man who has power over her.[30]

The *Newsweek* article provided a profile of the minister who strays sexually. In this profile he is usually middle-aged, disillusioned with his calling, neglecting his own marriage, and a lone ranger who is isolated from his clerical colleagues. His failure commenced when he met a woman who needed him.[31]

Glenn Gabbard, a psychiatrist who is the director of Menninger Hospital in Topeka, Kansas, identified a common characteristic of ministers which could lead to sexual infidelity. He referred to those ministers who go into the ministry with a longing to be loved, to be idealized, or to be godlike. This minister may become disappointed by the congregation's response to him. He wants to be idealized, but the congregation sees his human frailties. He is attracted to a young woman who comes to him for pastoral counseling. Gabbert observed that the minister sees in this woman the gratification of the minister's original wish to be loved like God is loved.[32]

Some persons are intentionally seductive and attempt to lure their minister into sexual activities. Among those who view the pastor as a person of power, this sense of power, or intimacy with a power figure, is itself attractive to them. For some emotionally insecure persons, to sexually seduce a minister gives a sense of pseudo-satisfaction. Some would feel that had established a more intimate relationship with God through intimate contact with a minister. George Parsons, of the Alban Institute in Washington, D. C., observed: "This notion, in effect, is that they can seduce God. It is an irrational dynamic, but it's there."[33]

Another reason for frequent sexual problems is that many ministers who counsel people do not understand the concept of transference and how to deal with it. Transference has been defined as "the process in which people project their own (often unmet) needs onto an idealized figure. Such transference can be 'positive' (affection, warmth, and so on) or 'negative' (anger, rejections, and so on)." Transference often involves dependency, romantic feelings, hostility feelings, and ambivalence about authority.[34] These feelings occur because of the role, not because of the personal attractiveness or qualities of the minister.

Countertransference can also occur. This is the tendency for the minister to project his or her unmet needs on someone else which can contribute to acting out sexual feelings. While marital dissatisfaction always does not explain ministerial sexual impropriety, it does make the minister more susceptible.[35] Most counselors are given training in understanding transference and countertransference. Ministers generally do not receive training in those areas, thus they are more vulnerable to them. In his book on ministerial infidelity, Tim LaHaye identified three "forces that can lead to sexual sin":

- the power of sexual attraction,
- the power of seductive women, and
- the power of emotional bonding.

In addition, he pointed out some "attitudes that can lead to a moral fall." These were

- pride,
- resistance to accountability, and
- anger.

To these he added

- the press for success,
- the drive to fulfill goals, and
- work, work, work

as "the values that corrode a pastor's moral life."[36]

In the *Leadership* magazine survey referred to earlier, the most common cause cited for sexual impropriety was physical and emotional attraction (78 percent). That leading cause for sexual impropriety was followed by marital dissatisfaction (41 percent).[37]

Researchers in the *Newsweek* article cited earlier also pointed to a possible cause in that many ministers are underpaid, overstressed workaholics who put in sixty to eighty hours per week. Peter Carnes, a pioneer researcher in sexual addiction, added that ministers are always on display, always on call, which makes them susceptible to a double life.[38]

In the *Leadership* survey the pastors who acknowledged sexual intercourse or sexual contact with persons other than their spouse were asked who the other person was. Their responses indicated that the sexual partners were

- a counselee (17 percent),
- a ministerial staff member (5 percent),
- other church staff member (8 percent),
- a church member in a teaching/leadership role (9 percent) ,
- someone else in the congregation (30 percent), and
- someone outside the congregation (31 percent).[39]

Consequences

In a parable about discipleship, Jesus urged people to count the cost before signing on as His followers (Luke 14:25-33). Before any minister engages in an act that could be considered a sexual indiscretion, he should count the cost. No matter what the extenuating circumstances, a choice has been made. That individual chooses to act in a manner that has serious consequences.

Robyn Warner (a pseudonym) pointed out the costs of irresponsible sexual behavior, in terms of personal loss. Warner experienced the loss of

- self-esteem,
- position,
- respect in the community,
- his children,
- financial security, and
- his partner.[40]

In view of these consequences, it is at great personal risk that a minister yields to sexual temptation. These losses detailed above do not include the damage to the church the minister served, the effect on the ministry at large, and the hindrance to the work of Christ. It really does not matter whether a minister whose sexual escapades are publicly revealed belongs to your denomination. All ministers are hurt when one minister fails. The loss of faith in ministers and the ministry affects all clergy.

The study of ministerial sexuality entitled *Sex in the Parish* by Karen Lebacqz and Ronald G. Barton grew out of the work of the Professional Ethics Group of the Center for Ethics and Social Policy at the Graduate Theological Union in Berkeley, California. Through surveys of ministers concerning sexuality three reasons emerged for why sexual intimacy with parishioners was wrong. These reasons were

- previous commitments, specifically the marriage covenants;
- professional obligations including their own sense of identity and their responsibility to guide people in their spiritual journey;
- past experiences of either their own or other people's pain arising from sexual involvement between pastor and parishioner.[41]

Sexual indiscretions have cost some ministers their ministry. More than one minister has confessed the affair to the church, counting on the congregation's forgiveness (a virtue he had often eloquently preached). But rather than forgive him, the church usually terminated him. Church people expect exemplary behavior from their ministers.

A minister who conceals sexual misconduct rarely is able to continue that duplitious behavior indefinitely. In most cases, in some way and at some time, the truth comes out. In the story about Peter Donovan, Marie Fortune indicated the frustrations felt by the women who were sexually exploited by their pastor. Their first frustration was due to the reluctance of people to believe their stories. The next frustration was the extremely slow response of denominational officials to believe their charges.

With keen insight Marie Fortune proposes that a significant aspect of the problem is the reality that the church functions as family. The family image, with God as Father and fellow believers as siblings, suggests a positive relationship of trust, intimacy, caring, commitment, and respect, which are the bases of human family life. Within the church there are also roles and responsibilities. Whether ministers or church members like it or not, the minister's role is one of authority in relation to laypersons. Just as the role of the parent can be misused, so can the role of the minister. Fortune then stated: "When the irresponsible pastor does engage in sexual activity with parishioners, the result is incest in the church family; the parallels to incestuous abuse are disturbing."[42]

Others have joined Fortune in likening the sexual abuse of church members to incest in the family. Some of the same traits occur in the church as in incestuous families. Among these traits, David R. Brubaker mentioned

- social isolation,
- blurred boundaries,
- the paradoxical feelings of inadequacy and perfectionism,
- the "no talk" rule which distorts communication, and
- unequal power.[43]

Respondents in Lebacqz and Barton's study likened the violation of trust by one in a ministerial role to the violation of trust that occurs in incest. One woman pastor expressed it by saying, "To be their savior and then to cross sexual boundaries is devastating to people." To that statement the authors added, "Because clergy represent God, Christ, and the church, to be violated by a member of the cloth is to feel violated by God, Christ, and the church."[44]

Prevention

Since ministers are human and have both hormones and sexual feelings, can such sexual indiscretions be prevented?

Marie Fortune suggested that prevention for the individual minister should begin during the preparation for ministry. Both seminary students and ministers serving in churches need information and clarification of ethical standards for ministry. They need to understand the nature and meaning of ethical behavior in sexual relationships. The author also asserted that a ministerial code of ethics would be helpful in clarifying ethical sexual behavior for ministers. Along with a code, Fortune suggested ministers "need to understand the nature of the power and authority of their role and the responsibility that goes with it. They need to learn how to maintain boundaries in relationships with parishioners and counselees. They need to learn to care for their own emotional and sexual needs in appropriate ways."[45]

With reference to a ministerial code of ethics, Archibald Hart proposed that a code of ethics should be established to help regulate ministry relationships. Unlike mental health professionals, ministers are only loosely bound by a commonly understood moral code that is subject to differing interpretations. Clearly articulated boundaries for ministry relationships would help to prevent many problems arising in the minister's sexual relationships with others.[46] The subject of a code of ethics for ministers will be addressed in chapter 7.

One of the best ways to ensure responsible sexual behavior is for the minister to build a strong marriage. Ministers should work to strengthen their own marriages.

Ministers should be very aware of their boundaries and always seek to maintain those boundaries. Lebacqz and Barton wrote: "Many pastors argue that, even if the *boundaries* for sexual intimacy are the same for pastor and lay person, the *responsibility* for maintaining those boundaries falls to the professional person. It is he or she who must establish and keep those boundaries."[47] With this in mind, Fortune dispelled the idea of "consenting adults" in pastor-parishioner sexual relationships. She insists that the responsibility always lies with the minister in keeping the relationship within moral bounds. "The dynamics of a pastor-parishioner or counselor-client relationship create a context such that any behavior moving beyond those bounds 'takes place in the absence of meaningful consent'—that is, without mutuality, equality, shared power, and a nonpunitive outcome."[48]

Ministers must develop a "warning system" of some kind that will alert them to when they are approaching unacceptable levels of intimacy with parishioners. Some of those warning signals will come from the minister's own feelings and actions, while other clues will come from the other person's actions. Lebacqz and Barton give a list of such warning signals which might include the following:

- the "publicity" test: what would others think?
- physical arousal — one's own or the other's;
- inordinate sexual fantasy;
- sexual gestures or body language;
- sexual innuendo in verbal exchange;
- intuition, instinct, or not feeling right;
- wanting to share intimacies that are not called for;

- a parishioner wanting too much time or attention;
- wanting to shift the focus to sexual subjects.[49]

Some practical, common sense principles can be followed which would aid ministers from getting into compromising situations. Billy Graham cited some of them. In an interview in *Time* magazine referenced earlier he mentioned sex as one of the areas where ministers are vulnerable.

> I learned . . . that I would be tempted in those areas. So I never rode in a car with a woman alone. I never have eaten a meal with my secretary alone or ridden in a car with her alone. If we sit in here and I dictate something to her, the door is open. And just little things like that, that people would think are so silly, but it was ingrained in me in those early years.[50]

Graham cited several sensible principles that a minister could follow. Other cautions that could be listed are:

- never be totally alone with a person of the opposite sex (in counseling another person could always be in an adjacent office);
- be careful about being in places that are questionable environments (take a deacon or another church member with you);
- be cautious about friendships that could be considered inappropriate;
- be aware of the risk of emotional bonding;
- be sure to avoid placing yourself in a place or a position where moral compromise could happen.

As the apostle Paul said, "Abstain from all appearance of evil" (1 Thess. 5:22, KJV).

Recognizing a minister's sexual vulnerability is vital to prevention. Each one of us should recognize that as human beings, we too, are vulnerable. Because of this, restraint and responsible sexuality are necessary. These practical, common sense guidelines can protect the minister from many serious pitfalls. Morality is intentional. A minister is a moral person because that minister intends to be moral and seeks to safeguard that morality throughout ministry.

Building a strong marriage and a healthy attitude toward sexuality is an ongoing process. One resource is ministerial accountability. Ministers are accountable to God, to the church, to the community, and their family. Ministers can also make themselves responsible to a support group, a church committee, or a mentor. Constant appeal to the Holy Spirit for strength and the good sense to practice proper behavior are also helpful resources.

Ministerial Restoration

When considering the moral failure of ministers, the question of restoration of a minister who has been guilty of sexual misbehavior must be addressed. Some denominations, which are more connectional in character, have specific procedures for the discipline and restoration of erring ministers. Independent churches and those denominations that emphasize the autonomy of the local church have no method to deal with the issue at the denominational level.

In preparing for his book, *If Ministers Fail, Can They Be Restored?*, Tim LaHaye prepared a questionnaire concerning restoration that was sent to fourteen well-known conservative evangelical leaders. All agreed that fallen leaders would need to repent of sexual sin and then work diligently to save their marriages. These leaders believed that any future service would depend on a reconciliation with family. All of the questioned leaders believed forgiveness of the fallen leader was possible and that God could use the restored minister in some place of service. They were not agreed on whether the person could return to a pastoral ministry. All counseled a delay in any return to ministry, as many as five years in some cases. All thought that the minister would have to prove himself or herself worthy of trust before resuming any public ministry.[51]

After advocating a Restoration Committee in the church served by an erring minister, LaHaye proposed an eight-step restoration process. These included

- genuine repentance;
- helping to rebuild the minister's spiritual life;
- helping to rebuild the minister's marriage;
- helping the minister to find work;
- the establishment of a waiting period;
- convening a restoration service;
- the consideration of the "open door" (the door that might open to him for ministry, possibly a ministry other than the pastorate);
- the establishment of ongoing voluntary accountability.[52]

Following an article dealing with a high-visibility pastor who resigned from the church he served because of sexual indiscretion, *Leadership* published the results of a forum between four ministerial leaders concerning recovery and restoration. They believed that sins that violated trust and invalidated the minister's ongoing ability to provide spiritual leadership, particularly sexual sins, required some sort of restoration process. The forum recommended a restoration committee that also included laypersons under the oversight of a church that also included laypersons. Each of them agreed that a minister could be returned to some type of ministry, though not normally in the same church previously served.[53]

Gordon MacDonald told the story of his recovery and restoration following a moral failure in the book *Rebuilding Your Broken World*. He was ultimately reordained and restored to ministry in the same church where he had previously served as pastor. MacDonald began the final chapter with a summation he called the bottom line: "When you have been pushed or have fallen to the ground, there can be only one useful resolve: GET UP AND FINISH THE RACE!"[54]

Persons recommending a minister to a church should be honest in these matters. Too many times, a person who has been guilty of sexual sin is recommended to another church with the idea that if he or she moves on to another place the problem will disappear. When a church is considering a person for a ministerial position who has been guilty of sexual indiscretions, the church should be aware of the failure. If that church chooses to call the individual even with that knowledge, then it has made the decision with full understanding; it has not been duped into calling a person whose integrity may later be questioned.

Interestingly enough, the Levitical code specifies certain stipulations applied to the sins of the priests including what sacrifice was to be made and how it was to be offered (Lev. 4:3-12). Recognizing the differences between an Old Testament priest and a New Testament minister, the implication is that through repentance, restoration, and recommitment a contemporary church leader could resume a ministry for God when restoration occurs openly and honestly.

Some consideration should be given to whether the minister's sexual indiscretion is a one-time occurrence or a pattern of life. Before the writing of this section was completed, a news story broke of the resignation of a pastor of a church near Dallas, Texas, who was guilty of sexual improprieties with female members of several churches. This minister had been showcased by Jerry Falwell on his television programs due to his amazing testimony about his life as a homeless youngster before his conversion. As a result of those appearances this minister had become nationally known. His sexual improprieties have been traced over a period of several years through four different churches.[55] Whether sexual impropriety is a pattern of life or a one-time occurrence surely must be considered when restoration is considered.

Marie Fortune differentiates between clergy sexual immorality that occurs outside the congregation and sexual involvement that abuses the role and authority of a pastor or Christian counselor. She noted that while Jimmy Swaggart's visiting a prostitute showed "a problem with his own sexuality" and created a dilemma for the church, he "evidently did not betray his pastoral relationship" with any individual congregational members. In contrast, "Jim Bakker used his position and power to coerce and manipulate" a woman within his own ministry into sexual involvement. She concluded: "There's an ethical distinction here most people don't make."[56] Both cases, however, indicate improper sexual activities that must be addressed.

Ministers' personal lives are distinct from their professional lives. In some personal areas, however, ministers should show unusual care. Historically the clergy have been uniquely vulnerable in these four categories: self, family, finances, and sexuality. In his farewell address to the leaders of the Ephesian church, Paul said, "Keep watch over yourselves and all the flock of which the Holy Spirit has made you overseers" (Acts 20:28). Most ministers have been faithful to keep watch over the flock. They must be as faithful to keep watch over themselves. Early in Christian history John Chrysostom (A.D. 347-407) counseled:

> The minister's shortcomings simply cannot be concealed. Even the most trivial soon get known. . . . However trifling their offenses, these little things seem great to others, since everyone measures sin, not by the size of the offense, but by the standing of the sinner.[57]

Now that we have viewed the minister's personal life and those areas of unique responsibility for ethical integrity, we see that integrity in those areas must be intentional rather than incidental. Integrity in ministry does not just happen.

From the minister's personal life, we will turn next to the minister and the congregation to determine what it may take in the relationships between the minister and the congregation to be a good minister in a not-so-good world. Each minister has both obligations and responsibilities to the congregation and the parishioners.

Suggested Readings

Fortune, Marie M. *Is Nothing Sacred: When Sex Invades the Pastoral Relationship.* San Francisco: Harper and Row, 1989.

Foster, Richard. *Money, Sex, and Power: The Challenge of the Disciplined Life.* San Francisco: Harper and Row, 1985.

MacDonald, Gordon. *Rebuilding Your Broken World.* Nashville: Oliver Nelson, 1988.

Mace, David and Vera. *What's Happening to Clergy Marriages?* Nashville: Abingdon Press, 1980.

Merrill, Dean. *Clergy Couples in Crisis.* Carol Stream, IL, and Waco, TX: Leadership/Word Books, 1965.

Rediger, G. Lloyd. *Ministry and Sexuality.* Minneapolis: Fortress Press, 1990.

Ministerial Ethics

Notes

[1]Theodore H. White, *Breach of Faith* (New York: Atheneum, 1975), 322.

[2]Richard Foster, *Money, Sex & Power: The Challenge of the Disciplined Life* (San Francisco: Harper and Row, 1985), 1.

[3]*Time* (May 28, 1990), 13.

[4]Walter E. Wiest and Elwyn A. Smith, *Ethics in Ministry* (Minneapolis: Fortress Press, 1990), 97.

[5]Kenneth Cooper, *The Aerobics Program for Total Well-Being* (New York: Bantam Books, 1982), 19.

[6]Charles Bugg, "Professional Ethics Among Ministers," *Review and Expositor* (Fall, 1989), 562-63.

[7]Dean Merrill, *Clergy Couples in Crisis* (Carol Stream, IL and Waco, TX: Leadership/Word Books, 1985), 9-10.

[8]Glenn R. Putnam, *An Investigation of the Relationship of Marital Pressures to the Marital Satisfaction of the Wives of Southern Baptist Ministers.* Unpublished Ed. D. dissertation, Mississippi State University, Starkville, MS, 1990, 44-46.

[9]Martha G. Washam, "Preacher's Kid's," *Your Church* (May/June, 1987), 22.

[10]J. Clark Hensley, *Preacher Behave!* (Jackson, MS: Dallas Printing Co., 1978), 9.

[11]David and Vera Mace, *What's Happening to Clergy Marriages?* (Nashville: Abingdon, 1980), 24-25.

[12]Ibid., 33.

[13]Keith Miller, *Habitation of Dragons* (Waco: Word Books, 1970), 138-140.

[14]Mace, 36.

[15]Helen Parmley, "Pastors' Pay in Area Leads U. S.," *The Dallas Morning News* (October, 1987), 15-A.

[16]David Briggs, "Clergy salaries lag rate of inflation," [Alexandria, LA] *Daily Town Talk* (March, 1992), C-8. For the complete report see the *1992 Church Compensation Report*, (Carol Stream, IL: Christianity Today, Inc., 1991).

[17]James D. Berkley, "What Pastors Are Paid," *Leadership* (Spring, 1992), 89.

[18]James E. Carter, *A Sourcebook for Stewardship Sermons* (Nashville: Broadman, 1972), 110.

[19]Foster, 20-23.

[20]Brenda Kent Paine, "NOBTS Graduates Told to 'Keep Your Vows," *Baptist Press* (May 7, 1991).

[21]"Gorman's Suit Against Swaggart Starts in NO," [Alexandria, LA] *Daily Town Talk*, (July 1991), D-1.

[22]Cited in Kenneth L. Woodward with Patricia King, "When a Pastor Turns Seducer," *Newsweek* (August, 1989), 48.

[23]The Editors, "How Common Is Pastoral Indiscretion?" *Leadership* (Winter, 1988), 12.

[24]Richard A. Blackmon and Archibald D. Hart, "Personal Growth for Clergy" in Richard A. Hunt, John E. Hinkle, Jr., and H. Newton Malony, ed., *Clergy Assessment and Career Development* (Nashville: Abingdon, 1990), 39.

[25]Cited in Joy Jordan-Lake, "Conduct Unbecoming a Preacher," *Christianity Today* (10 February 1992), 26.

[26]G. Lloyd Rediger, "Clergy Moral Malfeasance," *Church Management-The Clergy Journal* (May/June, 1991), 37-38.

[27]Marie M. Fortune, *Is Nothing Sacred? When Sex Invades the Pastoral Relationship* (San Francisco: Harper and Row, 1989), xv.

[28]*Newsweek* (28 August 1989), 49.

[29]David Briggs, "Church scandals shed light on taboo subject," [New Orleans, LA] *Times-Picayune* (24 May 1992), A-16.

[30]Peter Rutter, "Sex in the Forbidden Zone," *Ministry* (January, 1992), 6.

[31]*Newsweek*, 48.

[32]Ibid.

[33]Briggs, *Times-Picayune*, A-16.

[34]Blackmon and Hart, *Clergy Assessment and Career Development*, 40.

The Minister's Personal Life

[35]Ibid.

[36]Tim LaHaye, *If Ministers Fall, Can They Be Restored?* (Grand Rapids: Zondervan, 1990), 36-56.

[37]*Leadership*, 12.

[38]*Newsweek*, 49.

[39]*Leadership*, 12.

[40]Robyn Warner, "Are You Living a Double Life?" *Ministry* (November, 1990), 11-12.

[41]Karen Lebacqz and Ronald G. Barton, *Sex in the Parish* (Louisville: Westminster/John Knox Press, 1991), 47-51.

[42]Fortune, 103-106.

[43]David R. Brubaker, "Secret Sins in the Church Closet," *Christianity Today*, 30-32.

[44]Lebacqz and Barton, 104-5.

[45]Fortune, 106.

[46]Blackmon and Hart, 48.

[47]Lebacqz and Barton, 107-8.

[48]Quoted in Jordan-Lake, *Christianity Today*, 29.

[49]Lebacqz and Barton, 65.

[50]*Time*, 13.

[51]LaHaye, 154-55.

[52]Ibid., 171-184.

[53]"Creating a Restoration Process, A Leadership Forum," *Leadership* (Winter Quarter, 1992), 122-34.

[54]Gordon MacDonald, *Rebuilding Your Broken World* (Nashville: Oliver Nelson, 1988), 224.

[55]Allen Pusey and Rebecca Sherman, "Falwell protege quits amid charges of sexual offenses," [Alexandria, LA] *Daily Town Talk* (July 13, 1991), A-7.

[56]Quoted in Jordan-Lake, *Christianity Today*, 28

[57]"Pastoring Through the Ages," *Leadership Supplement*, 1.

4

THE MINISTER'S CONGREGATION:

Friend or Foe?

One of us was visiting in a theological seminary in another state when he chanced upon a friend who was a longtime professor of theology in that school. After an exchange of greeting and inquiries about each family, the professor brought up the problem of forced termination.

"Is the basic problem theology?" he asked.

"No," was the reply to the scholar who had spent most of his adult life teaching theology. "Churches have an amazing tolerance for bad theology. The basic problem is relational."

The relationships between the minister and the members of the congregation are essential. Does the minister view the congregation as friend or foe? Does the congregation look upon the minister as a friend who will care for them, laugh with them, cry with them, and share life with them, or as a foe whom they ought to resist and whose teachings, motives, and methods they ought to question?

The difference in the way the minister and the congregation view each other depends on the relationship that they have with each other. To a large degree, that relationship will depend on the ministry skills that the minister displays with them. Some of these skills are personal—the personal integrity of the minister. Others are professional—the ministering ability of the minister.

Relationships are more important in ministry than in any other profession. The morals of the carpenter who framed your house do not concern you greatly so long as the person can measure accurately, saw a straight board, and set a nail. You do not worry much about whether you like your dentist personally as long as the person is competent in dentistry. When you look for a surgeon, your primary concern is in the person's professional qualifications and competence, not in your personal evaluation of the surgeon's personality. In these areas, professional competence is of more importance than personal relationships.

That is not true in the ministry. No matter how competent church leaders may be in biblical exposition, the grasp of church growth principles, and the intricacies of organization, they cannot adequately minister without good relationships with the church people. Relationships determine whether the clerics and their congregations view one another as friends or foes. Many issues in churches will be decided by whether or not they love and trust their ministers, not on the issue itself.

Good relationships between ministers and congregations must be developed. How are they developed? They are developed in the normal course of ministry. As pastors bury the dead, visit the sick, comfort families, sit through troubles, walk through problems, counsel in tough times, laugh in good times, marry the children, and generally share in living with people, they build lasting relationships. A pastor once observed that a minister is building pastoral collateral during those times. That pastoral collateral is spent when the programs and projects are presented.

Knowing one another personally and sharing experiences of life aid in building good ministerial relationships between pastor and people. The shared experiences of life add to the building of good relationships between minister and member. By compassionate care and genuine concern a minister lets people know that they are meaningful and important. And all of that rests on the personal integrity of the minister.

How does the minister relate to the congregation? In this chapter we will examine this crucial question from the standpoint of ministerial leadership, ministerial duties, the transitions in ministry, and the difficult question of how to define success in the ministry. Being a good minister in a not-so-good world has a definite relationship to the way the minister relates to the congregation, ideally as friend and not as foe.

Ministerial Leadership—Authority and Power

Models for Ministery

All ministers have a model for ministerial leadership. That model may come from a previous pastor, or a respected professor, or it may be a conglomerate picture of persons they have known and characteristics they have observed that should be either emulated or avoided. Notice some of the contemporary models for ministry.

Some ministers model their ministry after a *chief executive officer.* Their model is the corporate executive, and they aspire to be a spiritual CEO. *Active* is the operative word for this style of ministerial

96

leadership. This leader makes things happen, no matter what it takes. Rather than actively doing ministry, this minister will often direct ministry rather like an executive leader or director. William F. May described the spiritual CEO model for ministry when he wrote:

> This model apparently offers the most powerful conception of leadership: the CEO leads the organization largely (but not exclusively) by command and obedience. . . . authority moved from the top down without the formal or substantive need to persuade. This mode of leadership obtains largely in the modern world in authoritarian governments and in the modern corporation, where the effort to persuade may exist but does not constitute the sine qua non of the enterprise.[1]

May believes that this model will not work in the church for reasons that are both extrinsic and intrinsic to church life. The extrinsic reason he pointed out is based on the democratic setting in America. In both political life and voluntary organizations, leadership depends on the consent of the governed. The intrinsic reason is that Christian churches believe in the lordship of Christ; Christ the Lord "rules the inward motions of the human spirit." May also observed that "salvation takes hold of the whole person, the deliberative processes included. . . . The notion of the CEO . . . foreshortens the deliberative process and therefore diminishes the reach of the salvation to which the faith testifies."[2]

A Baptist pastor asserted that "pastors who see themselves as chief executive officers and operate their churches like large corporations seem to have forgotten they were called by God to be servants."[3]

The *political dictator model* is another model for ministry that some have followed. The primary descriptive term for the political dictator model of ministry is *authoritative*. These ministers, authority figures who makes their desires known to the congregation, often couching these desires in terms of the will of God or the direction that God has revealed to them and expects them to carry out.

A well-known pastor of a First Church in a major city often said that people had accused him and the deacons of running the church. "There is not a word of truth in it," he would snort with tongue in cheek, "the deacons have nothing to do with it!"

Authority, as we shall see later in this chapter, is earned and not assumed. Simply because a person occupies the position of pastor does not automatically give that person the authority to order others around and to assume that the pastor is the only person in the church to whom God makes His will known. Dictatorship may be the most efficient form of government, but it leaves out the consent of the governed. May identified this model as "the leader of the republic."[4]

The Minister's Congregation

The office of the president in its U. S. political setting combines several ingredients, one of which we may wholly reject as germane to the ministry—the president as commander-in-chief. The pastor has no troops to command and very minimal power of command over subordinates on the executive side to his or her responsibilities.[5]

He then noted that the "more important substantive powers of the presidency lie in the powers of persuasion." These powers of persuasion, according to May, take the two forms of exemplary persuasion and deliberative persuasion.[6] Effective ministers do not order; they persuade.

A third model followed by some ministers is the *hired hand* model for ministry. The operative word for this ministry model is *passive*. Hired-hand type ministers simply do what they are told and go where they are directed. They exert little leadership and give no direction for the ministry. In a submissive manner, the hired-hand kind of ministry is subservient to the board, or the congregation, or to either an individual or group of individuals who exert power in the church. The negative effects of this type of ministry on both the church and the minister are apparent.

The better model for ministry is the *servant model*. The servant model was given by Jesus Christ who embodied this type of ministry: "the Son of Man did not come to be served, but to serve, and to give his life as a ransom for many" (Matt. 20:28). Jesus further exemplified this model when He tied the towel around His waist and washed the feet of His disciples when none of the twelve was willing to take on the servant role (John 13: 1-17).

In describing Jesus, Paul wrote that He took "the very nature of a servant, being made in human likeness" (Phil. 2:7). Concerning Jesus' model of the servant to us, Leonard Griffith observed: "He appeared on the stage of history in the role of a servant, the man for others, who asked nothing for himself—no home, no money, no leisure, no privacy. He had everything to give and he gave it freely."[7]

Responsiveness is the word that best describes the servant model of ministry. The minister who acts as a servant responds to the needs of the people, responds to the directives of God, and responds to the guidance of the Holy Spirit.

How do you function as a servant-minister? Based on the parable of the unworthy servant in Luke 17:7-10, a Bible expositor explained that a servant is someone who works in somebody else's house, who ministers to somebody else's needs, who works at somebody else's convenience, and who does not expect to be thanked.[8]

Of the many models for ministry that modern ministers may choose, the servant model carries with it the commendation of the

Lord as well as the Master's example. Franklin M. Segler pointed out that "in the teaching of his disciples Jesus emphasized serving as the fundamental quality of ministry. He pointed to himself as the *model* and the *example*."[9]

A friend of both of us preached a sermon to a gathering of ministers based on the event of Jesus' washing the feet of His disciples. In that sermon, he said that when we each appear before the Lord in the end, He will not ask, "What is your title?", but He will ask, "Where is your towel?" We serve God and His people as servants, responsive to His leadership in our lives and His guidance in our ministry.

Authority in Ministry

The authority of the minister is directly related to the model of ministry followed by a pastor. In recent years, the issue of ministerial authority, particularly pastoral authority, has become prominent.

The authority of the pastor is often asserted by citing the *King James Version* translation of Hebrew 13:17: "Obey them that have the rule over you, and submit yourselves: for they watch for your souls, as they that must give account, that they may do it with joy, and not with grief: for that is unprofitable to you."

Commenting on this verse, Herschel H. Hobbs observed:

> The Greek phrase is "the ones leading [or guiding] you." This suggests a shepherd (pastor) leading his flock.
> "Obey" translates a verb which has many usages. Arndt and Gingrich Lexicon (Greek Dictionary) cites the meaning in Hebrews 13:17 as "obey" or "follow." In light of "the ones leading you" it seems that "follow" is the preferred meaning. It is like the sheep following the Shepherd. "Submit" renders a verb meaning to yield, give way, submit to one's authority (Arndt and Gingrich). In terms of leadership, the first two seem preferable. If the shepherd leads one way and a sheep wants to go another way, the sheep should yield or give way to the shepherd's way.
> In terms of the pastor-church relationship, the sense is to follow the leader in carrying out the Lord's work.[10]

Hobbs concludes that the pastor's authority is earned, not conferred. That authority is found in leading the people of God to do the will and work of God, not in ruling over them. Hobbs also commented in the same article that "Nowhere in the New Testament is the pastor presented as a *ruler*."[11] Segler added, "Undoubtedly the phrase *'ministerial authority'* is an *oxymoron*, the combination of two ideas or terms that are incongruous or contradictory." He would prefer paradoxical terms like minister-leader or servant-leader. [12]

Jesus had authority. At the conclusion of the Sermon on the Mount, the Gospel indicated: "When Jesus had finished saying these things, the crowds were amazed at his teaching, because he taught as one who had authority, and not as a teacher of law" (Matt. 7:28-29). Charles Bugg commented on that reaction by stating, "The authority of Jesus did not come from sticking his finger between the eyes of people and saying, 'You must listen.' Rather, Jesus had a freshness in his message that caused people to say, 'This man has a word from God.'"[13]

Felix Montgomery worked toward a definition of authority in ministry.

> [T]he New Testament suggests a divine purpose and direction for ministry. Authority is important for the reason that it claims the right to do the ministry for which one has been called. Ministers hold a right, a legitimacy to fulfill the task the Holy Spirit sets before them. The church grants a part of ministerial authority by affirming the call and by providing a place of service. . . .
>
> Ministry's purpose and direction come from God, yet take place in terms of human interaction. We include both dimensions by defining ministerial authority as "the power or right the minister possesses and the church grants for the purpose of fulfilling God's call."[14]

The minister serves God in a human organization, the church. Samuel Southard recognized that a minister serving in a church must be authoritative in a variety of functions. The seminary professor identified these functions as

- maintenance of traditional values;
- sensitivity to personal feelings and community relationships to move the church organization toward specific goals;
- influence over the lives of persons so that they and the world in which they live may be changed toward God.[15]

> The authority of a minister will appear in prophetic and evangelistic forms when he is seeking to change men and movements; it will appear in pastoral emphasis when he is called upon to reflect feelings or understand group relationships; his authority as a priest or reminder of values comes through his preaching and sacramental ministry; organizational authority is manifested in his power to move the church toward a specific program of action.[16]

The designation of authority for these responsibilities has been given in some traditional ways. These traditional designations are

- the derived authority that the minister has received from church and community tradition;

- a legal responsibility to function as a representative of an established institution and to uphold the norms of that institution;
- the charismatic hold which a saintly or heroic individual has upon the hearers;
- the technical knowledge which a person offers without coercion to those who need his help.[17]

Taken together, these traditional designations give the minister authority.

Obviously, some authority goes with any leadership role, including ministerial roles in churches. One writer observed, "The fact of the matter is that the people expect their minister to exercise leadership both in and out of the pulpit. He is not called to 'lord it over them,' but the pastor is called to send a clear signal about what he thinks is important in the life and work of the church."[18] The minister's authority should be used and not abused, for "the real danger of authority is authoritarianism."[19] And the minister's authority should be used to build up the church, to strengthen and to teach the people, and to fulfill the ministry to which God has called him.

> Effectiveness in ministry depends greatly on a clear understanding of authority by ministers and churches. Real authority in ministry comes from affirmation of duties and rights (sacred office), personality and capability (human person), preparation and approval (human office), and personal encounter with God for mission or call (sacred person). Every minister needs to work out of these four dimensions to effect substantial results in serving.[20]

With that in mind, Felix Montgomery asked the question: "How much authority is enough?" He answered his own question by saying, "enough to be respected, accepted, believed, trusted, and followed."[21]

The Use of Power

The issue of power is closely related to the minister's authority. As a professional and as an authority figure, the minister has power over other persons. Karen Lebacqz observed that professionals have both power—the ability to influence behavior—and authority—legitimated and institutionalized power.[22] Ministers represent not only themselves and society, but also God. As a minister, by your very presence you exert a measure of power.

Power has been defined as "a measure of a person's potential to get others to do what he or she wants them to do, as well as to avoid being forced by others to do what he or she does not want to do."[23] With that as a working definition, ministers certainly have power as a part of their arsenal. From an ethical perspective, the use of that power is the key factor. Wayne Oates believes that the "integrity of a Christian leader is measured by his or her sense and use of power in relation to others."[24]

The major problem with power is what it does to relationships. Richard J. Foster observed that "power hits us in our relationships. Power profoundly impacts our interpersonal relationships, our social relationships, and our relationship with God."[25] When ministers use the power they possess in a destructive manner or to gain power over others, power has destroyed the relationship and hurt the person.

Ministers always live with the realization that they risk misusing the power they have with people. Marie M. Fortune was on target when she wrote:

> A healthy professional, pastoral relationship realizes the fact of pastoral power, acknowledging both the gift that it brings and the implication that the pastor is at risk to misuse that power. The laity are vulnerable to harm should that occur. The risk of misusing the power is a risk for all pastors. This risk is a function of the role itself, not just the character of the pastor.[26]

Power comes into play with the way that we view ourselves. When we view ourselves as persons of power who have the power to do what we want and get what we want, even if it is directed toward church goals or spiritual ends, we have misused power.

> When we are convinced that what we are doing is identical with the kingdom of God, anyone who opposes us *must* be wrong. When we are convinced that we always use our power to good ends, we believe we can never do wrong. But when this mentality possesses us, we are taking the power of God and using it to our ends.[27]

Simon Magus, you remember, attempted to buy the power of the Holy Spirit in order to use it for his own purposes. Simon Peter rebuked him for that (Acts 8:9-25). The attempt to use the power that one has as a minister for personal gain or for the display of personal strength must still be rebuked. Some ministers have bullied their families as well as abused their parishioners with their misuse of the power they have as persons.

Power, however, can be constructive. Foster described the creative use of power when he pointed out: "The power that creates gives life and joy and peace. . . . The power that creates restores relationship and gives the gift of wholeness to all."[28]

Creative power is the power that restores relationships. That is the power the pastor uses to bring unity to a divided fellowship, to heal the hurts between two friends, to help people work together rather than pull against one another. That is the power of moral persuasion rather than coercion. Martin Luther King, Jr. used his power to help bring civil rights to all Americans. A pastor may use his power to lead a church to direct involvement in a mission activity to a disadvantaged area by teaming with a church in that community for both worship, work, and witness.

As a minister you have power as a person, as a professional, and as a pastor. That power can be used wisely or unwisely, destructively or constructively. "The task of the pastor is to use the authority image that he carries as a professional and to use it properly. . . . It is his by virtue of his profession, and he is therefore responsible for its use."[29] That responsibility must be accepted.

Leadership

In a study of world leaders, former president Richard M. Nixon noted, "Great leadership is a unique form of art, requiring both force and vision to an extraordinary degree." He went on to say,

> Leadership is more than technique, though techniques are necessary. In a sense, management is prose; leadership is poetry. The leader necessarily deals to a large extent in symbols, in images, and in the sort of galvanizing idea that becomes a force of history. People are persuaded by reason, but moved by emotion; he must both persuade them and move them. The manager thinks of today and tomorrow. The leader must think of the day after tomorrow.[30]

Those same characteristics are necessary for ministerial leadership, for the minister functions as a leader in the church and among people. The leader convinces rather than coerces. The leader persuades rather than pressures.

Robert D. Dale asked the question, "What do leaders provide?" Defining leadership as an action-oriented, interpersonal influencing process, Dale answered his question by saying that leadership is roughly equal parts of vision and initiative. "Vision defines the task and provides the content for the leadership setting. Initiative allows followers to be approached and designs the interpersonal processes for the group or organization." He also observed that effective congregational leaders tend to be "visionary and people-approachers, dreamers and doers."[31]

One of the forms that leadership takes is leadership by example. Writing to Timothy, a younger minister, Paul advised: "Don't let anyone look down on you because you are young, but set an example for the believers in speech, in life, in love, in faith and in purity"

(1 Tim. 4:12). In the models chosen for ministry in the use of authority and power, the leader sets an example for the other believers. One of us learned from a Boy Scout leadership manual years ago that you should never ask anyone to do anything that you are unwilling to do yourself.

Two Baylor University management professors (who were also directors of the Baylor Center for Church Management) wrote that a balanced church leader must combine both active and passive leadership traits. Ministers who lead must be capable of making things happen through planning, budgeting, and programming; they must also have the patience to wait for things to happen as the result of prayer and congregational action. This type of leader also expands the leadership base to include people in the church. "The search for balanced leadership really involves creating a leadership team or body within which active and passive orientations complement one another."[32]

Dale strengthened that idea: "When leaders in ministry use one style of leadership exclusively, they discover they are ineffective in circumstances that do not mesh well with their rigid approach."[33] Good leaders are both balanced and flexible.

The way ministerial leadership is conducted helps to determine whether the minister and the congregation view each other as friend or foe. The task is so great and the interpersonal relationships so essential that the effective minister must work hard to develop good leadership skills.

Ministerial Duties—Roles and Responsibilities

Relationships between the minister and the congregation are formed as ministers fulfill their duties. In simply carrying out the roles and responsibilities of the ministry, ministers form lasting relationships with their congregations. Consider some of those key ministerial duties with regard to the ethical obligations involved.

Preaching

Most ministers, particularly pastors, consider preaching their primary responsibility. And well it is. More people are touched by a person's ministry through preaching than through any other ministerial activity. Many ministers identify themselves as "the preacher" and explain their commitment to a vocational Christian ministry as "a call to preach."

How ethical are ministers in their preaching?

"Ministerially speaking" is a phrase synonymous with gross exaggeration. The secular person, and many Christians, use "preachy" and "preaching" as pejoratives. . . . Should the congregation not be able to listen to persons who wear the mantle of spokespersons for God without weighing each bit of evidence?[34]

The most effective preaching is pastoral preaching done within the context of a pastoral relationship and with pastoral concerns for the people. Preaching then is not just a spiritual exercise, but a real attempt to apply the Word of God and the truth of God to the lives of persons with whom the preacher is intimately involved. Harry Emerson Fosdick's prayer as he got up to preach was always, "O God, some one person here needs what I am going to say. Help me to reach him!"[35]

One pastor answered a key question: "What does it mean to do pastoral care through preaching? It means taking the Bible and a basic understanding about a human problem and ministering to the folks in the pew." Pastoral preaching with that perspective also says something about the manner of preaching. "Using preaching as a means of doing pastoral care means always preaching in love and not using the pulpit as your Sunday whipping post. It means proclaiming God's Word with a caring heart."[36]

Pastoral preaching is done in the context of worship. Ministers see their sermons as an integral part of the whole worship service and not just as a time for them to perform. The prayer and the praise in the order of worship are not just preliminaries to the sermon. They all fit together as a planned expression of the worship of God.

Adequate preparation of the message is assumed. Each sermon should be thoughtfully planned, prayerfully prepared, and effectively delivered. Preaching is that moment when God's truth is delivered through a human personality. For the minister to just get up and "wing it," depending on the inspiration of the moment or the effectiveness of delivery, debases the preaching moment.

In a doctoral dissertation on clergy ethics, James Allen Reasons argued that ethical preaching is more than preaching on ethical issues, it is also preaching in an ethical way.[37] Two issues present themselves in an examination of preaching in an ethical way: the use of Scripture and plagiarism.

Although ethical responsibility to Scripture is not debated in many circles, it is still a vital issue in ministerial ethics because of its abuse. At some point in his ministry, the preacher must establish personal guidelines to ensure faithful interpretation of the text.[38]

Preachers can preach on ethical issues in unethical ways.

Preachers can also misrepresent the sermon text in the Scripture.

Lapsing into allegory, symbolism, or the spiritualization of the passage, skillful preachers can make Scripture texts mean whatever they want them to mean with little concern for the context or the intended meaning of the passage. J. Clark Hensley passed on some hermeneutical principles that were first formulated by D. P. Brooks. The minister should

- determine the exact meaning of the text,
- the literary form the writer used,
- the context,
- the historical and cultural setting,
- the meaning in the light of Christ, and
- what the passage means now.[39]

Eisegesis, reading into the text one's own meaning, is to be avoided.

Many preachers are guilty of plagiarizing. Of this clergy sin, Nolan B. Harmon noted: "Taking someone else's message and giving it as one's own is known as *plagiarism*. It is condemned by all ministers and defined differently by all. However, the honest minister will know when he or she takes what is in reality the work of another."[40]

How common is plagiarism? In 1989 three well-known, high-profile pastors of prominent churches in the Southwest were accused of plagiarism in their printed or taped materials.[41] An official of a publishing house that had produced both the original material and the plagiarized work in one of the incidents defended it by saying, "There's a whole oral tradition that exists that would be very complicated to try to trace down. . . . It's just drawing on that oral tradition that circulates."[42]

All preachers have been influenced by other people. In some cases, it would be difficult to trace the origin of a statement or a concept. For a person to get an idea from another person, research the concept, and develop it for himself, making it his own, would not be dishonest. Giving credit to others for the use of their material is also honest. Simply lifting material and preaching it as one's own ventures into the area of plagiarism. Too many preachers have followed the dictum of one well-known minister, now deceased, who often declared, "When better sermons are published, I will preach them!"

One of us visited a large urban church at Christmastime. The pastor's sermon for the morning was entitled: "Christmas Ho-Hum or Christmas Golly-Gee." That unique title together with the content of the message, which included two stories attributed to John Killinger, raised a suspicion that the sermon might not be original. A later search in a library uncovered a book of Christmas sermons by

John Killinger, including the one preached by the pastor as his own creation.

Two other areas where dishonesty is often practiced in preaching are confessional preaching and sermon illustrations. In confessional preaching, one may embellish the story and confess more than has actually been experienced. Early in 1992 a preacher in the Northwest claimed in his personal testimony that he had worked for Murder, Inc. for fifteen years. He claimed to have killed twenty-eight people as a Mafia hit man. The pastor claimed that he was counseled by Charles Colson, the convicted Watergate conspirator who now has a prison ministry, and by Billy Graham. According to his story, he found God on death row while reading a Bible in a prison cell. When the truth became known, his actual crime was violating his parole, after killing his wife and leaving his girlfriend for dead after choking and stabbing her. He was a murderer, but not in the way he claimed. Upon learning of his whereabouts, authorities from the state in which he had violated his parole arrested him.[43] That is carrying ministerial embellishment of a story a bit far!

Dishonesty may also occur in sermon illustrations. In personal illustrations you should not picture yourself smarter, better, or more spiritual than you really are. Neither should you claim for yourself experiences that were really someone else's. When both of us were in seminary, an executive of a national denominational agency spoke in the seminary chapel one morning. He concluded his message with a moving account of an experience that he had in India when a mother dropped a sore-encrusted baby into his lap through the open window of an automobile and said, "It's your baby now!" He applied it to the world mission task of evangelization.

The next Sunday a seminary student heard a fellow student preach. In that sermon he told of his military experience in North Africa where a mother dropped a sore-encrusted baby into his lap while he was in a Jeep and said, "It's your baby now!" He applied it to our world mission task.

Could both preachers have had the same experience, including the same wording to describe it? Possibly, but not probably. The student preacher's credibility was reduced for those who heard both messages.

In examining ethics in preaching, Raymond H. Bailey mentioned five other matters that he identified as "specious sermonic fallacies and persuasive devices" that are ethical concerns in preaching. The five fallacies are

- poor preparation and faulty exegesis,
- glittering generalities,

- loaded language and name calling,
- emotional manipulation, and
- misrepresentation and partial truth.[44]

Proclaimers of God's truth must always remember their own humanity:

> The authority leader is under constant temptation to self-aggrandizement and the use of power in the pulpit. He thinks of himself as God's "prophet," "spokesman," "ambassador"! He can easily be deceived into thinking his own word is the authority, that it is infallible. His use of pious and even ecstatic language, in order to gain power by means of emotional persuasion, may belie or undercut the word of God he is supposed to proclaim and exemplify.[45]

Teaching

Two ethics teachers, Walter E. Wiest and Elwyn A. Smith, remind us forcefully of the need for truthfulness in both our proclamation and our teaching.

> Truth—which includes both truthfulness and being true—is the key both to ministry and the ethics of ministry. Ministers of the gospel have something to be true to. We have a message to proclaim that is given to us, we do not make it up ourselves, and we are to witness to that truth faithfully and with integrity. This is a moral commitment.[46]

The teaching ministry of the church has always been considered an essential element in church life. Jesus came preaching, teaching, and healing. The contemporary church continues to preach the Word of God, to teach the truths of God, and to heal the brokenness of persons. A Yale ethics professor expressed the importance of the teaching function by saying, "The pastor shares an ethical obligation with other teachers: the quest for and sharing of truth and knowledge. Many an ordination ritual includes the joint assignment, to be 'pastor and teacher'."[47]

The competent ministerial leader does not fear truth. In a Christian context, teaching is more a matter of education than indoctrination. Passing on the religious heritage of the faith community is essential. Yet truth cannot be guarded so closely that only one approach or interpretation is presented. Freedom to think, to research, and to ask questions without fear of reprisal must be maintained.

A minister cannot protect the people from confrontation with other approaches to life or learning. The goal of teaching spiritual truths is to help people become mature Christians. This does not mean that all Christians must look alike and think alike.

Those who build a creed on a selected teaching of the Bible or on a narrow segment of Christian theology become defensive about testing the belief by the wider expanse of truth. This often results in an attempt to suppress teachings which threaten the fixed doctrine. Such authoritarian views of education may result in the molding of creedal clones as ministers for our churches.[48]

The credibility and the integrity of ministers is demonstrated by the way they teach. The Word of God must be handled responsibly and respectfully. The ones being taught must be treated with dignity. Neither the dignity nor the personhood of the individual should be trampled in the attempt to teach them.

Administration

The practical matter of the administration of the church is a part of the minister's duties. Many ministers consider this the most disagreeable part of their work, partly because administration usually turns out to be the most time-consuming aspect of their work. Ministers' leadership styles influence their approach to administration. "The chief moral expectation of any professional is self-discipline enough not to selfishly exploit the power that is entrusted to him or her. Ministerial ethics commands us to be most wary about the way we exercise leadership."[49]

How persons are viewed and treated is one ethical issue in church administration. Persons should always be viewed as having intrinsic worth and value. They are never to be exploited or manipulated.

Trust is a key ingredient. The trust that the minister and the congregation have in one another affects the way they work together. Neither the minister nor the church members should be defensive toward one another. Instead, they should be positive and supportive of one another.

Trust begins with openness to and acceptance of the person. Trust results when one person has respect for another as a person. They will accept those individuals, even when they may not accept their ideas. Trust extends to the belief that the person is capable of functioning in his position. Training, teaching, and instructing may be necessary to help that person become fully functional in the position. That responsibility is a part of both the teaching ministry of the church and the administrative function of the minister.

The motives for service or actions of other persons are also involved in trust. You should never judge another's motives for any action or activity as less than you would judge your own motives. To assume that another person operates out of motives less pure than your own is unfair.

Persons respond better to programs and promotions when they have some *ownership* in them. Many churches use the committee system to great advantage. One strong component of the committee system is that it not only allows for the individual expertise of committee members, and the strength of group decisions as contrasted with individual decisions, but it also involves church members in the decisions. People have greater ownership in those decisions in which they have been involved. People like to have a part in the decisions that affect their lives.

Good organizational practices should be followed. The minister exhibits leadership. But some management is also involved. Ernest White distinguished between leadership, management, and administration.

> I distinguish among three human relations functions: administration, management, and leadership. Administration concerns "over-all supervision." It exercises the "eyes-on" process of overseeing an organization. Management concerns the immediate direction and control of an organization or group. From the word *management* (*manus*-hand), it is the "hands-on" process.
>
> Leadership is much more than administration or management. Leadership is an influence process by which persons, organizations, communities, or nations are guided and make progress toward some goal other than where they were prior to the exercise of leadership. Leadership is the "moving on" process.[50]

All three of those processes are involved in administrating a church. A church that is properly organized and functioning can follow the leadership of its ministerial leaders. The ministerial leaders can both administer and manage that process better with good organization. This has ethical implications in its trust of persons, in the involvement of individuals in processes and programs that affect their lives, and in how ministers practice leadership and use power and authority.

The proper administration of *finances* is a key ethical factor in the administration of a church. Christian stewardship is more than a scheme to raise money for the church. It is the response of a Christian in love to God's grace.

Ministers can become involved in stewardship promotion in the church in several ways. They may do nothing, believing that the finances will take care of themselves. Or, they may emphasize money as the major basis of the church. They may see stewardship promotion as a necessity, not as a prominent ministry of the church but a means through which the other ministries are accomplished. A better option: they may view stewardship as a ministry of growth among the members and as an avenue through which to share commitment.[51]

How Christian stewardship is presented is one concern. Noyce advised, "Integrity, therefore, must be our byword; congruence of ends and means. Fund raising should be straightforward and not devious, open rather than secretive."[52] The author of *Pastoral Ethics* then outlined some of the ways that integrity is guarded in fund raising for Christian causes:

- by applying ethics in promotion;
- by avoiding the exploitation of vulnerable people;
- by applying the highest principles in promotional material;
- by avoiding "undue influence";
- by using the right method.[53]

How the money raised is used is another concern of ministerial ethics. In recent years the nation has been shocked by the misuse of funds given by faithful followers to highly visible Christian leaders, particularly televangelists. The money given to churches and other religious causes should always be scrupulously audited. The persons responsible for finances must be sure that the money is spent for the purposes for which it was given. Generally speaking, the best accounted dollar given for charitable or benevolent purposes is the dollar given to the local church. In churches with congregational government, the church itself has adopted the budget. A finance committee has the responsibility of overseeing the expenditure of the funds. Reports are made periodically to the church. Pastors who control a Pastor's Discretionary Fund should be particularly careful in using it. Such a fund is usually intended for benevolent purposes or for the entertainment of prospects for church membership or visiting personalities, but it is open to abuse. Too many ministers have not been discreet in using the discretionary fund and have had trouble telling the difference between their money and the church's money.

Who has access to church funds and the use of church accounts is also an issue. That access should be carefully guarded with checks and balances so that the honesty of each person is beyond question.

Openness in financial matters creates trust in the church and in the integrity of the ministers.

Counseling

Wayne Oates has pointed out that ministers, whatever their training, do not enjoy the privilege of deciding whether to counsel with people or not. "His choice," he said, "is not between counseling and not counseling, but between counseling in a disciplined and skilled way and counseling in an undisciplined and unskilled way."[54] Whenever people come to you for help, you are in a counseling situation. Inevitably people will bring their problems to their pastor for personal guidance and care.

One immediate ethical concern for counseling is whether you are prepared for it or not. For many counseling situations, no particular training is required. You can answer the question. You can listen to the concern. You can be a friend. You can provide reassurance. You can give encouragement. Much pastoral counseling is what Oates called "the brief pastoral dialogue." While this may not be considered counseling in the technical sense, it is typical pastoral counseling.[55]

Other counseling is on the level of what Oates called "the level of pastoral counseling and psychotherapy."[56] This type of counseling is what others have labeled "insight counseling." The difference has to do with short-term or long-term counseling. This type of counseling calls for appointments and multiple sessions. Many ministers without specialized training or clinical experience will not feel comfortable with long-term counseling and should refer persons needing counseling. Competency to perform the task undertaken is an ethical concern. Generally speaking, the minister's counseling should be confined to the area of relationships. Personality disorders should be referred. Knowing when to refer is a major factor in counseling. All ministers do some counseling in some form.

Confidentiality is a big issue in counseling. Clergy confidentiality in counseling and the confessional is a long tradition in Christian churches. Noyce observed, "That pastoral conversation be confidential and not subject to forced disclosure is as important for the clergy as for psychiatrists and psychotherapists, and it is rooted for us in a much longer tradition."[57]

From the legal standpoint, two issues are involved in clergy confidentiality. The first issue is the testimonial privilege, whether ministers can be compelled to testify in a judicial proceeding about matters that have been told them in confidence. The second issue involves the rights of privacy, whether the person who reveals confidential matters to a minister has a legal right to expect that these matters will not be revealed to others.[58]

With regard to the issue of testimonial privilege, generally the courts have held that the information given to a minister in counseling or as penitential communication, in confession, is privileged communication. These are confidential communications and the minister is protected from being forced to use them in testimony. Child abuse cases, particularly child sexual abuse cases, are exceptions. About this Buzzard and Hall reported, "Few privileges are absolute, the clergy-penitent privilege is no exception. Today, in some states members of the clergy are required by state child abuse 'reporting' statutes to report known or suspected cases of child abuse, even if confidentially disclosed to them."[59] Other legal responsibilities of the minister will be discussed in chapter 6.

Ministers must be able to keep confidences. Matters told them in confidence should not be shared with others. This is a reasonable expectation.

How could breaches of confidence occur? You should not take sermon illustrations from your counseling experiences. That violates the confidence of the person or persons involved; furthermore when parishioners hear the experiences of others used in sermons, they will not trust you to keep their confidences. You should guard casual conversations lest you leak something that has been told you in confidence. In church committee meetings you could break some confidence in commenting on the qualifications of an individual being considered to serve in a church responsibility. Discussing church problems with deacons, elders, or a church board is another vulnerable area for ministerial confidentiality. Confidential information must be kept inviolate, except in those cases where a minister is required to report information.

Another counseling issue has to do with counseling with persons of the opposite sex. "There is no more frequent and painful a ministry-wrecking blunder than sexual involvement growing out of cross-gender pastoral care. A minister 'falls in love' with a parishioner, and an affair or divorce ensues. What also ensues is a crisis for a congregation."[60] In the *Leadership* magazine survey concerning ministers' sexual indiscretions cited in chapter 3, 17 percent of the pastors who had intercourse or other forms of sexual contact with someone other than their spouse had the experience with a counselee.[61]

Noyes suggested some "rules of thumb to serve as reflexes in the pastor and pastoral counselor." These rules of thumb designed to protect the minister are:

- when a cross-gender church member issues repeated appeals for pastoral help and time that are unusually repetitive and persistent, look at the probability of romantic transference;
- discretion should be exaggerated in pastoral care rather than relaxed;
- while maintaining visual and acoustic privacy, cross-gender counseling should be done in the proximity of other staff or church people.[62]

The problems of transference and countertransference in counseling were treated in chapter 3.

Visitation

Personal visitation or pastoral calling has long been considered a primary responsibility of a minister. In an urban setting where there are more two-income families, personal visitation to the homes of church members has become very difficult. Today's society requires that more pastoral calling be done now by appointment. Personal contact is still important. In many church communities personal visits by the pastor are expected.

The purpose of visitation breaks down into several categories. Some pastoral calls are prospect or enlistment visitation. Other calls will be evangelistic. Visiting the sick is a necessary element of pastoral care. Some pastoral visits may be primarily social calls. Some pastors make it a priority to visit in each home in the church within a time period. Those who are homebound or institutionalized also need visits from the ministers.

In *hospital visitation* the minister is a part of the healing team. Even with that understanding, you should remember that you are a guest of the hospital; you must not take liberties with the privileges given you. Never interfere with treatment being given to a patient. Do not barge into the areas of the hospital where special permission is required, areas such as the intensive care unit or the surgical recovery room. Check with the nurses' station before entering any room. Hospital visits ordinarily should be brief, about five to ten minutes. Always keep in mind that you are neither God nor the physician. The answers to some questions are beyond your knowledge. Loud talk, too much levity, and boisterous behavior of any kind can be self-defeating. At some times prayer is appropriate, but it is often better to ask before offering the prayer.

Evangelistic visitation is for the purpose of presenting the claims of Jesus Christ on human hearts. The purpose is for the individual to make a personal decision to accept Jesus Christ as personal Savior. This decision should never be forced or coerced. The dignity of the individual should not be violated. The visit is not simply to count another decision but to introduce a new person into the family of God. That visit should be made in the spirit of prayer and with the power and presence of the Holy Spirit.

The minister must consider the ethical obligations to a member of another church. "Sheep stealing" is universally disdained. A position adopted by many ministers is not to personally visit a member of another local church unless that person takes the initiative by requesting a visit or indicating that they would appreciate a visit by the minister. After that individual has taken the initiative with the minister, then the minister will feel free to visit with them.

In all visits in homes, remember that you are an invited guest. Do not be a rude or ungracious guest. When one of us was a high school student, he was employed on Saturdays and during school vacations selling shoes. When being trained in how to sell shoes—how to measure the foot, where to find the shoes, and how to write the sales ticket—the assistant manager of that large department store emphasized that the store's business was built on repeat customers. The store would rather lose a sale than sell something that did not fit and lose a customer. The sales trainees were told always to leave a way for the customer to come back. That is also good advice for home visitation by ministers: always leave a way to come back to that home with the gospel of Christ or the care of a pastor.

The question of visiting members of the opposite sex, either in their homes or hospital rooms, is difficult. The same care should be taken in that setting as in the counseling of persons of the opposite sex. Appointments for visitation are helpful, so that other family members can arrange to be there. Having another person visit with you also helps. If no one but the opposite gender person is at home when you arrive, the visit can be done at the front door without entering the house itself. In a hospital room, the door should be left open. Rumors have been circulated, eyebrows raised, and reputations tarnished, when a minister has repeatedly visited in the home of church members of the opposite sex while no one else was present. That practice should be avoided.

Basic Duties

Weddings and funerals are two other basic ministerial duties that include ethical responsibilities. Strong relationships between the minister and the congregation are formed in the process of these two common ventures of life.

Marriage is one of the significant moments of one's life. From ancient times marriage has been considered a religious rite. Ministers were at one time the sole judge of who might be married, for there was no state license for marriage. When the state gained control of legitimizing marriage, that obligation was removed from the church. Nevertheless, ministers still have an important spiritual responsibility.

A church wedding is actually a private event done in a public place. The wedding is performed in the context of the church, the place for worship and witness, to give a spiritual emphasis to the marriage. For a marriage to be a Christian union requires more than a wedding ceremony in a church sanctuary.

The church should begin to prepare persons for marriage long before the wedding service occurs. Through Christian family emphases, special studies on human sexuality, sermons on the Christian home, and appropriate literature, the church prepares Christians for family life.

Most ministers insist on at least one, and often more, sessions of premarital counseling before performing a wedding ceremony. In those sessions the wedding itself is planned. Such topics as gender roles in the home, developing a routine and the use of time, work and vocation, finances and money management, relationship with parents-in-law, religious differences, and the birth of children are discussed.[63]

An ethical dilemma for many ministers concerns whose marriage ceremony they will perform. Some consider themselves "Marrying Sams" who will perform the ceremony for anyone who comes along with a license and the fee. Others will only perform the ceremony for members of the church they serve as minister. The choice becomes even more selective when considering whether to perform the marriage ceremony for a person who has been divorced.

Ministers usually have followed one of four approaches to performing the wedding for someone who has been divorced. Some, of course, make no distinction and will perform the ceremony for anyone with a valid license. Another approach is a blanket refusal. They will not perform the ceremony for one who has been divorced. The approach of others is to perform the ceremony only if the divorced person was the "innocent" party in the divorce. This approach is difficult to uphold, as there is usually no truly innocent partner in a divorce. The understanding of Jesus' word in Matthew 19:9 tends to become legalistic and to lack Jesus' spirit of forgiveness. The fourth approach is to consider each case on its own merits. This approach has difficulties also, but it does seem to use the example of Christ in accepting people where they are and helping them back into wholeness with God and with one another. If the church has a responsibility to that couple, then the ceremony is performed in an effort to be redemptive to the persons. Some denominations have guidelines for their ministers to follow in these cases.

One of us grew up under a pastor who had strict standards about divorce and remarriage. He absolutely refused to perform the marriage ceremony of anyone who had been divorced, whatever the reason. As a young man, this minister followed the guidance of his mentor. Probably it was more the mentor's conviction than the minister's belief. On several occasions he had refused to perform the wedding ceremony of a divorced person, even when that person was marrying the child of a prominent member of the church.

One day he was approached by the child of an active church family with the request to perform his wedding. This young man, it turned out, had been married briefly as a teenager and then divorced. Now he was a university student. For some reason, the minister was indecisive. He explained his normal practice, but did not give a definite answer at that time. Several days later, he called the young man to tell him that he felt compelled to stick by his position; he would not perform the ceremony. Then he said to the student, "If there is any other way that I can help you, please let me know." The icy answer was, "Don't worry. There won't ever be any other way." Then the young man hung up.

That evening the pastor preached from Jonah 4:1-11, the story of the prophet under the gourd vine complaining about the vine wilting while all the people of Nineveh were living in spiritual darkness. God reminded Jonah of that disparity. The point of the passage was the contrast between gourds and human souls. Was Jonah's concern for principle more important than God's regard for persons?

In that sermon the preacher was convicted. He had made his marriage principle more important than the persons involved. Following the evening service of the church, he rushed into his office, called the young man, and agreed to perform the wedding ceremony. That young man is still married, and is a leading professional person in his city, as well as a leader in his church. The minister often wonders what would have happened to this family had he stuck by his original position.

Whether a person has been divorced is not the only special condition a minister must consider. What will the cleric do about couples who have been living together, about a bride that is pregnant, about interfaith marriages even when one faith is not Christian, and about interracial marriages? Each minister has to make those decisions based on his understanding of the nature of the gospel, the nature of pastoral care, and the responsibility of the church for ministry.

The minister's responsibility does not end with pronouncing "I now pronounce you husband and wife." A follow-up visit to the home of the newly married couple is helpful. The minister should give them a copy of the wedding certificate and possibly a copy of the ceremony. The minister will have a continuing ministry to them if they remain in the community. Certainly the minister will be available for further counsel and help as that is needed. The marriage begins when the wedding is over; the ministry also continues after the wedding is over.

The *funeral* is another one of the basic duties of the minister. The ministry provided during the times of bereavement and through the funeral is a very personal one at a particularly meaningful time in the life of a family.

> A minister in charge of a funeral is often in one of the most difficult of situations. The pastor represents God, under whose watch-care all events, even death, take place. The minister represents humanity in its efforts to ease the bitterness of the hour, and at the same time represents an ecclesiastical organization and profession in conducting a public service.[64]

The funeral service has several functions. Through the funeral service the family

- faces the reality of death;
- expresses its grief in a socially acceptable manner;
- gives witness to the Christian faith celebrating both the life of the deceased and the promises of God;
- participates in a rite of closure.[65]

Each of these serves a distinct function.

How ministers guide the family through these functions and help them to find wholeness and healing rather than manipulating them or exploiting their feelings becomes an ethical issue. Some other ethical questions ministers face at funerals are the following:

- Will she be truthful about the person or bestow instant sainthood upon her at death?
- Should the minister accept fees for funerals?
- If fees are accepted, should they be discussed before the service?
- What is the distinction between a fee and a love gift?
- Will the minister conduct the funeral service for a non-Christian?
- Should the services be held in the place of worship or in a funeral home chapel?
- What about the involvement of fraternal organizations in the burial?

Each of these issues must be individually faced and answered.

A ministry at death is a priority ministry for a pastor. The pastor should get in touch with the family as soon as possible after being informed of the person's death, either by telephone or in person. A personal visit is best when possible. A ministry to the bereaved is begun immediately. In this ministry, the cleric should understand something about death, something about grief, and something about a grief ministry.

So far as possible, the minister should participate in planning the funeral service. Questions need to be answered: Where will the service be? Who will conduct the service? What will be included in the service?

Some basic guidelines for the ethical conduct of the funeral service itself are the following:

- make it positive;
- make it Christian;
- make it personal;
- make it helpful, strengthening;
- make it brief.

Through the entire service, the strengthening, encouraging, helping presence of God through the Holy Spirit should be emphasized.

The minister's responsibility does not end when the flowers have faded. By helping the bereaved do the grief work necessary, by sharing helpful literature with them, and by follow-up visits to the home and with the family, the minister can help those who have lost loved ones. Many churches do grief recovery work as a part of their ministry.

Should former pastors return to conduct weddings and funerals in a former church? Each minister will have to make that decision. In many cases, it is not feasible to do so. For the most part, the answer should be negative. The new minister should be given the opportunity to form the same kind of relationships with the people of the church that the former pastor had. These relationships were formed, for the most part, through the normal conduct of ministerial duties. If the former minister returns, it should definitely be with the full knowledge, blessing, and even invitation of the current pastor. Those relationships, too, must be maintained.

Ministerial Transitions—Beginning and Closure

The Committee

Ministers also do a lot of going back and forth. By the very nature of ministry, some mobility is required. New positions open, new challenges arise, and sometimes new approaches offer ministers the opportunity to change churches. Through it all, ministers move around a good bit.

Some denominations appoint ministers to a church. Many evangelical denominations do not; churches seek out and call their own ministers. Some religious groups operate with a combination of the two systems. By whatever means it comes about, most ministers feel that through a confluence of the leadership of the Holy Spirit, the desire of the church, and the willingness of a minister, a call is issued and another minister is off to another place of service.

In most cases, the prospective minister will deal with a committee. That committee may be a pastor search committee, a pastoral advisory committee, a personnel committee, or a specialized committee commissioned to recommend a minister for a particular position.

Search committees are unique creations. They begin to take on a life and personality of their own. In the case of search committees for church positions, they are normally composed of lay persons who have volunteered their services and donated their time to the church for this task.

The search committees get the names of persons to consider for the ministry position through the recommendations of others. This introduces the first ethical consideration. How honest should the recommendation be? We would expect that a letter of recommendation commending an individual for a position in ministry would be truthful. Simple truth-telling ought to suffice. Two Pittsburgh Theological Seminary professors state:

> It is expected that in a letter of recommendation one will say as much as possible that is positive and as few negative things as honesty allows. What is crucial is that the truth should be told where it really counts, as kindly as possible. Thus the failure to mention a negative factor that is crucial in the job consideration falls outside the range of the ethical.[66]

Many times the person who gives information about a minister will not be completely candid about the minister. Perhaps they think they are helping a friend. Possibly they feel that the people will discover "the whole truth" after the person is in the position. Maybe they are fearful that the complete truth will prohibit the minister from landing the position. Many churches have been hurt because the recommender or the person providing the reference was not completely truthful. Problem ministers have passed from church to church, some with severe personality problems. The answer is not to move them from position to position, or from place to place. A little honesty would help the whole situation.

Related to that, a minister is expected to be honest in the résumé. Few will outright fabricate degrees or falsify positions of service, though that has been known to occur. More will leave misleading impressions. By listing a school in the résumé, the impression will be left that this minister has graduated from that institution, when actually the minister has only attended there a short time.

Should divorced ministers reveal on their résumés that they are divorced and remarried? Not necessarily. That fact will often cause a committee to discard the résumé immediately without considering the details or other relevant factors. They should, however, tell the committee about the marital failure very early in the process, even in the first meeting. By telling them early they can be sure the committee knows it, as well as control how they know it and what they know about it.

The minister and the committee must deal with one another on the basis of honesty. The committee should be honest about their church and their community. The minister should be honest about personal experiences and abilities. Neither of them should be surprised by the truth later.

Both the committee and the minister should do their homework about each other. As location, location, location are the three most important factors in real estate, so investigation, investigation, investigation are the three most important factors for a search committee. The committee cannot know too much about the prospective minister; the prospective minister cannot know too much about the church. Never go past the clues. The clues about the character of the cleric and the church are always there.

Lyle Schaller has suggested a series of questions the prospective minister can ask the church. One group of them are *what* questions:

- What is the reason you are a member of that church?
- What does the church do best?
- What would you change?
- What are the church's major goals?
- What was the period of greatest strength of the church?

Another group of questions are *why* questions. These have to do with a study of the statistics of the church and the trends in the church. Then the question is, why is there a difference? Next come the *what's the type* questions dealing with the type of church, community, and people involved. The final group of questions are *what are your expectations* questions. These also deal with the priorities of the church.[67]

The Conditions

Both the committee and the minister should be clear about the conditions of the call. Agreement should be reached on the church's expectations. Ministers could go a long way toward eliminating forced terminations if both the minister and the church agreed on the expressed and unexpressed expectations of the people before the call.

The financial arrangements are conditions of the call. What is the base compensation? Does that include housing allowance and utility allowances? If a church-owned home is provided, who pays the utilities? The fringe benefits need to be detailed. Does it include retirement? insurance? Is the whole family or just the minister covered by the medical insurance? The minister's professional expenses should be outlined. Is there a car allowance or a reimbursement program? What about expenses for conventions, conferences, and continuing education? Will the church provide a book allowance?

The conditions that relate to time arrangements should also be specified. These include work schedules, days off, vacations, holidays, released time for revivals, leading or attending conferences or workshops, and participation in denominational meetings. Who will pay for the pulpit supply when the position must be filled during the minister's absence?

The final set of conditions concerns the timetable for the transition to take place. When will the minister come before the church for presentation and election? When will the minister resign from the current position? When will his new responsibilities begin?

While these questions may seem mundane, they must be answered for both the church and the minister to act ethically. By settling them before issuing the call and the making the move, churches and ministers alike eliminate many possibilities for misunderstanding and trouble. In churches with congregational government these agreements should be presented to the church by the committee and adopted by the church. The agreements will then be a part of the church's records. The prospective minister should receive a written copy of the minutes that spell out the agreements.

The Call

The committee has made its decision. Once the call has been issued, the prospective minister then faces the decision of whether or not to accept that call.

A number of factors go into the decision. Ministers should assay their capabilities. Can they handle that position? If it is a position as a minister of education, for instance, that calls for a person who is interested in detail work. Candidates who are given to directing broad, sweeping programs, leaving the details to others, obviously would have a difficult time in this position. Ministers should also consider the ministry goals. Under what church leaders have interpreted as the will of God for their lives, will this position help to fulfill those goals? Self-fulfillment in ministry must be considered. As persons work toward what they feel is God's will according to calling, background, and experience, they come to interpret the will of God for their lives.

The Closure

By accepting a call to a new place, ministers must bring their ministry at their present places to a close. Although the excitement of new possibilities may seem attractive, the actual move may be trau-matic. The future promises new friends, new vistas, new approaches, and new experiences; but the present means leaving behind old places, old friends, familiar scenes, and the known. The unknown can be scary.

The church shepherd must first resign the present position. In many cases, the church by-laws will specify the amount of advance notice required. Two weeks is the minimum usually. The time should be long enough to enable an orderly exit but not so long that the work is crippled or the people begin to wonder when the "ex-pastor" is ever going to leave. A month is probably maximum, unless unique circumstances exist.

Courtesy demands that some advance notice be given to selective persons. A pastor might want to discuss it with a trusted advisor, the leader of the deacons, or the whole board before announcing it to the church. A staff minister should let the immediate supervisor know. In some cases, the resignation may be made to the supervi-sor, who then makes it known to the proper body or the church as a whole.

An exit interview or series of interviews is helpful. Departing ministers can reflect on their ministries and churches can evaluate their relation to their ministers. Whether this is done formally or informally, the exit interview helps to evaluate the person's ministry and the church's program.

The departing minister begins to disengage from both the people, the place, and the position. The last days should be spent in an effort to make an orderly exit and to clear the way for the on-going ministry. In the next chapter we examine the relationship between the de-parted minster and the former congregation, as well as the relation-ship with both the predecessor and successor in that ministry position.

The Challenge

When ministers move on to accept new challenges in the Lord's work, they do not come to new positions with all the answers and a ready-made program. The new shepherd discovers a different com-munity, and adapts to a new ministry.

Any new ministry is begun with anxiety. This new minister will have to get acquainted with new policies, new procedures, and the established customs of the new place. "We never did it that way before" may be the seven last words of the church, but they may also be the seven first words the new minister hears.

A new support system for the minister will have to be established.

If it is a multistaff congregation, each minister will have to carve out a niche among other clergy. In single-staff churches, each will have to discover who the power brokers are in that church and learn how to relate to them. The initial nagging question is whether the minister will be adequate for the task.

New beginnings are difficult. From an ethical perspective, new pastors will show integrity by the way they move into the position and among the people. They will prove their honesty with the search committee by a ministry consistent with what was offered and what was received. Major changes in the church should not be made during those first months. Instead, minister and congregation should establish and nurture the relationship that will carry them through the years.

Ministerial Success

The Measure of Success

How do you measure success in ministry? As professionals and as Americans, ministers are success oriented; but knowing how to properly measure that success is more difficult. Richard Bondi wrote, "[S]uccess or failure forces us to examine the standards by which we measure either one. We may well fear to discover that our standards have more to do with the story of the world than the story of the Church."[68]

Three methods of measuring success are often used. The first of these measures of success is the *bottom-line approach*. This is basically the approach used by businesses. The bottom-line definition of success goes strictly by numbers. Are statistics better this year than last year? Is the count up? The measurement may be of the three B's: buildings, budgets, and baptisms. Or the measurement may be of the three S's: membership size, amount of salary, and number of staff.[69]

The second way to measure success is by *personal satisfaction*. How satisfied have you been with yourself and your ministry? Has the ministry been fulfilling to you? Have you given your best to God and to His people? The answers you give to these questions indicate your personal satisfaction with your ministry.

The third measure of success is a *spiritual approach that evaluates commitment and faithfulness*. Do you remember Isaiah's response to the vision of God in the temple when he was called and commissioned?

Then I said, "For how long, O Lord?" And he answered: "Until the cities lie ruined and without inhabitant, until the houses are left deserted and the fields ruined and ravaged, until the Lord has sent everyone far away and the land is utterly forsaken. And though a tenth remains in the land, it will again be laid waste. But as the terebinth and oak leave stumps when they are cut down, so the holy seed will be the stump in the land" (Isa. 6:11-13).

The standard of success was not measured in results, but in faithfulness to God.

In an article in *Context*, Martin Marty referred to another publication in which a pastor and his wife were discussing success in ministry. They remembered the seminary commencement speaker who had concluded his message with a text of his own: "You have heard that it was said, 'God does not call you to be successful but to be faithful.' But I say to you that in God's eyes faithfulness is success. Down here success is the sign of faithfulness, but up there the only sign of success is faithfulness." The pastor's wife cross-stitched and framed a piece for her husband with these words: "Up there the only sign of success is faithfulness."[70] Good ministers need to remember that.

A pastor and wife, Kent and Barbara Hughes, wrote a book which grew out of their achievement of a sense of success after feeling despondency when the new church with great promise that they served did not grow. They included this testimony: "We found success in a small church that was not growing. We found success in the midst of what the world would call failure." From their study of Scripture they came to the conclusion that "we are not called to success, as the world fancies it, but to *faithfulness*. We realized that the results are for God and eternity to reveal."[71]

They shared what they called "the basic plan for biblical success" by which they were liberated from the success syndrome, which they testified was their success. To the best of their ability they were striving:

- To be faithful (obedient to God's Word and hardworking);
- To serve God and others;
- To love God;
- To believe He *is* (to believe what we believe);
- To pray;
- To pursue holiness;
- To develop a positive attitude.[72]

Success Is a Moving Target

Robert Raines wrote it: "Success is a moving target." He explained, "our goals change by reason of age, circumstance, growth and experience."[73] These four factors are certainly involved in any ethical assessment of success. With growth and maturity, the standards for success usually change.

That must be what Richard Bondi had in mind when he observed, "[I]t is when we forget the story that called us into ministry in the first place that we place a misguided importance on our own success or failure, or the expectations placed on us by people in a particular time and place."[74]

The Goal for Christians

A denominational executive once wrote about measuring the pastor's success. He asked if success could be measured with one element, and he concluded that the pastor's main goal should be to disciple the church into Christlikeness. He defined functional Christlikeness in terms of three activities that characterized Jesus' life: "He prayed, He bore faithful witness of His Father's love, and He shepherded His Father's sheep."[75] In addition to that, Jesus challenged the social injustices of His day by His very life.

Jesus Himself called us to be godlike and mature disciples when He said, "Be perfect, therefore, as your heavenly Father is perfect" (Matt. 5:48). Our standard of success can never be based on one another or our own accomplishments. Our standard of measurement is Christ Jesus. Our success is determined by obedient faithfulness to Him and our progress toward Christlikeness. Christlikeness is the goal for the minister, as it is for all Christians. As both minister and congregation progress toward that goal they can be friends, not foes.

Being a good minister in a not-so-good-world means being an ethical minister who serves the congregation with effectiveness and integrity. The relationship they develop together determines whether the minister and the congregation view one another as friend or foe.

After looking at some of the ways the minister relates ethically to the congregation, we will next consider how the minister relates to colleagues; this will be the subject of the next chapter.

Suggested Reading

Bondi, Richard. *Leading God's People: Ethics for the Practice of Ministry.* Nashville: Abingdon, 1989.

Brister, C. W. *Pastoral Care in the Church.* 3d. ed., revised and expanded. San Francisco: Harper, 1992.

Carroll, Jackson W. *As One with Authority.* Louisville: Westminster/John Knox Press, 1991.

Dale, Robert D. *Ministers as Leaders.* Nashville: Broadman Press, 1984.

Harbin, J. William. *When a Search Committee Comes . . . or Doesn't.* Nashville: Broadman Press, 1985.

Ministerial Ethics

Hughes, Kent and Barbara. *Liberating Ministry from the Success Syndrome.* Wheaton, IL: Tyndale House Publishers, 1987.

Peterson, Eugene H. *Working the Angles: The Shape of Pastoral Integrity.* Grand Rapids: William B. Eerdmans Co., 1987.

Segler, Franklin M. *A Theology of Church and Ministry.* Nashville: Broadman Press, 1960.

Notes

[1]William F. May, "Images that Shape the Public Obligations of the Minister," *Clergy Ethics in a Changing Society,* James P. Wind, Russell Burck, Paul F. Camenisch, and Dennis P. McCann, eds. (Louisville: Westminster/John Knox Press, 1991), 79-80.

[2]Ibid., 80.

[3]Terri Lackey, "'CEO' pastors forget calling to be servants," *Baptist Standard* (18 March 1992), 12.

[4]May, 81.

[5]Ibid.

[6]Ibid.

[7]Leonard Griffith, *We Have This Ministry* (Waco: Word Books, 1973), 48.

[8]Ibid., 50-58.

[9]Franklin M. Segler, "Theological Foundations for Ministry," *Southwestern Journal of Theology* (Spring, 1978), 7.

[10]Herschel H. Hobbs, "The Role of the Pastor," *Baptist Standard* (July, 1988), 23.

[11]Ibid., 27.

[12]Segler, 5-6.

[13]Charles Bugg, "Professional Ethics Among Ministers," *Review and Expositor* (Fall, 1989), 565.

[14]Felix Montgomery, "Authority in Ministry: Meaning and Sources," *Church Administration* (June, 1990), 26.

[15]Samuel Southard, *Pastoral Authority in Personal Relationships* (Nashville: Abingdon 1969), 13-14.

[16]Ibid., 14.

[17]Ibid., 14-15.

[18]Bugg, 565.

[19]Ibid.

[20]Montgomery, 28.

[21]Ibid.

[22]Karen Lebacqz, *Professional Ethics: Power and Paradox* (Nashville: Abindgon, 1985), 113.

[23]John P. Kotter, *Power in Management* (New York: AMACOM, 1979), i.

[24]Wayne Oates, "The Marks of a Christian Leader," *Southwestern Journal of Theology* (Spring, 1987), 19.

[25]Richard Foster, *Money, Sex, and Power: The Challenge of the Disciplined Life* (San Francisco: Harper and Row, 1985).

[26]Marie M. Fortune, *Is Nothing Sacred? When Sex Invades the Pastoral Relationship* (San Francisco: Harper and Row, 1989), 102.

[27]Foster, 178.

[28]Ibid., 196.

[29]David C. Jacobsen, *The Positive Use of the Minister's Role* (Philadelphia: Westminster Press, 1967), 107.

[30]Richard M. Nixon, *Leaders* (New York: Warner Books, 1982), 4.

[31]Robert D. Dale, "Leadership-Followership: The Church's Challenge," *Southwestern Journal of Theology* (Spring, 1987), 23.

[32]Philip M. Van Auken and Sharon G. Johnson, "Balanced Christian Leadership," *The Baptist Program* (November, 1984), 13.

[33]Dale, 23.

[34]Raymond H. Bailey, "Ethics in Preaching," *Review and Expositor* (Fall, 1989), 533.

[35]Harry Emerson Fosdick, *The Living of These Days* (New York: Harper and Brothers, 1956), 7

[36]Glenn W. Mollette, "Doing Pastoral Care Through Preaching," *Proclaim* (April, May, June, 1987), 41.

[37]James Allen Reasons, *The Biblical Concept of Integrity and Professional Codes of Ethics in Ministerial Ethics*, unpublished Ph. D. dissertation, Southwestern Baptist Theological Seminary, Fort Worth, Texas, 1990, 154-55.

[38]Ibid., 157.

[39]J. Clark Hensley, *Preacher Behave!* (Jackson, MS: Christian Action Commission, 1978), 57-58.

[40]Nolan B. Harmon, *Ministerial Ethics and Etiquette* (Nashville: Abingdon, 1928; rev. 1987), 145.

[41]Darrell Turner, "Third Pastor Accused of 'Lifting' Another's Work," *Baptist Messenger* (August 24, 1989), 10.

[42]Ibid.

[43]Nicholas K. Geranios, "Pastor Confuses Flock," [Alexandria, LA] *Daily Town Talk* (January 8, 1992), A-3.

[44]Bailey, 536.

[45]Segler, 16.

[46]Walter E. Wiest and Elwyn A. Smith, *Ethics in Ministry* (Minneapolis: Fortress Press, 1990), 21.

[47]Gaylord Noyce, *Pastoral Ethics* (Nashville: Abingdon, 1988), 53.

[48]Segler, 18.

[49]Noyce, 34.

[50]Ernest White, "The Crisis in Christian Leadership," *Review and Expositor* (Fall, 1986), 546.

[51]Lee A. Davis and Ernest D. Standerfer, *Christian Stewardship in Action* (Nashville: Convention Press, 1983), 13.

[52]Noyce, 122.

[53]Ibid., 123-125.

[54]Wayne Oates, "Editor's Preface" in *An Introduction to Pastoral Counseling*, ed. Wayne Oates (Nashville: Broadman, 1959), vi.

[55]Wayne Oates, *The Christian Pastor* (Philadelphia: Westminster, 1964 rev. ed.), 181-84.

[56]Ibid., 184-219.

[57]Noyce, 92.

[58]Lynn R. Buzzard and Dan Hall, *Clergy Confidentiality* (Diamond Bar, CA: Christian Ministries Management Association, 1988), 4-5.

[59]Ibid., 25.

[60]Noyes, 99.

[61]Editors, "How Common is Pastoral Indiscretion?," *Leadership* (Winter, 1988), 13.

[62]Noyes, 103-104.

[63]These topics are outlined in Wayne Oates, *Premarital Pastoral Care and Counseling* (Nashville: Broadman Press, 1958), 22-34, an older but still helpful book on premarital pastoral care and counseling.

[64]Harmon, 149.

[65]James E. Carter, *Facing the Final Foe* (Nashville: Broadman, 1986), 30-33.

[66]Wiest and Smith, 42.

[67]Lyle Schaller, *The Pastor and the People* (Nashville: Abingdon, 1973), 32-44.

[68]Richard Bondi, *Leading God's People: Ethics for the Practice of Ministry* (Nashville: Abingdon Press, 1989), 102.

[69]Morton F. Rose, "Ministerial Success," *Search* (Fall, 1985), 18.

[70]"How do you spell success," *Context* (Nov. 15, 1991), 3-4.

[71]Kent and Barbara Hughes, *Liberating Ministry from the Success Syndrome* (Wheaton, IL: Tyndale House Publishers, 1987), 106.

[72]Ibid., 106-7.
[73]Robert Raines, *Success Is a Moving Target* (Waco: Word Books, 1975), 15.
[74]Bondi, 107.
[75]Jay Gallimore, "Measuring the Pastor's Success," *Ministry* (May, 1990), 12-14.

5

THE MINISTER'S COLLEAGUES:

Cooperation or Competition?

John Donne, a minister and poet, once wrote: "No man is an island entire of itself; every man is a piece of the continent, a part of the main."[1] While Donne was actually referring to the fact that each person's death diminishes each one of us, he also enunciated a principle for ministry: no one of us performs ministry entirely alone. Each one ministers in collegiality with others. How do we view the others with whom we minister? Are the ministers colleagues who compete to achieve a spiritual goal, or are they competitors who try to outdo one another?

Could ministers actually compete with one another? Consider these scenarios.

John Jones has just been called as pastor of Mt. Pisgah Church. He has particular expectations of what he will accomplish during his ministry in that church. He will lead the church to new heights in church growth; he will lead in building the fellowship hall that some of the people on the Pastor Search Committee assured him the church wanted; he will develop a stewardship program that will involve all the church members and set new giving records for the church. John Jones, however, did not reckon on Uncle Jack. Uncle Jack is a long-time member of the church. He is a deacon and chairman of the Finance Committee, but other than that he holds no official position in the church. Uncle Jack, however, has functioned in Mt. Pisgah Church for years as a subterranean pastor or permission-giver in the church. No matter whose name is on the church sign as pastor, Uncle Jack is actually the one who gives permission for church programs to be adopted or, once adopted, to be followed to completion. He does not mind church growth; he just does not want all those new people in the church. Rather than build a new fellowship hall, he would prefer to increase the cash reserves of the church by swelling the certificates of deposit owned by Mt. Pisgah Church in the local bank. As far as giving to the church goes, he determined years ago the amount of money he would give each year, and it has never varied. Considering the expectations with which John Jones came to the pastorate of Mt. Pisgah Church, does the minister have competition in this church?

Mary Jacobs was a staff addition to First Church as minister to single adults. That responsibility had previously been covered by Joe Smith who had the staff position of minister to students including ministry to youth, university students, and single adults. Since he was a single adult, he felt as though he had been cut off from his own group by the addition of Mary Jacobs to the staff. In conversation with other single adults, he often sharply questioned Mary's approaches to ministry. In staff meetings, he would play the devil's advocate—often with an edge to it—on any issue involving Mary. When he and the pastor talked together, Joe would inquire about Mary's loyalty to the pastor. At the times when he treated the church business administrator to lunch, he would ask how Mary Jacobs handled the financial accounts for which she was responsible in her ministry. Joe Smith would also muse that since Mary Jacobs was female she might not have much background for keeping up with her accounts and could easily become overdrawn. On the staff of First Church, was Joe Smith a cooperating colleague or a competitor with Mary Jacobs?

At the denomination's monthly pastor's conference, Rev. Fred Friendly always let it be known that his church had gained many new members the past month. Dr. Sam Cureton, a fellow pastor, often observed Reverend Friendly—whom he privately called Friendly Fred—and his braggadocio, his manner with the parishioners of other churches, and his desire to be known as the most aggressive advocate of outreach in the area. Dr. Cureton computed that if all the persons Friendly claimed had joined his church and had maintained membership there, that church would now have two hundred more people in worship each Sunday than the statistics indicated. Cureton also observed a steady drain of persons moving from other neighboring churches to the church served by Reverend Friendly. Most of the other pastors were convinced that Fred Friendly was a renowned "sheep stealer." Was Fred Friendly in cooperation or in competition with the other pastors of his denomination in his area?

Jesse DeWitt insisted on injecting his denominational distinctives into every discussion in the General Minister's Association of Casual County. At times, he questioned the degree of Christian faith and even the salvation of the pastors in other denominations. The church served by Jesse DeWitt never participated in the community services, such as a community Thanksgiving service, a community hymn sing, or a community prayer effort for peace during Desert Storm. Would the other churches in the community consider him a cooperating colleague or a competitor?

Every minister serves with other ministers. We are indeed "a part of the main." We relate to one another, either cooperatively or in competition. We work together, either willingly or grudgingly, either with one another or against one another.

Ministers are accountable to God for their personal lives and ministry. They are also accountable to other ministers. Accountability applies to the profession of ministry as a whole. What one minister does can impact the ministry of many others even though they may not serve in the same denomination. Ministerial accountability to one another and to the ministerial profession as well as to God is vital to the total ministry and to the work of the Kingdom of God.

The relationship to your peers is an ethical concern. Many codes of ethics among professionals make peer relationships a primary concern. Being a good minister in a not-so-good world involves your colleagues. Will you relate to your colleagues in cooperation or in competition?

Local Church Leaders

The Foundational Relationship of Trust

Obviously, relationships between ministers and local church leaders are crucial. Trust is essential for these relationships to survive and for ministers to cooperate with the leadership of the church rather than compete with them. The changes that must be made in a church can be made because the people trust the pastor to lead them properly. They trust the leader to be sensitive to the Holy Spirit's leadership, to be concerned about their spiritual welfare rather than his ministerial reputation, and to be a trustworthy person of integrity.

Church work is different from any other kind of work. In a church, the members are not only the "clients" or "customers," they are also colleagues. The clergy minister to church members, but they also work with them. In a single staff church, where the pastor is the only staff person, many church officers actually function as a church staff would function. These members become the colleagues with the minister. In churches of all sizes, the members form the committees, teach Sunday School, and perform the work of the church between Sundays as well as on Sundays. In these ways, church members are colleagues as well as clients.

How important is trust? The Book of Ruth is the beautiful story of Ruth the Moabitess who followed her mother-in-law Naomi home to Israel. As she pledged her love to Naomi, Ruth said that Naomi's people would be her people, Naomi's home would be her home, and Naomi's God would be her God (Ruth 1:16). Ruth believed in Naomi's God because she had first believed in Naomi. People will believe in the minister's program or project or preaching because they have first believed in him.

When Trust Is Broken

Forced termination is every minister's nightmare. The event may come in the form of a group from the church, a committee of deacons, or members of the board, who say, "Pastor, we feel that your effectiveness in this church is over. We think you ought to resign." Or the nightmare may take the shape of a stormy church business meeting when the crowd has been swelled by calls and contacts from each side, some supporting the minister and others calling for dismissal. In churches with a congregational form of church government, the incident may occur by someone standing up at some business meeting night and saying, "I move that we declare the pulpit vacant."

Just what is forced termination? The Church Administration Department of The Sunday School Board of the Southern Baptist Convention uses the working definition that forced termination is "the severing of the formal relationship between the minister and the church either by coercion or by vote."[2]

In 1984, the Research Department of the Sunday School Board made a study of forced termination. At that time, eighty-eight ministers were being fired each month. The two primary causes cited were the disunity of the congregation and the interpersonal skills of the pastor. The pastors claimed that they were terminated by a small powerful minority who controlled the decision-making process of the church. The churches insisted that the pastor could not get along with church members, especially church leaders.

In 1988, another study was released which showed an alarming increase in forced terminations. Within four years, forced terminations among Southern Baptist ministers had increased from an average of eighty-eight a month to one hundred sixteen per month. A different set of causes emerged. The leading cause was the lack of communication between the minister and the church leaders. The second leading cause was immorality.[3]

Norris Smith, a consultant in the Church Administration Department of the Sunday School Board who is an authority on the subject of forced termination, observed: "Research . . . seems to declare that forced termination is no respecter of place. No area seemed to be more susceptible to terminations than any other."[4]

From these two studies the importance of the relationship between the minister and the church members who are quasi-colleagues is evident. Everyone suffers when a forced termination occurs. The fellowship of the church is fractured. Individuals in the church experience a wide range of emotions. The church assumes a defensive posture rather than an aggressive pursuit of its mission. The reputation of the church is sullied in the community. The minister's feeling of self-worth is deeply affected. The minister's wife is shaken by insecurity, and the minister's children are badly hurt. "[Forced termination] leaves the minister's family and the congregation devastated. Everyone loses something. No one really wins."[5]

Baptists are not the only ones who are subject to forced terminations. Because of their congregational form of church government and the autonomy of the local church, Baptists can force the termination of a minister more easily than some other churches. Many denominations have procedures that must be followed when a minister is terminated. All ministers, however, face the possibility of the breakdown of relationships and the sundering of the bond between the minister and the church.

A number of ethical issues are grouped around the forced termination of ministers. The issues include:

- the minister's personal integrity,
- the acceptance of the worth of the individual as reflected in the way persons are treated,
- the responsibility to develop pastoral skills and competence in ministry.

One minister who had experienced forced termination indicated that ethics, the sense of right and wrong and the exercise thereof, play a primary role in forced terminations. He presented biblical guidelines and principles that relate to forced termination:

- showing the reverence for the minister and the church demanded by the Bible,
- practicing loving forthrightness and communication in relationships,
- understanding the issues before undertaking any course of action,
- practicing *agape*,
- resisting using the secular legal system to settle disputes in the church.[6]

Avoiding Forced Termination

The good minister in a not-so-good world is not concerned simply with avoiding forced termination. That is a negative approach to life

134

Ministerial Ethics

and ministry. The positive approach is to develop the ministry skills to the degree that the minister is so competent and effective that forced termination never becomes an issue.

Ministerial competence involves developing the pastoral skills necessary to minister effectively. In the previous discussion on professionalism, the professional was defined as one having particular skills for specific responsibilities. Ministerial competence is developed through the educational process, through continuing education, through reading, and through on-the-job training. Many of the necessary ministerial skills cannot be taught. They are acquired by doing. Learning to preach, for instance, is done by preaching. You can learn the theory and study the methods, but you never really learn to preach until you actually preach. Developing pastoral skills is a lifelong process. No one ever finally arrives at total perfection in every area. Ministers are ethically obligated to continue to develop the skills in ministry as long as they minister to others in God's name.

Ministerial competence also involves developing personal skills. The need for developing interpersonal skills is evident from the studies previously cited. Speed Leas of the Alban Institute, a recognized authority on church conflicts and conflict management, conducted a study which showed that minister's lack of interpersonal skills caused 46 percent of involuntary terminations.[7] In ministry, a great deal rides on interpersonal relationships.

Knowing and agreeing on the expectations helps clergy and avoids forced termination. Edward B. Bratcher argued that incompetence in ministry is unnecessary. Stressing the involvement of both clergy and laity, he wrote: "Both must have a sense of direction for the church and its ministry. Both must be prepared to set goals, to seek to achieve them, and to be open to negotiation when differences arise."[8] The Southern Baptist Theological Seminary and the Lily Foundation conducted a study on "Quality in Southern Baptist Pastoral Ministry." One of the discoveries was that some differences exist in what was emphasized as quality between those who lead the churches and those who are in the pew. "This research would point to the need for greater sensitivity to the expectations of laity, if ministers are to function with greater effectiveness in the future."[9]

Both ministers and church leaders should be open and honest with one another. If lack of communication is a major cause of forced termination, the practice of clear, open, and honest communication would be a major factor in avoiding forced termination. While "communication" is often a buzz word, it is also of significant importance in a church setting.

In churches, communication occurs on two levels: the formal level and the informal. The formal level of communication involves those ways in which someone intentionally and consciously attempts to communicate materials and matters to the church folks. These include such things as:

- public announcements,
- posters,
- signs,
- church papers,
- bulletins,
- advertisements.

The informal means of communication involve:

- telephone conversations,
- hall discussions,
- coffee break snippets,
- discussions between friends,
- the little groups that gather on the parking lot.

Which level of communication is more effective? Probably the informal. Many formal messages are stopped before they ever get out. Clear communication is essential. One characteristic of churches in conflict is that information is hoarded and decisions are made by a few.[10]

Becoming a healthy minister helps in avoiding forced termination. Healthy wholeness as a person and a parson is a goal for all ministers. Brooks Faulkner has stated "Being a healthy minister will not prevent forced termination. The reason is simple: Not all churches are healthy, and some churches that have the potential of being healthy have unhealthy and/or unsteady influences." Faulkner indicated that being a healthy minister was essential for self-preservation, effectiveness, personal growth, and dealing with the possibility of forced termination. Both physical and spiritual health are necessary.[11] From Titus 3:15 Faulkner derived characteristics of a healthy minister. Healthy ministers:

- respect authority,
- are ready for every good deed,
- malign no one,
- are not contentious,
- are gentle,
- are kind.[12]

Based on several lines of research, Faulkner, the church administration authority, summarized good health in a minister by asserting that healthy ministers:

- grow,
- have a place for retreat,
- have a sense of humor,
- can live with not knowing,
- are not preoccupied with suspicion and resentment,
- have learned the art of forgiveness.[13]

Bratcher contends that "ministers are not miracle-workers—they cannot walk on water; but they can learn to swim."[14]

Church Staff

Much of ministry is performed in multistaff churches. Some churches have a ministerial staff comprised of a number of ministers who function in specialized ministries. Even single staff churches have volunteer church staff persons. How do the various ministers who comprise the staff of a particular church relate to one another? Are they colleagues or competitors? "Attitude toward and treatment of one's fellow staff workers are indicators of one's theology. The practice of ministry is intrinsically involved in one's understanding of theological truth. Relationships . . . with fellow staff members become theological action."[15] Relationships with fellow staff members also become ethical actions.

An incident from the Hebrews' exodus experience related in Exodus 18:13-23 gives a biblical model for how church staff people are called to serve together. After the Hebrews crossed the Red Sea and were camped near Mount Sinai, Jethro, Moses' father-in-law, came to visit him. Observing how Moses was both leader and judge of the people and noting the personal toll this took on him, Jethro made a suggestion. Jethro counseled Moses that he should select persons from among the people who would serve as judges over groups numbering one thousand, one hundred, fifty, and ten. These persons would decide over the minor disputes. Moses would teach the people and make decisions over major matters that were referred to him by the others. Notice what this biblical story teaches us about staff relation ships and serving the Lord together.

Called

The people who served with Moses were called from among the congregation. All ministers, whatever their function in ministry, have been called by God from among the congregation. This is one distinctive that is shared by all—all have been called from among the people of God to serve God.

Both Romans 12 and 1 Corinthians 12 indicate that Christians are gifted in different ways. All gifts are gifts of the Holy Spirit. And all gifts are to be used for the building up of the church. Responsibilities may vary and functions may differ, but each minister on a church staff is a real minister, and each ministry is a valid ministry. "What these other ministers do is just as surely ministry as that which a pastor might do. Ministry is ministry because of what is done rather than by whom it is done."[16]

Generally speaking, the staff ministers are called by the church and not by the senior minister. Charles A. Tidwell suggested, "Let all of a church's ministers be called by church action, not just employed by an individual or committee acting independently or alone. If the church requires evidence of a call of God to qualify one of its ministers, then it seems wise to have the church endorse the minister's call by church action."[17]

The practice of "cleaning out" a staff when the senior minister moves to another church or retires fails to recognize that each person on the church staff was at some time presented to that church as the person whom God had called to that position. Did the call of God to the senior minister to another position or to retirement rescind the call of God to the other staff ministers to that place of service? Allowing a senior minister to choose his own staff may result in more efficiency and a closer initial relationship between staff members, but it does not give sufficient recognition to the call of all staff persons to that church to serve. Neither does it allow time or effort for the staff and senior minister to learn to work together. That practice creates a sense of "my staff" on the part of the senior minister rather than "our staff ministers" on the part of the church.

Collegiality

Collegiality is a second concept gleaned from Moses' experience. The ministers serve God together. They serve as colleagues in the Lord's service. One pastor commented, "Each minister understands that his or her ministry is significant as a part of the team, but, due to the variety in talents, experience, and training, responsibility may not always be totally equal."[18] The pastor also said that the senior minister is the key to creating a climate of cooperation, trust, support, communication, mutual love, and understanding.

The idea of a ministering team comes from the concept of collegiality. A pastor who used the team ministry approach in one church for nearly two decades found the scriptural basis for that approach in 1 Corinthians 3:9 (GNB): "We are partners working together for God." Two matters particularly in this verse demonstrate a team ministry.

First," work for God." All the members of the church work for God in ministry as do the staff ministers. The second matter leads directly from that concept: "We are partners working *together.*" This pastor observed, "If one feels jealous when a colleague experiences success or achieves recognition, the problem is not likely with the colleague. The solution is not in the suppression of a colleague's individuality, but in one's becoming more secure in one's own ministries under God."[19]

Understanding staff ministry as collegiality in ministry fits in well with Jesus' teachings about servanthood. Collegiality in ministry follows a team model rather than an hierarchial model for organization. It also follows a servant model for expression. Jesus challenged the leadership of His day when He taught His followers that the mark of effective leadership was not lording it over others, but serving others (Mark 10:42-45). His servants rule only by serving. Another pastor stated:

> The ministers on a church staff can provide the congregation with a model of servant ministry through their relationships with each other and by their performances of their responsibilities. . . . If church members see staff workers who are constantly putting each other down, circumventing each other for a place of greater recognition in the church, and unable to relate well with their fellow ministers, they will have great difficulty in understanding what it means to be servants in Christ's name. . . . The servant image provides a model which is patterned after our Lord's own ministry. When the staff is committed to this kind of ministry, they can serve as a catalyst for the whole congregation.[20]

Characteristics

A description of the characteristics expected of a minister comes from the Exodus passage referred to earlier (Ex. 8:13-23). The description of the kind of persons chosen to aid Moses in his ministry in verse 21 describes the basic characteristics of a minister. Notice these four traits.

The first characteristic is *capability.* The person who serves in any ministering task must be capable of doing the job. Capability comes through (1) God-given spiritual gifts, (2) the natural gifts the person possesses, and (3) the acquired skills the individual gains through education and experience. Persons are not called to church staff positions just because they are nice, but because they have the capability of performing that specified ministerial task.

The second characteristic is *commitment.* These leaders were described as those "who fear God." Christian commitment is expected of each staff minister, not just the pastor or senior minister. The

Christian minister is committed to Christ, to the church, and to the kingdom of God. "The minister's calling is linked to a vision of the kingdom that so dominates one's life that all other concerns become peripheral."[21]

Competence is a third characteristic of the minister. The Exodus account called for "trustworthy" leaders. Trustworthy people are worthy of trust. They are competent to the task to which God and the church have called them. Competence is an ethical imperative for each person ministering with a church staff.

Each position on a church staff should have a description that outlines the major responsibilities of the position as well as the accountabilities for that position. The description will present the expectations for the performance of that job, and it will determine the competence of the individual for that position. The major goal is doing the Lord's work through the church. Being so tied to one's position description that a minister will never attempt anything else is detrimental to good staff relationships. Each person at times will be called on to perform ministries that may not be specifically covered by the position description. Those tasks should be cheerfully and competently executed.

The fourth characteristic mentioned to Moses was *character*, a more general term. Jethro described persons with character as those "who hate a bribe." That is a negative expression. The more positive expression would be "persons of character." A retired professor of Christian ethics noted that the most frequently mentioned essential of the minister in the Lyman Beecher Lectures at Yale is character. This may be true, he continued, because people are more impressed by a preacher's life than by sermons. They hear the person more than the sermon. "Ministers of good character incarnate into their lives the spirit of Christ."[22]

These four characteristics apply to all persons who minister in the name of the Lord Jesus Christ. It is not a matter of some more visible ministers possessing these characteristics and other ministers' being immune to them. Whatever an individual's function on a church staff, the positive characteristics of a minister are necessary.

Consequences

Do ethical staff relationships make a difference in a church? Look back again to the account in the Book of Exodus. Two consequences occur.

One consequence relates to the minister as a person himself. Jethro told Moses, "You will be able to stand the strain" (Ex. 18:23). Ethical and fulfilling relationships on a church staff enable the staff to work more effectively. Creating a climate where each staff person can do his or her best work is a responsibility of the staff leader, usually the pastor or senior minister. Removing some of the stress from the ministry and challenging the minister to the highest standards of work can accomplish this.

A study conducted by the Research Services Department of the Baptist Sunday School Board in 1977 reported that most staff members feel accepted, affirmed, and appreciated by each other. "Staff members feel personally accepted (94.7%), loved and cared for (93.2%) by other staff members all or most of the time. They also feel their opinions are important to other staff members all or most of the time (90.3%)."[23] This kind of ethical relationship between staff members enables them to "stand the strain" as they minister together.

The second consequence of ethical staff relationships relates to the church. Jethro expressed it to Moses by saying, "All these people will go home satisfied" (v. 23). That kind of ethical relationship helps perform the ministry, meet the needs of the people, exemplifies the servant model of ministry, and satisfies and contents the congregation rather than dissatisfy and discontent them.

A pastor turned professor shared some "rules of the road" related to ethical staff relationships.

- Respect each other as persons and ministers;
- Give each other the gift of attention;
- Recognize that every staff has problems and see these as opportunities for growth and not division;
- Handle conflict fairly;
- Have some time when the staff can get away from the pressures of the church and get to know each other as persons;
- As church staffs we need to remember that we model relationships for the rest of the church.[24]

Following these "rules of the road" would enable a church staff to serve God together as colleagues rather than as competitors, enabling those ministers to be good ministers in a not-so-good world. The church would benefit greatly from it; and the ministry would be exalted rather than debased by their effective ministry together. The main concern is getting the work of the church done without worrying about who gets the credit. Working as a team with a spirit of collegiality accomplishes that goal.

Other Ministers

Few ministries begin with the person currently serving in that ministry. We all have both predecessors and successors. We all serve in the same area with other ministers of our own as well as other denominations. How do we relate to these other ministers?

The Predecessor

Consider, first, your relationship with your predecessor. Often, departed ministers, like deceased husbands, assume sainthood. The incoming pastor hears nothing but good reports of the excellent work of the former pastor. After awhile, he may wonder if the predecessor ever did anything wrong. One of us followed pastors with long tenures in two successive pastorates. After hearing nothing but glowing reports of all the preceding minister had accomplished, a civic club meeting brought humorous relief. One of the members told a story about the former pastor running out of gas on a bridge in the middle of town. While others at the table laughed at the minister's embarrassing situation, the response of the newer, younger minister to the story was, "I'm just glad to know that he ever ran out of gas." Memories are selective. The former minister's failures, disappointments, and discouragements were probably at about the same rate as the current minister's; but they were not so fresh in other people's memories.

Generally speaking, the incoming minister does not need to fear those who speak well of the predecessor. Those who loved, appreciated, respected, and supported the former minister will likely do the same with the new minister. The church member of whom the minister should be wary is the one who speaks ill of the previous minister. Those who criticize, find fault with, and express disappointment in the former minister will probably react to the new minister in a similar way over time.

We all build on the foundation that others have laid. We are the recipients of the ministry of our predecessors. In 1894, Bishop Charles Galloway of the Methodist Episcopal Church spoke to a conference at Boston University on "ministerial ethics." In that address Galloway said:

> Much of our work is to reap where others have sown. Their sowing should have equal honor with our reaping. A circuit, station, or district may be served full term without the earnest pastor's noting much fruit of his labor. Another comes whose mission is to gather golden sheaves and whose joy it is to sing a harvest song. Though possibly much honored, credited with being a more successful workman, he really enjoys the fruit of another's planting. . . . He that planteth and he that watereth are one.[25]

Honor and respect the minister who preceded you. After all, you have more in common with that minister than with most other ministers. You never exalt yourself by debasing someone else. You do not look good, nor act ethically, when you criticize or question the character of the those who preceded you. Encourage the church members to love and respect your predecessors. Their ministry impacted the lives of those church members.

Invite former ministers back for special occasions in the church. Perhaps a building is completed that a former minister helped to plan or led in the acquisition of the property on which it is located. Invite the former minister to deliver the dedicatory message when the building is dedicated. Another option is to invite the former minister to speak at a banquet or to lead in a series of special services. If you never involve former ministers in the life or affairs of your church, it only reveals your insecurities by failing to recognize his contributions.

Keep former church leaders informed of events in the life of the church. The church newsletter lists the major events in church life, but never tells the whole story. Significant events also occur in the lives of church members that do not appear in the newsletter. A letter or a telephone call to reveal those occurrences will mean a lot to the person who invested a portion of their lives with those people.

One of us was the pastor of a church when several teenage girls were injured by being struck by a car when crossing a street. One girl was reported brain dead, but six years later when this girl walked across the stage to a standing ovation to receive her high school diploma, her former pastor greatly appreciated a telephone call telling of the girl's graduation and describing the joyous event.

Events in the life of the family of the former minister could be shared with the church. These were the people who taught the minister's children in Sunday School, who watched them advance through school, who attended their weddings, and cheered their achievements. Their interest in the minister's family continues. Informing them of the major events in that family's life—marriages, graduations, births—honors them through the years. Continued interest in the family of the former minister will not diminish their love or interest in the present minister's family.

The Successor

What about when you are the predecessor? What is your relationship to your successor?

In a book on ministerial ethics and etiquette first published in 1928, Nolan B. Harmon's comments still ring true:

> Above all, when a man leaves a charge, let him leave it. No minister should be constantly going back to gossip with the brethren or hear

comments on the work of his successor. Great harm has been done in this way by some ministers. The outgoing pastor should get all his supplies, trunks, boxes, barrels, the piano, the bread box, the garden hose and Willie's shotgun—everything loaded at one time, should give a good-by, making it as tearful as desired, but having started the moving van, don't look back! . . . "Get out and stay out" is the injunction here.[26]

Obviously, a minister will leave behind friends. Interest in them and concern for them will continue. However, the work of that church is now in the hands of another. The other person should be given the freedom to conduct that ministry without the interference of a predecessor.

Invitations will likely come to go back to the former place of service for funerals and weddings. The common wisdom among ministers is not to accept those invitations or, if accepting them, to accept them judiciously. The problem is whether some people are offended when others have been affirmed. Charles B. Bugg asked a significant question, "Whose needs are being met, the minister's or the church's?"[27]

The current minister needs to get to know the people, to form close relationships with them, and to become a part of their lives. The best way to do this is through sharing the major milestones of life with them. For the former minister to continue those functions cheats the current minister out of developing those relationships. That is how the former minister grew so close to the people in the first place and the present pastor needs those same opportunities. Pastoral relationships are deeply personal. Each pastor should have unrestrained access to allow those relationships to form through the giving of ministry to persons.

At the very least, when returning to a former place of service for a wedding or a funeral, have the invitation come through the present minister. When possible the present pastor should have the primary role and the former pastor should serve as assistant.

Leadership journal formed a panel of Christian leaders to discuss eight ethical choices among ministers. The question was introduced with these words, "Courtesy of one's predecessor and successor in a pastorate extends beyond matters of backbiting or malpractice." Then this question was asked: "When can a pastor return to a prior pastorate to preach or perform weddings, funerals, or baptisms/dedications?" Three members of the panel answered "never." Six thought it permissible upon the invitation or permission by the successor. Two panel members felt good about returning at any time, saying that they were not engaged in some kind of competition. One minister explained, "If the present pastor has difficulty with my returning, then it's his problem. He doesn't have to 'establish himself'; the Lord establishes a pastor."[28]

A Yale Divinity School professor of pastoral theology passed on a list of negative influences on a congregation by former clergy compiled by the Alban Institute:

- Contacts between a former minister and church members cause whatever negative emotions were present at the pastor's departure to continue to surface. [These emotions may be regret, guilt, anger, frustration, or relief.]
- Continued contacts deny members the opportunity to work through those emotions of grief directly and constructively and the contacts encourage their futile grappling with ghosts.
- Contacts discourage members' working through their feelings within the community ("I'd better not tell my deacon that I called the old pastor") and encourage a rivalry among members ("The pastor called *me*!").
- Private contacts with individuals deprive the community of the opportunity to share grief and loneliness, to build the strength that comes from shared suffering, to discover resurrection hope that emerges from shared struggles.
- Contacts with former ministers focus member energy outside the congregation at a time when that energy may be needed most within the community.
- Private communications encourage "holding on" to the past and fighting former battles—but this time with the invisible contenders; they decrease a person's ability to struggle with present realities and diminish hope for the future.
- Contacts confuse persons as to where and how to direct their commitment to new leadership; they make that difficult task even more difficult for members.
- Each contact places the resident pastor in the awkward position of interloper. Interim specialists are trained to deal with negativism so that the installed pastor can begin positive building at the earliest opportunity.
- By surfacing implicit comparisons between new and old, contacts between the former minister and church members undermine the choice of a new pastor and inhibit a wholehearted commitment to the new relationship.
- Contacts keep the new pastor on the defensive and subvert that pastor's morale and effectiveness. The new pastor can never successfully compete with the old pastor's "ghost" as long as that ghost is actively present.[29]

Retired Ministers

Another group of clergy with which a minister deals are retired ministers. Sometimes, they may be ministers who have retired from the very church served by the minister, continuing to live in that community. "One can think of pitiful situations in which the retiring minister's own sense of human worth and identify hinges heavily on the pastoral status. If that minister stays on in a neighborhood near enough to be accessible to or active in the last congregation, the pressures flood in, coming from parishioners and the retired pastor alike."[30]

One obvious matter for retired ministers to face is to secure their self worth in their own selfhood rather than in their ministry. Some ministers find it difficult to separate themselves from their ministry. The sense of personal identity should be strong enough by the time of retirement to enable one to function as a person when no longer able to function as a minister.

Active ministers should remember that retired ministers no longer have a church to love and to return love. Ministers have the ongoing contact with people from which they draw strength. The current minister needs to be sensitive to the needs and feelings of the retired minister. A sensitive, caring relationship between the two of them can bring satisfaction to both. [31]

Retired ministers should be recognized, appreciated, and allowed to be a full and contributing part of their church. Some churches bestow a title like "Pastor Emeritus" on these ministers, perhaps providing a small stipend, and an office space. Retired ministers can assist in funerals and weddings on occasion. New pastors who sponsor these programs show that they are not threatened by the presence of retired ministers. The counsel older, experienced ministers give to a younger, inexperienced minister is helpful. In times of congregational crisis their insight and active help is invaluable. That person becomes a source for pulpit supply preaching or the work of an interim pastor in other churches. Above all, no effort should be made to discredit the retired minister or to wean the congregation away from the retiree.

> If they have much love for him, be assured that they have enough to go around and their hearts can be stretched to love you, too. Just thank God that he taught them to love their pastor or enabled them by being loving to thus love you, their present pastor. An unloving attitude by the new pastor toward the retired pastor can hinder the congregation from loving the new one.[32]

All ministers deal with other ministers in a variety of relationships. Ministry is much better served and the Christian faith is advanced when ministers view themselves as colleagues rather than as competitors.

Other Churches

Some of the other clergy with whom a minister relates are ministers in churches of other denominations. Even though it is not always admitted, the other ministers in a community are the people with whom the minister has the most in common. The relationship between ministers of other denominations, however, is not always exemplary.

In earlier times denominational distinctives were emphasized more than at the present. Denominational loyalty is now shrinking. When people seek a church home, they now look for a church which meets their personal and family needs rather than a church of their denominational family. Because of particular emphases in church life—charismatic experiences, for instance, or a celebrative style of worship—more might be found in common between churches of other denominations than in churches of the same denomination. Many strong churches have no denominational ties. Since the churches no longer hold Saturday afternoon debates on the courthouse square defending their positions and deriding others' positions, what is the relationship between ministers of differing denominations? Noyce affirmed, "We are called on to encourage and affirm, not denigrate, the work of other pastors."[33]

Proselytism, or sheep stealing, is no more acceptable between denominations than between churches of the same denomination. In calling on new families in a community, on learning that the newcomers are of a denomination other than one's own, the least that a parson can do is to inform them of the churches of their denominational family.

A general practice is to let the person or the family of another denomination make the first move toward joining another church. While ethical ministers would hardly go out looking for people of other churches to enlist for membership in their church, they will often be contacted by people who want to switch denominations. Answer the questions about your church family honestly. Point out differences, but do not use that as an occasion to be derisive about other people's beliefs. Most ministers feel comfortable in talking with the families only after they have made the initial approach.

When a person from another denomination unites with a church, the pastor or the church should inform the other church of that person's decision. Letters of recommendation or letters of dismissal or certificates of transfer are often exchanged between churches of the same denomination, but not between churches of other denominations. A simple note to the other church informing them of the individual's decision would be courteous, and it would allow them to adjust their records.

Ministers within a community should know one another personally. They will have church members who are related to one another. They will work together on projects of community interest. In hospitals they will bump into one another. The better they know one another personally, the better they can serve together. This is often achieved through a general minister's association in the community formed by the ministers in all of the churches regardless of denomination. Another avenue is an interdenominational study group, support group, or fellowship group, in which ministers of various denominations share their commonalities, their community interest, and their fellowship.

The pastor who is already present in a community should visit the incoming pastor of a neighboring church, no matter what the denomination. If a reception or a welcoming party is held to introduce the minister to the community, other ministers should attend. Not only would they meet one another, this would also show mutual support to the community.

Who ministers to the minister in time of need? Ministers can respond to the spiritual needs of other ministers without regard to denomination when they are hospitalized, when they have personal tragedies or family traumas, or when they have been recognized through a personal achievement.

Ecumenism is often looked for in the wrong places. Many denominational groups or independent churches have opted not to become a part of organized national or international ecumenical movements. Yet on the local scene, churches of these denominations often work well with other churches to relieve human hurts and to advance the cause of Christ. Shelters for the homeless, food for the hungry, clothes for the needy, and aid for transients are often provided in a community through the efforts of churches of several denominations working together. Moral concerns such as gambling, abortion, the sale of alcoholic beverages to minors, the abuse of drugs, or detrimental business practices have been addressed through the cooperation of churches of many denominations.

The contemporary minister always lives with the tension between being priest and prophet. When the prophetic prevails, the minister often needs the support of other prophets to make an impact on the community. At times, the community must be called into account for its actions and be reminded of the Christian values. Hear Ernest Campbell, former pastor of the Riverside Church, New York City:

> I have held to the view that a preacher, to be prophetic, must live out of phase with his times. Our prototypes in Israel and Judah seemed impossible to please. When the nation was consumed with delight over its accomplishments the prophets predicted disaster and called for repentance. Conversely, when the spirit of the nation was low (as in the Babylonian Captivity) the prophets came through with words of hope and the promise of a better day.
>
> The time has come for ministers in this country to counter the despair that has gripped the nation. To live out of phase in these days is to point to a better way. As in recent years we warned about American pride and pointed out the injustices that mock our public rhetoric, so now the hour has come to lift this people up.
>
> It is when we are weak that we can be strong. It is when the false gods fail that the God of grace and glory has a chance. It is when old balances of power shift and leave us vulnerable that the power of the Spirit can give us the vision of a world at peace. It is when we have spent and spent for that which cannot satisfy that the bread of life, proclaimed in love, can nourish a weary people back to health.
>
> To believe in God is to believe that in every situation, personal and collective, there is an alternative to despair. We may be dead, but God isn't. Our sins may have done us in but there is a grace greater than our sin.[34]

To live "out of phase with his times" is a part of the prophetic presence of the preacher. Richard Bondi argued for the personal presence of the minister when he said there is "no substitute for the personal presence." He went on to claim, "The leader must remain on the edge in order to lead. . . . But the leader must also have an active presence with the community in order to claim solidarity with it."[35] Remaining on the edge, living out of phase with the times, while living in solidarity with the community, are challenges to the minister. As a moral leader the minister must speak prophetically but also must work redemptively as a priest. Ministers who work with other ministers on moral issues help the Christian faith to address the contemporary world with a more united front.

A wholesome, healthy relationship with ministers of other denominations is desirable. Life is enriched and ministry is expanded when a minister knows, respects, and appreciates ministers of other faith groups. While denominational distinctives are not compromised, nor all the methods of others approved, the person can be affirmed, appreciated, and counted as an ally on many issues. Harmon concluded, "When a person is found to be genuine, whatever the methods, others neither fear nor are jealous; they rejoice to have another worker for Christ in their community."[36]

The Minister's Colleagues
Other Professionals

A Professional Among Professionals

Chapter 1 revealed that the minister functions as a professional among professionals. Many ministers carry a certain ambivalence about the concept of the ministry as a profession. One writer found this ambivalence centered in the minister's search for a vocational role:

> The concept of the professional is not that of a person who acts out an image for the public twenty-four hours a day. A minister can retain his integrity and proper self-identity at the same time that he carries his role with professional concern for the good of those to whom he ministers. There is no reason for him to feel guilty for carrying himself with professional competence.[37]

Ministers should be professionals without being mere professionals. They should always be competent in practicing their ministry, exemplary in their personal conduct, capable of meeting the demands placed upon them, and responsive to calls for ministry. *Professional* should never mean a cold, calculating, uncaring person.

"Each of the classic professions—medicine, law, and the church—carries an implicit profession of faith. The very word 'profession' has significance because it implies a profession of faith in some person or concept."[38] The medical person has placed faith in the healing arts, the lawyer has faith in the system of law that operates in the state, and the minister has faith in God as a Christian and in the visible church as clergy.[39] Or, as Karen Lebacqz put it, "A professional is called not simply to *do* something but to *be* something. A professional 'professes.'"[40] Professionalism involves both being and doing, what a person is and what that person does. Ministers profess faith in God through Jesus Christ whom they serve through the church. If ministers act in a manner that is unbecoming to a minister, they are said to have behaved unprofessionally.

The concept of ministry as a profession is both freedom-producing and anxiety-producing. By being involved in a vocation that calls for loyalty to a visible body of believers, the minister has a specific, defined task. Knowing what the job is and what is expected in terms of competence, capability, and character can be freedom-producing. There are times when a person's understanding of God's will and love conflicts with the good of the institution, the church. In those cases, ministry as a profession is anxiety-producing.[41]

Another way that ministry produces anxiety is in knowing how to relate to other professionals in the church and the community. The minister should show respect for the other professionals in the community. Each of them has also prepared for work, professed faith in that field, and acted professionally. These professionals are to be respected and honored for who they are and what they do. The ethical minister acts toward them in such a way that they are recognized and appreciated.

Ministers relate to the doctors, lawyers, and other professionals in the community by not encroaching on their fields. Concerned ministers spend a lot of time in hospitals; but that does not qualify them to prescribe medicine or pass judgment on the treatment being given. While pastors counsel persons, they are not psychiatrists, but pastoral counselors. Legal matters become too complicated, too technical, and too risky for ministers to hand out legal advice freely. Each person operates out of their experience. In some instances, they may have had an experience similar to another persons and believe they know some of the answers. That, however, is telling one's story, not prescribing or advising. The physician, lawyer, and minister—members of the "learned professions"—should know where the work of one starts and the work of the other stops.

The minister functions in the community as a professional among professionals, yet it is normal to feel somewhat uncomfortable about it. "Yes, the ordained ministry is a profession. It is also a gift, and a vocation, a calling. By holding on to some ambivalence about the word *profession*, we can move toward a deeper understanding of our work."[42]

A Part of the Community Team

The minister works with other professionals in the community to form a community team to meet the needs of persons. Not every need the minister faces is a spiritual need. Some of them are needs that can be better met by other trained persons. A minister may not be able to give a job to a person desperately seeking employment, but he can introduce that individual to someone else in the community who can provide the employment needed.

Wayne Oates suggests that a Christian pastor's first responsibility to a new community is to become friends with fellow shepherds, other pastors of all denominations. After that ministers should become acquainted with the medical community, physicians of both general practice and specialties. The third group they should get to know are the social workers, heads of institutions, and public-school teachers. Another important group for new ministers to know are the parent-teacher organizations and the child-care agencies. Certainly the parents of the children in the church need to become friends.

"These," Oates observes, "are all members of a 'community team' of healing helpfulness to people. As a general rule, they, like the minister, are passionately devoted to what they are doing."[43]

Ministers often helps persons best by referring them to people who can help them with a particular problem. This referral becomes a primary means of helping people. Ministers are functioning and valuable members of the community team that is dedicated to meeting human needs and helping persons. Wiest and Smith are of the opinion that "pastors cannot perform their pastoral duties at maximum effectiveness if they have not worked out some way to communicate with doctors, attorneys, law enforcement personnel, and many others."[44]

A Member of the Healing Team

A specific community team composed of professionals attempting to meet human need is the healing team. Most ministers spend a lot of time around hospitals and ministering to persons who are sick and dying. This not only follows Jesus' injunction to visit the sick, but also plays a part in the healing of persons. The minister is a part of the healing team. When ministers visit a hospital room, they bring hope and help to others and guide them in spiritual development. Ministers are not an extra ingredient spliced into the hospital setting. Instead, spiritual ministry is an integral part of the healing process.

Howard Clinebell, a recognized authority in pastoral care and counseling commented on this truth.

> During the time I served as a hospital chaplain, I often felt frustrated by some hospital personnel who perceived my role as exclusively that of bringing religious resources, anxiety-reduction, and comfort to patients —especially when medical treatment had done all it could and failed. Although I regarded those traditional functions as valuable, I sensed that a minister's role with the sick also had another significant dimension—to help enable healing. Experience in recent years has increased my appreciation of the great importance of this second aspect of the minister's role with the sick. The skillful use of listening, caring, and counseling methods with those who are ill can help them become more open to the God-given healing resources within their bodies, minds, spirits, and relationships. When those counseling skills have a vertical dimension and use religious resources appropriately, they can be particularly helpful in enabling people to help people open themselves to experience the healing energies of the ever-present love of God—the ultimate source of all healing.[45]

Clinebell reminded us that the words "health, heal, hale, whole, and holy are all derived from the same or closely related Old English root words,"[46] which underscores the role of religion in healing.

Healing is what we are about in ministry. As a minister you are a part of the healing team. You are helping the people of your church and community find and experience wholeness. You are essential to that process, not ancillary to it.

For ministers to relate properly to their colleagues, they must be emotionally mature. Yet what does it take to be emotionally mature? A longtime professor of Christian ethics, now retired, indicated that a minister must be a model of emotional maturity. He identified ten marks of emotional maturity:

- the capacity for healthy self-acceptance;
- the capacity to maintain durable relationships;
- the ability to work with people holding different value orientations;
- the capacity to delay present gratification for future and more permanent satisfactions;
- the ability to cope with indecision or mental paralysis;
- the ability to achieve a large measure of objectivity;
- the ability to get along with other people, to tolerate their views and values without becoming dogmatic and defensive about one's own;
- a sense of humor;
- love;
- the capacity to care.[47]

Each of these marks of maturity helps a person to be a good minister in a not-so-good world. In the next chapter we shall see how these principles apply in the minister's community.

Suggested Reading

Bratcher, Edward B. *The Walk-On-Water Syndrome*. Waco: Word Books, 1984.
Brister, C. W. *Caring for the Caregivers*. Nashville: Broadman, 1985.
Chandler, Charles. *Minister's Support Group: Alternative to Burnout*. Nashville: Broadman, 1987.
Faulkner, Brooks. *Forced Termination*. Nashville: Broadman, 1986.
Griffith, Leonard. *We Have This Ministry*. Waco: Word Books, 1973.
Lebacqz, Karen. *Professional Ethics: Power and Paradox*. Nashville: Abingdon, 1985.

Notes

[1]John Donne, *Devotions Upon Emergent Occasions*, in *Handbook of Preaching Resources from Literature*, James D. Robertson, ed. (Grand Rapids: Baker Book House, 1962), 87.
[2]Norris Smith, "Forced Termination: Scope and Response," *Search* (Fall, 1990), 6.

The Minister's Colleagues

[3]Ibid.

[4]Ibid.

[5]Ibid., 7.

[6]Lee Morris, "Ethical Factors in Forced Termination," *Search* (Fall, 1990), 50-58.

[7]"Inside Church Fights: An Interview with Speed Leas, *Leadership* (Winter, 1989), 15.

[8]Edward B. Bratcher, *The Walk-On-Water Syndrome* (Waco: Word Books, 1984), 165.

[9]*Quality in Southern Baptist Pastoral Ministry.* Summary and Conclusions, Phase One Research (Louisville: The Southern Baptist Theological Seminary, n. d.), 16-17.

[10]Smith, 7.

[11]Brooks Faulkner, "Healthy Ministers, *Search* (Fall, 1990), 30-31.

[12]Ibid., 32-34.

[13]Ibid., 34-35.

[14]Bratcher, 11.

[15]William P. Tuck, "A Theology for Healthy Church Staff Relations, *Review and Expositor* (Winter, 1981), 5-6.

[16]Charles A. Tidwell, "The Church Staff as a Ministering Team," *Southwestern Journal of Theology* (Spring, 1987), 29.

[17]Ibid., 33.

[18]Ibid., 12.

[19]Hardy Clemons, "The Pastor Staff as Ministry Team," *Review and Expositor* (Winter, 1990), 52-53.

[20]Tuck, 12.

[21]Paul D. Simmons, "Priorities in Christian Ministry," *Review and Expositor* (Fall, 1986), 539.

[22]Henlee H. Barnette, "The Minister as a Moral Role-Model," *Review and Expositor* (Fall, 1989), 514.

[23]"Church Staff Survey" (November, 1977), prepared by Research Services Department, The Sunday School Board of the Southern Baptist Convention, 5, quoted in Brooks Faulkner, "Ethics and Staff Relations," *Review and Expositor* (Fall, 1989), 555.

[24]Charles B. Bugg, "Professional Ethics Among Ministers," *Review and Expositor* (Fall, 1989), 567.

[25]Quoted in Nolan Harmon, *Ministerial Ethics and Etiquette* (Nashville: Abingdon, 1928), 66.

[26]Ibid., 72.

[27]Bugg, 568.

[28]James D. Berkley, "Turning Points: Eight Ethical Choices," *Leadership* (Spring, 1988), 38-39.

[29]Cited in Gaylord Noyce, *Pastoral Ethics* (Nashville: Abingdon, 1928), 137-38.

[30]Ibid., 134.

[31]Bugg, 569.

[32]Hensley, 92.

[33]Noyce, 139.

[34]Ernest T. Campbell, "Preaching Out of Phase," *Campbell's Notebook* (vol. XII, no. 1: January, 1992), 1.

[35]Richard Bondi, *Leading God's People: Ethics for the Practice of Ministry* (Nashville: Abingdon, 1989), 110.

[36]Harmon, 80.

[37]David C. Jacobsen, *The Positive Use of the Minister's Role* (Philadelphia: Westminster, 1967), 20.

[38]Ibid., 21.

[39]Ibid., 21-22.

[40]Karen Lebacqz, *Professional Ethics: Power and Paradox* (Nashville: Abingdon, 1985), 71.

[41]Jacobsen, 23.

[42]Noyce, 208.

[43]Wayne Oates, *The Christian Pastor* (Philadelphia: Westminster, 1964, rev. and enlarged ed.), 224.

[44]Walter E. Wiest and Elwin A. Smith, *Ethics in Ministry* (Minneapolis: Fortress, 1990), 176.

[45]Howard Clinebell, *Basic Types of Pastoral Care and Counseling* (Nashville: Abingdon, 1984 rev. and enlarged ed.), 210-211.

[46]Ibid., 210.

[47]Barnette, 510-513.

6

THE MINISTER'S COMMUNITY:
Threat or Opportunity?

Walker Percy's *Thanatos Syndrome* is an apocalyptic tale set in Feliciana, Louisiana, during the late twentieth-century. A psychiatrist discovers that well-intentioned but misguided medical researchers have slipped a Sodium 24 ion into the water supply. The drug has made a measureable impact on deviant behavior in Feliciana. By inhibiting certain activities of the brain, the invisible drug has caused a significant decline in crime, the spread of AIDS, wife and child abuse, teenage suicide, and other social maladies.

Unfortunately, the drug has side effects: dramatic emotional, linguistic, and sexual changes. The Felicianans may be better behaved, but the price is high—the loss of human traits.

Father Simon Smith, the priest who plays a prominent role in the novel, perches like a postmodern Simeon Stylites (the fifth-century pillar saint who spent his lifetime "above" the world) in a fire tower on the outskirts of town. Father Smith fled to the tower in despair over the success of the Qualitarian Movement, which proposed quick and painless death for those suffering in hospitals. Once a hospice director, this priest has given up on conventional attempts to stop this mercy killing, hoping his absurd act might raise questions. When a psychiatrist does ask the priest why, his response resembles that of the eighth-century prophets of the Old Testament.

> You are a member of the first generation of doctors in the history of medicine to turn their backs on the oath of Hippocrates and kill millions of old useless people, unborn children, born malformed children for the good of mankind—and to do so without a single murmur from one of you. Not a single letter of protest in the august New England Journal of Medicine. And do you know what you're going to end up doing? You a graduate of Harvard and a reader of The New York Times and a member of the Ford Foundation's Program for the Third World? . . . You're going to end up killing Jews.[1]

Percy's critique of our unquestioning trust in technology and science also offers insight about pastoral ethics, and what James Wind

155

calls "our ministerial moment."[2] Like Jeremiah or Jonah, there are times when the modern minister is called upon to engage in hand-to-hand combat.

Yet, the public role of the minister is not just that of a prophet, but also that of a pastor. The shepherd of God is concerned about community needs and ministry opportunities as well as public morality. Along with congregation building and pastoral caring, the minister does have a public ministry that is larger than the claims of a particular church.

The role of the minister in society is mandated by both biblical tradition and professional responsibility. Just how to interact with the world has been the basis of much theological debate and the occasion for many historical movements. Perhaps no one has better portrayed the struggle of Christianity to relate to the world than H. Richard Niebuhr in his classic work, *Christ and Culture*.[3]

The Yale Divinity School professor set forth a question every generation of Christians must answer. In the midst of the proximate loyalties in every society (family, state, church), how does the believer judge between loyalty to Christ and the many loyalties of culture?

The ethics teacher outlined five patterns of this relationship between culture and the church that have occurred throughout history. The first two are what he terms, "radical answers."

Christ *against* culture is the response of sectarian groups that condemn culture and separate themselves from it. Partly due to persecution from an immoral and pagan Roman society, early Christians like Tertullian took this stance. Later groups like the ascetics, the monastics, and modern Amish communities illustrate this same rejection of culture.

The second radical answer is termed Christ *of* culture. As the name indicates, early Christian Gnostics and modern cultural Protestants selectively identified certain aspects of culture and Christ. For them culture interprets Christ; the best insights of civilization (science, philosophy) harmonize with revelation.

What do these two approaches say to the modern minister? The danger still exists for Christian leaders today to relate to the community in one of these two ways. A pastor may give up on the world and withdraw from society, assuming it is sold out to Satan and sin and is totally beyond redemption. Many conservative Christians in this century have sought to separate themselves from evil by renouncing "worldliness."

Evangelicals in the 1990s more often identify themselves with culture. Many would see in the Religious Right Movement and the trend toward civil religion, a repetition of that age-old strategy of "Christian-izing" some part of culture. Today it might be a political party or a some social movement. The mistakes of the Social Gospel Movement of the early 1900s may be repeated in the many religious-political movements of the latter part of this century.

Niebuhr correctly rejects both of these extreme positions for several basic theological reasons. Both separate nature from culture, denying that God the Creator is also God the Governor. The "against" position moves only toward Christ; the other only toward culture. The Yale theologian prefers another alternative: the "Church of the Center," which works to change society by properly relating Christ to culture.

Three types represent this preferred approach of the church to the world. Christ *above* culture is a synthesist response which affirms both the world and faith, but gives superior value to Christ over culture. Christians like Thomas Aquinas believed the natural world revealed much truth about God and life, a base on which a supernatural revelation could be added to this foundation of natural knowledge.

Christ and culture in *paradox* is a dualistic approach to life in community. Martin Luther taught that a person lives in two king-doms: the state has the final word on secular matters; the church has authority in spiritual concerns. The Christian lives in paradoxical tension, for the two worlds do not always agree, but both must always be obeyed.

The preferred approach discussed by Niebuhr is Christ the *trans-former* of culture. This "conversionist" approach seeks to transform the world into conformity to the will of God. It works from the conviction that the claims of Christ extend to all of life and society. Christian thinkers like Augustine and John Calvin, as well as some modern leaders of the Great Awakenings (1726-1810) and the Social Gospel Movement represent this strategy.

What do these historical examples teach contemporary clergy about life in community? They obviously warn Christian leaders to beware of withdrawal from the world or of a utopian identification of the gospel with culture. To seize Niebuhr's theme, the Christian minister must affirm absolute loyalty to Jesus Christ while accomodating his loyalties to culture.

God is Creator, Governor, and Redeemer; but sin is also radical and universal. Christian involvement in the community must always be realistic—every culture is corrupted by sin. At the same time, the gospel of Jesus Christ is powerful—societies can be transformed. These two realities create a healthy tension between Christian ideals and social action and ministry.[4]

One fact remains: the church is in the world, and the world is also in the church. The community poses for the minister both a threat and an opportunity. At times a pastor leads the congregation to minister in the community, as friend to friend. At other times, when social evils raise their dragonic heads, the prophet must go forth like a medieval knight to battle the forces that ravage human life. To be God's minister in the world is ethically demanding, for it requires of the clergy a dual role of pastor and prophet.

Basis for Ethical Involvement

What biblical and theological basis do ministers have for ethical involvement in the community? One of the first revelations of Scripture is that God is Creator of all that is: "God saw all that he had made, and it was very good" (Gen. 1:31). This good creation, both the world of nature and the the world of culture, is governed by a sovereign Lord to whom humankind is responsible (Gen. 2; Matt. 25:31-46). God's created order did not long remain. Sin and evil quickly entered the picture, corrupting the earth and all persons upon it (Gen. 3).

The ultimate revelation of Scripture, however, is not about ruin, but redemption. God the Creator and Governor of the world is also God the Redeemer. The story of the Bible, from the Red Sea to Golgotha, is the narrative of the one and only Redeemer who works and is working to transform the kingdoms of this earth into the kingdom of God (Rev. 21).

The Old Testament prophets walked out into their world to proclaim the need for social justice and community righteousness (Amos 5:21-24). Isaiah condemned the religious festivals and meaningless offerings of Judah because their religion was ethically deficient; it did not work in the marketplace.

> Stop doing wrong, learn to do right!
> Seek justice, encourage the oppressed.
> Defend the cause of the fatherless,
> plead the case of the widow (Isa. 1:16-17).

Perhaps Micah summarizes best the call of the Old Testament messengers for social righteousness:

> He has told you, O mortal, what is good;
> and what does the Lord require of you
> but to do justly and to love mercy
> and to walk humbly with your God? (Mic. 6:8, NRSV).

The New Testament continues concern for social justice expressed in the Old Covenant. The Gospels witness this prophetic emphasis through the life and teachings of Jesus, who often confirmed His intent not to "abolish the Law or the Prophets . . . but to fulfill them" (Matt. 5:17)." Christ explained in the Sermon on the Mount that His followers were citizens of a new kingdom and lived by a new law—the law of righteousness (Matt. 5:20). As "salt of the earth" and the "light of the world," disciples of Jesus were mandated to exercise a positive influence on a darkened and decaying society (Matt. 5: 13-16). His followers are called to live in the world (Matt. 5:21-28) according to the ethical ideals inherent in the moral character of God: "Be perfect, therefore, as your heavenly Father is perfect" (Matt. 5:48).

As God's new covenant community, the Christian church is not an end in itself; disciples of Jesus are the body of Christ in the world. The Christian community is to be involved in doing what Jesus did, for the Lord said, "As the Father has sent me, I am sending you" (John 20:21). The position of the "called out ones," like that of Israel, is one of service, not of privilege.

In two respects the church differs from Israel. For the Hebrews, church and state were the same; the religious and political communities were identical. However this was not the case with Christianity, for the Roman emperor was never the Davidic king. This reality means that Christians must never expect political rulers to impose their faith or morals. The church must never become a political power broker.

> Whatever may be said for the Constantinian establishment of Christianity and for the cultural achievements of the medieval church in the West, the state-established church cannot be the norm of Christian ethics.[5]

Does this "separation of church and state" mean that ministers should never get involved in economic issues or politics? What did Jesus teach about the state? Although Christ lived under an imperial dictatorship, He accepted the authority of the state and recognized its legitimate functions (Matt. 17:24-25; Mark 12:17). Christ's classic statement about God and government came in response to the Pharisees' question about Roman taxes. Taking a Roman coin between His fingers, Jesus replied, "Give to Caesar what is Caesar's, and to God what is God's" (Matt. 22:21). Jesus did reject the Zealot way of violent revolution, but not on the ground that God's kingdom is socially irrelevant, but because the methods were not God's kingdom way.

As the Teacher of an ethical kingdom, Jesus continually challenged the social order of His time.[6] He was crucified not for being a nice fellow, but because He threatened the social and political powers of the first century, both Jewish and Roman. Jesus was radical in many of His actions: he identified with the poor, the oppressed, and the outcasts of His society. He outraged many by associating with women in public, treating them as equals. His concern for the weak was a challenge to Rome's unjust treatment of the "worthless" and Israel's many social distinctions.

Paul's realization that all are equal, that "there is neither Jew nor Greek, slave nor free, male nor female, for you are all one in Christ Jesus" (Gal. 3:23), became a first-century battlecry for breaking down the social walls that divide and destroy human worth and dignity. The apostle to the Gentiles acknowledged civil authority as God-ordained and worthy of respect and obedience (Rom. 13:1-7); however, his life reflected the words of Simon Peter that God always comes first before the will of the state (Acts 4:18-20).

How do these biblical teachings and theological understandings relate to the ethical conduct of the clergy in society today? A graduate student once commented that if neither Jesus nor early Christianity attacked the institution of slavery in the Roman world, why should we today be involved in social action?

Two main reasons come to mind. First, as a result of Jesus' life and teachings, the early church did create a slave-free distinction in its own community. One of the first acts of slave owners, after becoming Christians, was to hold a service of manumission in which their slaves were freed, since masters and slaves were now "brothers and sisters in the Lord." Christian cemeteries of that era made no distinction between the burial plots of slaves and free, as was normally done.

A second reason for the lack of social involvement in early Christianity was their lack of effective social and political influence. The world of Caesar was pagan, immoral, and hostile. Christianity was initially a very small minority sect, having less than 1 percent of the population. To try to exert Christian influence on the empire that was already persecuting followers of the Nazarene would have been futile indeed.

In light of the teachings of the Bible and the witness of Christian tradition, modern disciples cannot withdraw from the arena of politics and economics by saying the world is too wicked for Christians to get involved. Neither can we blind our eyes to the brokenness in society by saying there is no need for the church to minister to any but its own.

At the same time, as moral leaders of the church, Christian ministers must be the first to admit that the way of the world is not the way of the cross. The Christian witness in the community must always be Christian. Whenever the church gets in a position of influence, due to its own economic wealth or political power, it is then most vulnerable to the twin temptations of greed and pride.

In short, the church is to be in the world where God put us. Conversely, the world of material and spiritual resources are in the church, also because God put them there. Every minister therefore, faces a basic ethical question in social ministry and action: How can I be salt and light in the community without losing my savor and radiance?

Community Service

Clergy often have the competence and the professional freedom for considerable community service beyond the demands of the congregation. Public ministry can be very satisfying, but also a seductively time-consuming enterprise. A community-involved minister should never neglect pastoral duties to serve the general public. At the same time, a unique opportunity to benefit the community, such as membership on the school board, is a ministerial service the church normally affirms. The wise pastor will listen carefully to parish leaders to be sure church duties are never slighted to do community service.

Numerous are the ways a minister is able to serve her community. From fund raising to civic speeches, the church leader has opportunity to represent the church and the Lord of the church in the community. The motive should always be love of neighbor and selfless service in the name of Christ. If a moral issue emerges in the district, the pastor who has been involved in a positive way in community service will have greater credibility in supporting public morality.

Should a minister join a civic organization? What pastor has not felt the pressure from parishioners to become a member of the Lions, Kiwanis, or Civitan? Certainly advantages, both personal and professional, come with membership in a service club. Some clergy prefer a personal growth organization like Toastmasters. This decision remains largely a personal matter. Membership in a civic club is time consuming, but it often becomes a good outlet for the semicloistered minister. No parson should ever join any group just to please parishioners.

How should a preacher respond to an invitation to serve on a public board, council, or agency? Unpaid service on a public advisory commission or some other short-term appointive office, such as a city council, is appropriate service. There is an important distinction, however, between those volunteer positions and paid ones, such as appointment to a bank board of directors. The minister's power and influence should be in the interest of the whole public, not just a preferred few. The minister should never be among those who are working to gain public advantage for vested interests. Public service for the clergy means commitment to the ethical principle of justice.[7]

Many times the call of the community to the ordained is for their service as religious leaders. Quite commonly the clergy is asked to pronounce an invocation at a public gathering. For an occasion like a monthly P.T.A. meeting, it might be wise for the cleric to suggest the school group use a layperson—after all, the public should learn pastors are not the only ones who can pray. At an occasion like the Mayor's Prayer Breakfast, the invocator-minister should recognize the religious pluralism of the audience and plan a prayer that is sensitive to all religious convictions, but one that affirms the spiritual purpose of the meeting.

Gaylord Noyce points out that in several respects, the clergy serve as "chaplains" to the society at large. As ministers invoke God's blessing and offer grace at meals, let them guard against that bland "civil religion" which implies God's acceptance of all things American, from labor unions to the Ku Klux Klan. It may be wise to turn down some invitations.[8]

As a religious authority, the minister is sometimes called upon to teach in the public sector. Public schools and universities may invite the clergy to explain religious beliefs, discuss ethical values, or speak to a contemporary social issue. While a pastor in Austin, Texas, one of us regularly spoke to a high school home economics class on the subject of preparing for marriage and family. With the renewed interest in teaching moral values to students, ministers will probably have opportunity to address many groups about personal ethics. Again, the minister must respect the religious diversity in her audience and be sure to refrain from any hint of sectarianism.

Political Involvement

The 1960s witnessed a remarkable increase in political involvement by the clergy.[9] The civil rights movement led many local pastors to pack their bags and leave for Selma or Jackson or Washington D.C. Some sought approval from their congregations; some did not. Not a few ended up in jail. The antiwar movement followed, receiving much of its verve and method from the civil rights marchers. By and large these ministers came from mainline denominations of a more liberal political persuasion. Conservative ministers criticized this effort as a "social gospel," claiming the true gospel of Christ focuses on changing hearts, not society.

The movements of the 1960s and 1970s to effect social change toward justice were partially rooted in the Social Gospel Movement, which occurred around the turn of the century. Rapid industrialization in the late nineteenth century brought thousands to the already over-crowded cities. Factory workers were exploited: low wages, long hours, and horrendous working conditions increased poverty. Crime, prostitution, alcohol abuse, and subhuman living conditions infested urban slums.

Preachers in England and America cried out against these social ills. Religious leaders worked in the political arena to enact legislation which improved working conditions and protected the weak from economic exploitation. Although the Social Gospel Movement was naive about human nature and utopian about society, it was an attempt to get the church involved in applying the ethical teachings of Christ to modern society.[10]

Evangelical ministers today, fearful of political and theological "liberalism," have been slow to become involved in social ministry or action. Evangelist Billy Graham upset many conservatives by refusing to tolerate segregated audiences in his crusades, as well as being a foremost advocate for nuclear disarmament and response to world hunger. In the latter half of the twentieth century a growing number of evangelicals have become concerned about political response to social needs, forming organizations like JustLife and the Sojourner Community. Denominational social action committees, usually more progressive than churches, have often been on the "cutting edge" of social issues.

An amazing turnaround occurred in the 1980s. Led by Jerry Falwell's "Moral Majority" organization, religious elements of the most conservative type reversed the older evangelical opposition to political social action. A new force called the "religious right" brought fundamentalist American Christianity into politics. Although this movement was weakened by its penchant for "civil religion" and its tendency to baptize all conservative political views as "Christian," it was an attempt to get conservative ministers involved in the political processes.

A prime example of the political involvement of ministers during the latter half of this century is Martin Luther King, Jr. On April 16, 1963, from a Birmingham jail, the Baptist minister wrote an open letter[11] to eight white clergymen who had written him in January, declaring King's strategy disturbing and his tactics inflammatory.

Martin Luther King, Jr., began his reply with "My dear Fellow Clergymen." His closing remarks opened with "I hope this letter finds you strong in the faith." In between he explains why he has come to Birmingham from Atlanta, saying that as Paul went out from Tarsus, "I too am compelled to carry the gospel of freedom beyond my particular hometown. Like Paul, I must constantly respond to the Macedonian call for aid."[12]

King wrote that his greatest disappointment was with the leadership of the white churches; for among them, as ministers of the gospel, he had hoped to find his strongest support. Instead he found the country "moving toward the exit of the twentieth century with a religious community largely adjusted to the status quo." He reported traveling over the South, admiring "her beautiful churches with their lofty spires pointing heavenward," but he mused, "Over and over again I have found myself asking, 'What kind of people worship here? Who is their God?' . . . Yes, I see the church as the body of Christ. But, oh! How we have blemished and scarred that body through social neglect and fear of being nonconformists." King concluded,

> If I have said anything in this letter that is an overstatement of the truth and is indicative of an unreasonable impatience, I beg you to forgive me. If I have said anything in this letter that is an understatement of the truth and is indicative of my having a patience that makes me patient with anything less than brotherhood, I beg God to forgive me.[13]

With this historical overview in mind, what can be said about the ethical obligations of the minister in politics? Walter Winchell liked to call it "politricks." Many ministers agreed, refusing to participate in politics for fear of corrupting their ministry. The Scriptures have no such negative view. The word itself comes from the Greek term *politeusthe*, and is quoted by Paul when he wrote, "Let your citizenship [*politeusthe*] be worthy of the gospel of Christ" (Phil. 1:27, authors' translation).

At the level of Christian citizenship, the church shepherd certainly will obey the law, pay taxes, pray for public officials, and participate in supporting good government. This responsibility may sound mundane, but even ministers need to be reminded of these essentials. For example, many clergy have chosen not to pay Social Security taxes by signing a statement of exemption based on "individual religious considerations." Conversation with some ministers reveals their main motive is financial, not religious. Not only is this reason unethical, it is also illegal (as the agreement clearly indicates) and possibly jeopardizes the minister's future decisions about government programs such as Veteran's Administration loans and Medicare.

Beyond these basic duties to government, how politically active should a minister be? The public sometimes reacts to ministers "meddling" in community issues by appealing to separation of church and state. The Scriptures do teach, by implication, that the two institutions should be separate (Matt. 22:21). Neither church nor state should be controlled by the other or dependent on the other.

That does not prohibit each from being open to the other's views so that respect and influence may flow between the two. The First Amendment doctrine as articulated by Thomas Jefferson never meant to separate God from government—no one can do that. Nor does it mean the separation of religion from politics—no one should do that.[14]

Can a pastor run for public office or become actively involved in a political campaign? A tombstone in a cemetery in Palestine, Texas, reads: "J. D. DuPuy, December 13, 1853-December 19, 1927. He loved relatives, friends and country; was fond of games and sports; believed in God and Christianity, but denounced political preachers."[15]

Partisan politics is definitely a high-risk avocation for the pastor. Noyce contends, "Style is part of the answer. The minister cannot [be partisan], if his or her way of politicking is primarily to condemn the other side as evil, un-Christian, or vicious."[16] The Vatican has recently written against all public office for its clergy. Historically, Protestant ministers have served in appointive or electoral office without losing their ministerial standing.

Active political life is the right of all citizens. At the same time, a minister must remember that the line separating personal life from vocation is blurred for the professional. The life of the church pastor is even more open and available to "clients" than in other professionals, so much so that a member of the congregation of an opposing political persuasion may take offense at the pastor's stance.

One rule of thumb for the minister has been to focus on issues that are clearly moral, rather than on partisan politics. Most congregations will support a pastor who takes a courageous stand on the basis of moral convictions. At the same time, the fear of disagreement among church members should never lead a minister to conceal ethical convictions in the name of "church harmony." In the late 1930s Martin Niemoller, a German Protestant minister confessed his own failure.

In Germany they came first for the communists, and I didn't speak up because I wasn't a communist. Then they came for the Jews, and I didn't speak up because I wasn't a Jew. Then they came for the trade unionists, and I didn't speak up because I wasn't a trade unionist. Then they came for the Catholics, and I didn't speak up because I was a Protestant. Then they came for me, but by that time, no one was left to speak up.[17]

Another present danger for ministers active in politics is "civil religion." Richard V. Pierard defines the term as "the use of commonly accepted religious sentiments, concepts and symbols by the state for its own purposes . . . a blurring of religion and patriotism and of religious values with national values."[18]

A renowned television minister who pastors a church preached a patriotic sermon from the Book of Nehemiah. His message asserted that just as Israel was God's hope for the world then, the United States is God's hope for the world today. The walls modern believers must help build are the "Star Wars" defense systems. He preached that to oppose funding for "Star Wars" is to oppose God's will for the protection of Christian America.

The modern minister must beware of confusing God and country. Civil religion is dangerous because it assumes that the United States is a Christian nation and that Americans are God's chosen people. The temptation is to align Americanism and Christianity with a certain political point of view. The modern prophet of God, like Nathan of ancient Israel, must always keep a healthy distance from the king in order to say, "You are the man!" (2 Sam. 12:7).

Should the minister be involved in organized protests and civil disobedience? In a pluralistic democracy like ours, books will be written, films produced, and even laws passed that offend Christian moral values. As citizens, we can protest in many ways: private and public conversation, letter writing, contacting public officials, picketing, boycotting, and civil obedience. With such a range of options (you can think of more), how does a minister determine what is acceptable and what is best?

In an editorial in *Christianity Today*, Terry Muck urged Christians to ask four vital questions before they joined an organized protest:

(1) How serious is the issue?
(2) How reasonable and clear are the goals of the protest?
(3) How effective will the protest be and with what side effects?
(4) What will be the long-range consequences?

Christian social action often fails because these questions are never raised.

For example, television reporters asked "Operation Rescue" leaders why they staged their sit-ins. Answers ranged from "rescuing babies" to "changing abortion laws" to "raising public consciousness" to "closing down the clinics" to "helping mothers seek other alternatives." Without debating the validity of any of these goals, it is obvious that confusion over the purpose of this protest limits its effectiveness. In fact, Muck asks "Will the public perception of what we are doing through the protest so poison people's perceptions of Christians that the cause of Christ will be hurt?"[19]

The Minister's Community

Beyond these initial questions about the practicality and prudence of organized protests, a larger one emerges: Is civil disobedience ever right for Christians? On the one hand, the Bible instructs believers to obey the government (Rom. 13:1) and to "submit yourselves for the Lord's sake to every authority instituted among men" (1 Pet. 2:13). At the same time, the Word of God lauds persons who were not submissive: Rahab (Jos. 6:22-25), Hebrew midwives (Ex. 1:16-2:10), Daniel (Dan. 6), and Simon Peter and John (Acts 4; 5:12-42).

How do we reconcile these seeming contradictions? As we previously noted, the Scriptures teach that God instituted government for society's good—to maintain order, punish evil, and provide services to the citizenry (Rom. 13:1-7). The Christian is to be a supportive citizen (1 Tim. 2:2).

One exception does emerge. If the state requires obedience to a law which clearly violates the higher law of God, then it may be God's will to resist. Those who decide to become lawbreakers in the name of God choose many forms: blocking access to abortion clinics, withholding income tax as a protest against militarism, offering sanctuary to political refugees, and the illegal interference of environmental polluters. Civil disobedience is always a strategy of last resort and can only be justified if certain criteria are met:

1. The law being resisted is clearly unjust and contrary to God's will.
2. Legal means to change the law have been exhausted.
3. The act of civil disobedience is public, not clandestine.
4. There should be some likelihood of success.
5. Participants should willingly and nonviolently accept the penalty for breaking the law.[20]

Civil disobedience is different from revolution. True civil disobedience affirms the authority of the state by using nonviolent resistence and submitting to arrest.

> It is inconsistent for the civilly disobedient, after breaking the law to make their point, to then flee arrest, jump bail, hide from the authorities, or harbor personal bitterness as the state proceeds with its vocation to order.[21]

The minister should always work for justice. Civil disobedience may be permissible in some unique circumstances, but even then, however, it is an exception to the norm of lawful obedience to government. The purpose of such law breaking is consciousness-raising, education, and the focusing of public concern on an unjust law.

Is it ever appropriate for a minister to endorse a political candidate?

Ministerial Ethics

In a particularly passionate presidential election, a nominee visited the worship services of the largest church of a leading Protestant denomination. After the service, the renowned pastor stood on the front steps of the church and endorsed the visitor for president. The minister defended his actions, stating that outside the sanctuary he had the right as a private citizen to support whomever he chooses. The newspapers, however, did not identify him as a private citizen, but as the pastor of the church on whose steps he stood.

Political candidates yearn to list the names of local pastors among their supporters, for religious leaders garner widespread support among their constituencies. Ministers often find it difficult not to support public politicians who are good candidates and who take a strong stand on a crucial moral issue.

In private conversation, ministers are free to share political convictions, if they so choose. Public endorsement, on the other hand, is rarely (if ever) the right thing to do. Ministers should be especially cautious about inviting candidates to speak before their churches. In the 1992 presidential primaries, the newspapers reported weekly about churches where the politicians appeared, usually to bring a campaign message. This is partisan politics. Allowing the church to be a forum for all the candidates, particularly to discuss issues of concern to the church, is another matter.

Most ministers have received a letter from a fellow cleric (often printed on church stationery), asking for their support and vote. This kind of public endorsement of a candidate not only alienates some members who disagree, it is undoubtedly a misuse of the pastor's position of power and influence. The conscientious prophet of God must continue to speak to moral issues, but at the same time he must resist undue entanglement with a particular politician or party. This guideline will protect the cleric from present pressures and future embarrassments.

Churches and other tax-exempt charitable organizations should think twice before endorsing or opposing political candidates after 1992. The IRS investigation into the Jimmy Swaggart Ministries ruled that Swaggart's endorsement of Pat Robertson for president in a 1986 church service and a later publication violated the Internal Revenue Code. To maintain tax exemption, churches are prohibited from supporting or opposing candidates for public office. Individual ministers and employees may become involved in campaigns as long as no resources, personnel, or facilities of the organization are involved and as long as the individual makes it clear that he or she is not acting on behalf of the organization.[22]

Public Morality

Richard John Neuhaus is alarmed about what he calls "the naked public square" in America. By that he means "the result of political doctrine and practice that would exclude religion and religiously-grounded values from the conduct of public business."[23] If Neuhaus is correct in his belief that public policy has been divorced from religious belief, what should the contemporary clergy do to influence public morality?

Prophetic Proclamation

One obvious way that ministers contribute to public morality is through prophetic proclamation. Being prophetic involves more than vigorous preaching, angry denunciation of social vices, or a therapeutic venting of frustrations over the sinful conditions of society. Sometimes "prophetic" poses as moral indignation toward people whom both the prophets and Jesus defended. The biblical prophet spoke for God delivering a message not shallow or selective, but a proclamation of God's concern for the unborn and the aged, the poor and the powerful, the environment and the economy, health care and racial equality, personal morality and social righteousness.[24]

Not many years ago, while one of us served as pastor of a downtown First Baptist Church in a large metropolitan city, a community crisis arose. Unknown to business and professional leaders, a state senator secretly met with the president of the Chamber of Commerce and his executive committee to get their support for legislation he was sponsoring. Two days later, on a Friday, the senator introduced a bill to legalize casino gambling in this community bordering Mexico. Rumors spread that organized crime was involved, for this urban sprawl of over two million persons would be an ideal international location for "money laundering."

Immediate response from the religious community was vital. Within a few hours, ministers representing several major Protestant denominations, a Jewish rabbi, and an envoy from the Roman Catholic archbishop met at First Baptist Church to construct a joint statement. Before the day was over, a press conference was called for the purpose of reading a statement prepared and signed by all of the clergy. The religious community in this city unified to oppose a threat to the moral and social well-being of all citizens.

The next seven days were hectic. On the Sunday following the state senator's surprise legislation, one of the pastors preached a televised sermon on the moral issue. Evidently a large audience from the community listened and joined the opposition to the gambling legislation. The newspapers claimed that the unified response of the religious community, coupled with this televised sermon which was widely quoted in the media, were among major reasons this legislation was quickly defeated.

Prophetic preaching on ethical issues builds a foundation for Christian involvement in community moral issues. The minister may be hesitant to address moral issues in sermons because of their variety and their complexity. The potential negative reaction of the congregation, partly due to the church's conformity to culture, is another obstacle. In spite of these difficulties, the faithful proclaimer of God's Word will preach on ethical issues because of the needs of people, the demands of the gospel, and the example of the prophets and Jesus.

Before a minister preaches on ethical issues, however, a certain amount of preparation is required.[25] The prophet who speaks for God must know and understand God's character, for ethical preaching must be rooted in the moral nature of Jehovah. The proclaimer must also be an ethical model who correctly applies and interprets the teachings of the Scripture.

Those who declare a message from God on a moral issue must also know their limits. Because most ethical issues are complicated, thorough research is a must. The preacher may discover some subjects require more than is available. Remember also that every moral problem does not require a pastoral comment.

Three Greek words summarize the theological principles upon which ethical preaching stands: kerygma (gospel message), koinonia (fellowship), and kairos (time). The first word defines what to preach from: the Christian kerygma, the good news of the gospel. Focusing on the biblical story gives the preacher spiritual vision and corrects cultural blind spots. The second word defines whom to preach through: the Christian koinonia, the people of God. The pastor not only speaks to the church, but also speaks for the church as God's moral witness to the world. The last word kairos indicates to the minister when to preach. Ethical preaching requires a fine sense of timing. One pastor listed five key ethical preaching moments: when the issue is (1) in the canon, (2) on the calendar, (3) before the congregation, (4) an imminent crisis, and (5) a deep conviction.[26]

Charles Swindoll once recalled the words of Wilbur Reece, which may express our generation's reluctance to face the demands of discipleship and the ethical implications of the gospel:

> I would like to buy $3 worth of God—not enough to explode my soul or disturb my sleep, but just enough to equal a cup of warm milk or a

snooze in the sunshine. I don't want enough of God to make me love a black man or pick beets with a migrant. I want ectasy, not transformation. I want the warmth of the womb, not a new birth. I want about a pound of the eternal in a paper sack. I would like to buy $3 worth of God, please.[27]

Organized Participation

Another way a church prophet addresses public morality is through organized participation in addressing community needs. Why were the churches and their ministers able to unify the metropolitan city against the threat of casino gambling? One of the major reasons for their success was the involvement of the ministers and their churches in the community before this crisis arose. For years the churches had sponsored multiple ministries in the city, responding to a host of social needs.

Downtown churches had developed a comprehensive benevolence program that included counseling, food assistance, shelter, job assistance, and literacy classes. Along the international border churches sponsored medical clinics where doctors and nurses gave of their time to minister to the sick. Several churches sponsored an orphanage in Mexico. During winter months, clothes, blankets, and medicine were donated and taken into Mexico for distribution. Pastors who led their churches to minister to social needs in this community earned the right to be heard when other moral issues arose.

The first contact of Christian love with social action is what John Stott calls a "simple uncomplicated compassion" that spontaneously serves wherever need arises.[28] The story of the good Samaritan (Luke 10:25-37) could have had a second chapter. Suppose that every time the Samaritan walked the road from Jerusalem to Jericho, he found injured people who had been robbed by bandits. If he did nothing to prevent the robberies along this highway, would his love have been perfect?

Genuine love often motivates a person to engage in social action. Troeltsch argues that this is what happened in the ancient church. Though primarily concerned with social problems affecting its own life, the early church soon realized that those problems (such as slavery and injustice) all had to do with social institutions that were part of the state. Thus the church was forced to confront the state with the demands of the gospel of Jesus Christ.[29]

Moral Leadership

The key ingredient in the church's response to public morality is the moral leadership of the minister. The issues are seldom simple.

The pastor may hear two voices when faced with an issue of public morality. One voice is that of the prophet, who calls for a faithful witness; the other is the pastoral voice pleading for church unity. Pastoral ethics never backs away from controversy, but it also has a mandate to nurture the growth of a congregation—growth in faith, in compassionate concern, and in prophetic witness.[30]

According to Richard Bondi, the minister as a moral leader must live on the edge but remain connected to the center. In a sense, the church leader is "suspended" between center and edge.

> The edge and the center are paired in a difficult bond. There is movement and vitality on the edge, but power and stability at the center. Leaders who live only at the edge can become detached from their communities and unable to lead, whereas leaders who commandeer the center can end up protecting its interests from the dangerous opportunities of the edge. Nonetheless, trying to live always at the center is the more dangerous temptation, for stability without movement leads to stagnation and eventual collapse.[31]

Pronouncements from the denomination can support the pastor's leadership as a moral force. A church should be a community of moral discourse and, as such, should study and deliberate convention resolutions and statements by church groups on ethical issues such as abortion, nuclear arms, ecology, homosexuality, and the AIDS crisis.[32]

Once the decision has been made to become involved in a public morality issue, the question of strategy is primary. Community problems are complex and require battle on several fronts. A teacher of Christian ethics has compiled an excellent resource for aiding ministers to organize churches for community action, titled *Applying the Gospel*.[33] Any minister contemplating social action should study this resource carefully.

In conclusion, for the pastor-prophet to lead the church into community ministry and social action demands certain essentials.[34] First, and foremost, there must be a free pulpit. Though this freedom to preach God's message is assumed when a pastor is called, it must often be clarified by the clergy. The Spirit must be free to speak through God's messenger, or else the people will perish in the wilderness for lack of manna from God.

At the same time, the freedom of the pulpit is not license. Therefore a second axiom follows: the minister as a moral leader is part of a covenant community and always represents that larger body. A prophetic, public ministry should never be isolated from dialogue with the company of believers whose counsel and support is vital. This reality poses several obligations. It means the minister must give pastoral care of the congregation top priority. It means the basis for social action must always be theological, not based on the latest political or social fad. It means the minister may not have all the answers, and also, it means at times he has the wrong answer. It means the pastor will recognize that the laity have moral convictions worthy of respect, and often their insights may be superior to the clergy's. It means denominational pronouncements must be seriously received, as they are usually more prophetic than the congregation's position. It means, finally, that the needs of people in the community do have a claim on ministers, as they did on Jesus when He announced His ministry:

> The Spirit of the Lord is on me,
>   because he has anointed me
>   to preach good news to the poor.
> He has sent me to proclaim freedom for the prisoners
>   and recovery of sight for the blind,
>   to release the oppressed,
>   to proclaim the year of the Lord's favor (Luke 4:18-19).

Legal Responsibilities

In the city where one of us lives, a well-known local minister sued a television evangelist for $90 million for alleged defamation. The accuser claimed the TV preacher spread false statements about his sexual life, which brought down his own budding television ministry. After a nine-week trial, the jury awarded the wronged pastor $1 million in personal damages and $9 million to his bankrupt ministry.[35]

Ours is an increasingly lawsuit-prone society. Gone is the day when churches and preachers were immune to legal action. Government agencies are scrutinizing churches for infractions of tax laws. Clergy malpractice suits are increasing. "The Minister, Churches, and the Law" is a new topic for discussion at religious meetings.

Clergy malpractice suits usually involve allegations against ministers and churches in one of five areas: counseling, sexual misconduct, defamation, breach of confidentiality, and child care. The term *malpractice* means falling below the established standards of conduct for a particular profession.

Counseling

Oliver Thomas, general counsel for the Baptist Joint Committee on Public Affairs and an expert in this area, has noted that clergy malpractice "is one of the most challenging legal concepts to face church and state in recent years."[36] In a paper presented to the University of Virginia Law School, Thomas discussed a number of key issues related to clergy malpractice suits, the "victims" of ministerial malfeasance, and traditional crimes that plaintiffs might use against the clergy.

The watershed Nally case in 1980 involved the suicide of a bright young student who told his church counselors (none of whom were trained therapists) that he intended to commit suicide. The counselors neither informed the family nor tried to get Nally to a psychiatrist. The parents later sued, alleging both clergy malpractice and outrageous conduct. Ultimately, the appeals courts decided that for the courts to interfere in the counseling activities of the church is wrong; to set standards of competence and standards of training of church counselors would be excessive entanglement of church and state.

The Supreme Court of Colorado has similarly ruled against "clergy malpractice," stating that the "tort" (crime) is fundamentally flawed on two counts. First, it would secularize various forms of sectarian religious counseling entitled to constitutional protection. Second, it would deter some ministers, priests, and rabbis from engaging in marriage counseling in order to avoid liability.[37] With one exception, various other state courts have rejected the clergy malpractice theory.

The Ohio Court of Appeals, however, has accepted a clergy malpractice suit against a pastoral counselor. The case involved a couple who sought marital counseling from a Seventh-Day Adventist pastor, who induced the wife to engage in sex with him against her will. Thomas observed:

> When a couple is in marriage counseling and the counselor begins having sex with one of the counselees, the counselor should expect to be held liable. The fact that the counselor happens to be a minister is irrelevant. These cases, however, should not be termed "clergy malpractice."[38]

This last statement refers to the First Amendment question about the right of the courts to establish standards for pastoral counseling, which Thomas argues the Constitution forbids. Other constitutional questions convince the Baptist Joint Committee lawyer of the demise of clergy malpractice suits in counseling.

Should a church minister abdicate counseling for fear of litigation? Any pastor or church staff member lacking formal training in the field should question his or her ability to adequately counsel persons. Ministers sometimes make mistakes because they know neither the basic techniques of counseling nor their legal and ethical obligations.

In this era of specialization, it seems wise for the average minister to refer all serious counseling needs to a trained professional. Ministers who plan to specialize in church-related counseling should receive training in the discipline from a seminary, university, or some accredited entity. It is unethical to assume competence in counseling when you have no training.

Sexual Misconduct

As counsel Thomas noted, ministers are not immune from all criminal liability, nor should they be.[39] For example, the recent rash of lawsuits involving sexual improprieties should not be defended on First Amendment grounds, for no *bona fide* religious organization holds beliefs that affirm seduction, rape, or other sexual misconduct. Rather, traditional tort theories should be used as alternative means of recovery for those who have been mistreated.

For nonconsensual acts by a minister, sexual assault or sexual battery is a possible charge. For consensual acts, ministers have been held liable in three different ways: alienation of affection,[40] breach of fiduciary duty or confidential relations,[41] and intentional infliction of emotional distress or outrageous conduct.[42]

Defamation

Second in frequency to claims of sexual misconduct by ministers are those involving the publication of false or defamatory statements, usually arising from church disciplinary proceedings.[43] Like the press, churches and clergy enjoy a qualified privilege in regard to defamation, if the communication is made in the exercise of ministry and without malice. The privilege can be lost if the minister's statements concern nonmembers or former members,[44] or if defamatory statements are made outside or beyond the membership of the church.[45]

Confidentiality and Privacy

A third traditional tort means of recovery used in ministerial misconduct suits is the disclosure of confidential communications and other private facts.[46] The clergy probably receive as much confidential information as any other group of professionals in society. Disclosure of this information has severe ramifications for the congregant, and conversely, the risks for the minister are extremely high.[47]

The most common example is breach of confidentiality. All fifty states now grant a statutory privilege for certain information communicated to clergy which, in most states, cannot be breached except by waiver from the communicant or due to a special law. (Some states require ministers, for example, to report incidents of suspected child abuse even if received through confidential communications.)

Several limitations apply. Only a select group of persons are bound by the privilege, usually those who have been licensed, commissioned, or ordained by a religious body. Only certain communications are privileged. Casual conversations or business discussions are not covered, but only those in which the congregant is seeking spiritual advice. In addition to the presence of third parties, the duty of confidentiality may also be limited by (1) statutory provisions, (2) the doctrine and practices of the religious organization involved, (3) the common law duty to warn third parties of imminent bodily harm, and (4) places where the minister is given the discretion to decide if and when the privilege applies.

Violation of privacy is a second claim in disclosure of confidential information lawsuits. Three types of privacy violations apply to clergy: unreasonable publicity given to another's private life, unreasonable intrusion upon another's seclusion, and publicity that places another in false light.[48]

The first of these is the most likely to be filed against a minister and simply requires (1) public disclosure; (2) private facts; and (3) matter highly offensive and objectionable to a reasonable person. Truth is not a defense.

In the case of Marian Gwinn involving church discipline proceeding from alleged sexual misconduct, the church insisted on bringing the matter before the entire congregation. The facts were also publicized to area churches. Although liability was imposed on the Church of Christ at Collinsville, Oklahoma, for statements about the plaintiff publicized after her resignation from the church, the Supreme Court recognized that the church was shielded from liability by the First Amendment as long as she was a member. By joining the church, Ms. Gwinn consented to the church's discipline.[49]

As in the case of defamation, the minister's privilege to disclose private facts is not absolute and may be lost if the minister intends harm to the plaintiff, publicizes the information to persons outside the church, or continues to publicize the information after the plaintiff has resigned membership.

Unreasonable intrusion upon another's seclusion, the second type of privacy violations, does not require publicity, but only invasion of privacy that would be considered highly offensive to a reasonable person. One minister entered a plaintiff's home under the guise of helping their family through counseling, but his true motive was to harm the couple through information obtained. The minister was held liable.[50] To avoid liability a minister should make sure that permission is obtained before entering a house or private area and that the purpose of the visit is neither underhanded nor secretive.

The final version of privacy violations likely to affect ministers is publicity that places a person in a false light. Conviction in such cases requires (1) that the publicity be highly offensive to a reasonable person and (2) that the minister act intentionally or with reckless disregard for the truth. To make false accusations about a person in a sermon is not only unethical, it could result in a day in court.

Child Care

In addition to lawsuits related to clergy counseling, defamation, and confidentiality, child care is a sensitive area in the courts today. A mother brought suit against a Memphis church and its staff, claiming that her child had been sexually molested in the church day-care center. An aggressive prosecutor spearheaded the case, which dragged on for over five years. The church was finally exonerated of all charges, but the legal fees alone cost the congregation over $500,000.

Church leaders in the future must be just as careful as any secular institution in knowing the law, screening all who work with children, and supervising all child-care programs. Church ministers must be familiar with the law. Many states, for example, have very strict regulations about reporting evidence of child abuse discovered by a teacher or care giver. The church is also responsible, and should be, for all of its organizational activities involving children: Sunday School, youth meetings, outings, and study groups. If violations occur, the burden of proof is on church leaders to prove they did everything humanly possible to protect the young and the vulnerable against mistreatment.

Attorney William Colbert told participants in the Church and the Law Conference at Stetson University that church leaders are not helpless in today's lawsuit-prone society. He listed several preventive measures as examples:

1. Against inadequate supervision charges, churches should have written policies.
2. Against grounds and building liability, be alert to hazards and do adequate maintenance.
3. Against hazardous activities, take extra precautions, use common sense and consider something less hazardous. Parent-consent and waiver-of-liability forms ensure a parent knows what the child is doing, but it does not absolve the church of responsibility.

4. Against vehicle liability, have the vehicle inspected often, keep it in top condition, be certain the driver is licensed and has a good driving record, and check insurance coverage.
5. Against employee negligence, be careful who is hired, check references and arrest records, use a written application, have job descriptions, and dismiss any employee not doing the job.
6. In sexual harassment cases, remember it is not what is actually said or done, but how the victim perceives it.
7. Against inadequate insurance coverage, follow these guidelines: (1) know what church assets are and what replacement costs would be; (2) identify potential liabilities; (3) be sure everyone is covered; (4) add a rider covering ministerial counseling liability, personal property on church premises, and special coverages such as disability and accident.[51]

Even after taking all precautions, church officials should be aware that lawsuits are increasingly common against ministers and the church.[52] At the present time, professional liability insurance for the minister is inexpensive, while the costs of litigation can be enormous. For church insurance to be adequate, professional liability insurance for every staff minister should be included.

Yes, the church is in the world. Modern ministers cannot transform their congregations into medieval monasteries and busy themselves in spiritual exercises. The biblical mandate from Christ is to be salt and light, to penetrate society with the purifying and illuminating gospel. As both pastor and prophet, the contemporary cleric must be involved in the human community that God created for His glory. Life in community for God-called ministers will probably include community service, political participation, legal responsibility, and promotion of public morality. In every one of these areas, the minister's ethical practices will be tested. Because the community is basically "foreign territory" for most church ministers, they will walk cautiously, upholding those ethical obligations that are vital to a ministry of integrity.

An old Scottish professor liked to say that there were just three qualifications for the ministry: the grace of God, knowledge of the Scriptures in the original languages, and gumption. The first, he said, is available if we pray for it; the second can be ours if we work for it; but the last is a gift of nature. He was not sure that either prayer or labor could produce it.[53] For ministers to be ethically involved in their communities requires ample grace, adequate knowledge of the Scriptures, and no small amount of gumption.

We have now arrived at our final transition. In the first two chapters we established the minister's vocation as a called-of-God professional and the importance of the cleric's character, conduct, and moral vision in making good moral choices. On this foundation we then explored the ethical obligations of the church minister in relation to personal life, congregation, colleagues, and community. Our final chapter introduces a practical possibility—that of applying all that has been learned thus far in a ministerial code of ethics.

Suggested Reading

Hughes, Philip E. *Christian Ethics in a Secular Society.* Grand Rapids: Baker Book House, 1983.

Jerisild, Paul T. and Dale A. Johnson, eds. *Moral Issues and Christian Response: Third/Fourth Editions.* New York: Holt, Rinehart, and Winston, 1983/1988.

Mott, Stephan Charles. *Biblical Ethics and Social Change.* New York: Oxford Press, 1982.

Niebuhr, H. Richard. *Christ and Culture.* New York: Harper & Row, 1951.

Niebuhr, Reinhold. *Moral Man and Immoral Society: A Study in Ethics and Politics.* New York: Scribners, 1932.

Parham, Robert. *Loving Neighbors Across Time.* Birmingham: New Hope, 1991.

What Shall We Do in a Hungry World? Birmingham: New Hope, 1988.

Simon, Arthur. *Christian Faith and Public Policy: No Grounds for Divorce.* Grand Rapids: William B. Eerdmans, 1987.

Smedes, Lewis. *Mere Morality.* Grand Rapids: Eerdmans, 1983.

Notes

[1]Walker Percy, *Thanatos Syndrome* (New York: Farrar, Straus and Giraux, 1987), 127-28.

[2]James P. Wind, (Russell Burk, Paul F. Camenisch, and Dennis P. McCann, eds., *Clergy Ethics in a Changing Society* [Louisville: Westminster/John Knox, 1991], 102-04) uses Percy's novel to illustrate one of four clergy ethical situations, which he calls "Ministry in the Extreme Case."

[3]H. Richard Niebuhr, *Christ and Culture* (New York: Harper & Row, 1951).

[4]See T. B. Maston, *Why Live the Christian Life?* (Nashville, Broadman, 1974), 174-87, for a discussion of the "Tension Strategy."

[5]Walter E. Wiest and Elwyn A. Smith, *Ethics in Ministry* (Minneapolis: Fortress, 1990), 144.

[6]See John Yoder, *The Politics of Jesus* (Grand Rapids: Eerdmans, 1972), for the proposal that Jesus' public ministry was primarily a political statement.

[7]Wiest and Smith, 172-73.

[8]Gaylord Noyce, *Pastoral Ethics* (Nashville: Abingdon, 1988), 168.

[9]Ibid., 151-154.

[10]See Walter Rauschenbusch, *Christianizing the Social Order* (New York: Macmillan, 1912). Charles Sheldon's novel, *In His Steps* (Chicago: Advance Pub. Co., 1899) reflects the idealism of that era from an evangelical viewpoint.

[11]See Martin Luther King, Jr., *Why We Can't Wait* (New York: NAL, 1988), 76-95.

[12]Richard Bondi, *Leading God's People: Ethics for the Practice of Ministry* (Nashville: Abingdon, 1988), 73.

[13]Ibid., 73-74.

Ministerial Ethics

[14]Oliver S. Thomas, "Church and State: Matthew 22:15-22," *Theological Educator* (Fall, 1987): 35-43.

[15]*Light* (July, 1984), 6.

[16]Noyce, 166.

[17]Cited by Henlee H. Barnette, "The Minister as a Moral Role-Model," *Review and Expositor* (Fall, 1989): 514.

[18]Richard V. Pierard, "One Nation Under God: Judgment or Jingoism?" in *Christian Social Ethics*, Perry C. Cotham, ed. (Grand Rapids: Baker Book House, 1979), 81.

[19]Terry Muck, "Holy Indignation," *Christianity Today* (21 October 1988), 14-15.

[20]See Stephan Charles Mott, *Biblical Ethics and Social Change* (New York: Oxford Press, 1982), 161-65, for a discussion of these critieria.

[21]Noyce, 164.

[22]Glenn Brown, "Electioneering Off Limits to Churches," *Baptist Message* (5 March 1992), 2.

[23]Richard John Neuhaus, *The Naked Public Square: Religion and Democracy in America*, 2nd ed. (Grand Rapids: Eerdmans, 1984), ix.

[24]Paul Simmons, "The Pastor as Prophet: How Naked the Public Square?" *Review & Expositor* (Fall, 1989): 519.

[25]Cecil Sherman, "Preaching on Ethical Issues," *Light* (December, 1981), 9-10.

[26]Don B. Harbuck, "Preaching on Ethical Issues in the Context of the Pastor's Total Ministry," *Light* (December, 1981), 11-16.

[27]Charles Swindoll, "Discipleship and Ethics," unpublished speech delivered at the Christian Life Commission Seminar, Nashville, May, 1983.

[28]Stephen Charles Mott, *Biblical Ethics and Social Change* (New York: Oxford, 1982), 57.

[29]Ernst Troeltsch, *The Social Teachings of the Christian Churches*, 2 vols. (Chicago: University of Chicago Press, 1960), 112.

[30]Noyce, 168.

[31]Bondi, 17.

[32]See for example "To Meet AIDS with Grace and Truth," a statement adopted by the 200th General Assembly (1988) of the Presbyterian Church—U.S.A.

[33]William M. Pinson, Jr., *Applying the Gospel* (Nashville: Broadman, 1975), 68-87.

[34]Noyce, 157-162.

[35]"Swaggart, others are guilty of defaming rival preacher," *Richmond Times-Dispatch* (13 September 1991), A-8.

[36]Oliver Thomas, "Clergy Malpractice After *Nally v. Grace Community Church*: Where Do We Go From Here?", an unpublished paper delivered to the University of Virginia Law School in l991, 2, and the basis for much of the material in this section.

[37]*Destafano*, 729 P.2d at 290 (Quinn, C.J., concurring).

[38]"State court upholds filing of clergy malpractice suits," *The Baptist Message* (9 November 1989), 2.

[39]Thomas, "Clergy Malpractice," 14-16.

[40]*Hester v. Barnett*, 723 S.W.2d 544, 555 (1987).

[41]*Destafano v. Grabrian*, 763 F.2d 275 (Colo. 1988), and *Erickson v. Christenson*, 99 Or. App. 104, P.2d (1989) in which the court ruled "the harm to plaintiff stemmed from Christenson's misuse of his position of trust, not from the seduction as such...."

[42]Thomas, "Clergy Malpractice," 16-29.

[43]Ibid., 29-34.

[44]*Guinn v. Church of Christ of Collinsville*, 775 P.2d at 878, 883.

[45]524 So.2d 915 (La. App. 1988).

[46]Thomas, "Clergy Malpractice," 34-52.

[47]As has been noted before, the clergy counselor should inform all counselees that confidentiality may be broken if the information would (1) prevent a person harming himself; (2) prevent a person harming others; (3) prevent a crime; (4) or if required by court or law.

[48]Thomas, "Clergy Malpractice," 47-52.

[49]775 P.2d 766 (Okla. 1989).

[50]*Hester*, 723 S.W.2d 544 (Mo. App. 1987).

[51]Jacqueline Kersh, "Attorney cites measures to cut church liability," *Baptist Press* Release, May 31, 1989.

[52]As legal responsibilities which apply to the clergy vary from state to state, a minister should be familiar with the laws in his or her locale which are applicable.

[53]John Oman, *Concerning the Ministry* (New York: Harper & Brothers, 1937), 9.

7

A MINISTERIAL CODE OF ETHICS:
Help or Hindrance?

In the pastorate a very complex situation raised several ethical questions. Over a period of many months, a single college student made homosexual advances to several church youth, all under sixteen years of age. To further complicate the matter, the college student also served as a part-time minister on the church staff.

After one young person told his parents of an episode, the family confided in an associate minister. Other incidents soon came to light. Finally, two staff ministers came to the pastor with the revelation. When confronted with the facts, the college student broke down emotionally and admitted his guilt. Although he expressed deep sorrow over the pains he had caused, he refused to accept advice or seek counseling, stating that his problem was "incurable." Immediately he moved to a distant city, where he soon found employment as a student-minister in another church.

This crisis also raised several questions concerning ministerial ethics. First, the issue of confidentiality. One youth confided with the minister of music, who was unsure about how to handle the information. Should he tell the parents? The pastor? The youth minister? How far does confidentiality extend, and under what conditions can a promise of confidentiality be broken?

A second question concerned obligations to colleagues. What responsibility does one minister have to another, especially if that other is his or her supervisor? One difficult decision came in relation to the homosexual student after he moved. After much discussion, the church ministers decided to inform the student's new pastor of the incidents, both to protect against recurrences and to open the door for ministry to the student.

Another ministerial ethics question concerned how to share this incident. What should be told? To whom? Should the deacons or the personnel committee be informed? How would this affect the parents who were still in the church? Should anything be shared with the church youth, especially since some of them knew of the encounters?

Most ministers have never sat down to reason through a professional dilemma like this one or to develop guiding principles for those involved. Ordinarily church leaders simply respond to career problems as they happen, hoping their ability to think clearly will carry them through. This approach sometimes works, particularly if the minister is mature, experienced, or well-trained. Too often, however, tragic mistakes are made that create vocational headaches and personal heartaches.

Is there a way for the clergy to be prepared for ethical questions inherent to their profession? Are there obligations that are basic to the role of the ordained? Can a code of ethics for ministers be developed to guide and motivate them as they make professional decisions?

In chapter 1 we noted that almost all functional definitions of a professional included self-regulation, usually in the form of a code such as the Hippocratic Oath or the Code of Professional Responsibility of the American Bar Association.[1] Virtually every profession has a written code to guarantee ethical performance in the marketplace.

It seems enigmatic that in the one profession expected to model morality, very few codes of ethics are found. Although some religious denominations have written codes for their clergy, their number has decreased in this century. Nolan Harmon's classic text on ministerial ethics contained sample codes adopted by five major denominations between 1926 and 1944 (appendix I), but none of these are in current use.[2] A recent search among these same five denominations uncovered only two with contemporary standards, the Disciples of Christ and the Unitarian-Universalist churches (appendix II). Occasionly a smaller group of ministers will develop a written code.[3]

As we have seen in earlier chapters, the call to Christian ministry leads to many ethical dilemmas. The complex role of the modern minister and the structure of the contemporary church make it very difficult to be a "good minister in a not-so-good world." The contemporary cleric often feels like a person driving through a large city who makes a wrong turn on the freeway and gets lost. After several detours and dead-end streets, the traveler searches for a map.

One possible "road map" to assist ministers in their professional conduct is a code of ethics. Although such codes by themselves never develop an ethical person, they can give guidance. Codes inherently promote personal responsibility by encouraging a moral leader of the church to think about ethics in ministry.

At his daughter's graduation ceremony, Arthur Becker heard the class of veterinarians pledge compliance to a code of ethics. The

Lutheran teacher wondered why we didn't have something similar for ministers. "I think *we* need to have underscored for us the fact that being a professional in large part means being accountable to a set of values which guide our behavior as ministers."[4]

The credibility of church shepherds is contingent on their ability to control their own ethical conduct. James Reasons's thorough study on the role of codes in ministerial ethics began by stating, "It is crucial that the minister be able to discern the ethical difficulties unique to his profession and act on them in a biblical manner."[5] In a recent book dealing with sexual exploitation in the pastoral relationship, Marie Fortune calls for "the establishment of clear ethical guidelines concerning clergy misconduct by each denominational body" and urges church leaders to develop "unequivocal policies and procedural safeguards."[6]

The question raised by this chapter is this: Is a ministerial code of ethics a help or a hindrance? A second question is related. Is it possible to write such a code for ministers? Some clergy oppose a written code for theoretical and practical reasons. Liberal clergy may feel the strong deontological bent of professional codes inevitably leads to legalism.[7] Conservative clerics may fear that a denominational hierarchy will use the code as a club to keep disloyal ministers in line and out of significant churches. Ministers of every stripe are nervous about any document that could threaten their pastoral autonomy.

Developing a code of ethics for any professional group poses three major problems: authorship, instruction, and enforcement.[8] Who writes the code: the professionals, the clients, or third parties? Who teaches the code: someone outside the profession or a colleague from within? Who enforces the code: the professionals themselves or others?

There are lesser problems. What subjects should be addressed in a code? Should the document consist of rules, principles, or both? How is the code distributed? Are the sanctions fair? What process is used to enforce the code? To lead a group of ministers through that wilderness might require another Moses!

Although developing and implementing a code of ethics for ministers is an arduous task with many risks, we are convinced that it is worthwhile. Still it will not be a panacea for every ministerial problem nor will it guarantee safe passage through every ethical maze of ministry.

It is our firm belief, nevertheless, that a written code of ethics will assist the Christian minister as a guide and as a goal; it should both teach and inspire. The apostle Paul explained that "the law was our tutor to bring us to Christ" (Gal. 3:24, NKJV). The word for "tutor" was *paidagogas*, a Greek word that identified a custodian, usually a slave who had charge of a child from six to sixteen years old. This servant was to discipline the child.[9] In like manner, a code of ethics is no substitute for Christ, but it can discipline and direct ministers toward a Christlike ministry.

Let us now explore that possibility. First, we want to look at how codes function in the secular professions. The way doctors, lawyers, and other professionals use codes can help us understand their potential for ministers.

This overview will prepare us to address the heart of this chapter: the value of a ministerial code of ethics. A related task, how to write a code of ethics, will be our third major concern. One practical result of this study can be for you, the reader, to write your own personal code of ethics.

Codes in the Professions

Visiting professor Amitai Etzioni thought he was overprepared to teach ethics to a group of MBA's at Harvard Business School. He had just completed a book on ethics, after thirty years of teaching at Columbia, Berkeley, and George Washington Universities. Etzioni was loaded with material.

He soon discovered that these business-leaders-to-be were not easily swayed. In one class period, after presenting a case study, the professor asked, "Is that ethical?" One student responded, "I'm not sure there is such a thing as the subconscious."

Later the subject of "binding moral duties" was introduced with the analogy, "I would *like* to go to a movie but *ought* to visit a friend in the hospital." The students challenged the idea, saying, "The real reason is that you are just trying to impress your friends," or "It makes you feel good." In the mind of the students there were no noble acts in human behavior; moral goodness was always due to baser motives, such as self-interest.

The teacher noted that these MBA's were joining an age-old tradition called reductionism, denying the existence of morality. In so doing they also diluted its significance. Although Etzioni indicated that his teaching was not a complete failure, he confessed that he "had not found a way to help classes full of MBA's see that there is more to life than money, power, fame and self-interest."[10]

The 1980s and 1990s have witnessed a growing concern about the ethical values of professionals. Blatant moral misbehavior has tarnished the image of the New York Stock Exchange, the banking industry, the Congress, the White House, the health-care system, and even churches.

As we noted in chapter 1, this crisis in professional life has been caused primarily by a loss of common values. Alasdair MacIntyre thinks discussing professional ethics in a pluralistic society is impossible because of this lack of shared moral values.[11] Three major movements in Western culture have precipitated the crisis: secularization, pluralism, and relativism. Like a swarm of termites, these forces have eaten away the foundations of professionalism.

The mood today among professionals is in the direction of self-interest and away from altruistic service and moral commitments. Countering this tide are two trends: a surge of interest in professional ethics and the reintroduction of ethics studies in schools of law, medicine, business, and other professional institutions.[12]

Not everyone is convinced this will help. Concerning professional codes, many are negative, believing that codes are basically self-serving and contribute to unethical conduct. Michael Bayles strongly disagrees, stating that professionals engage in unethical behavior for the same reasons others do: financial gain, fame, desire to benefit clients or employers, and the simple failure to reflect on the ethical import of one's conduct.[13]

Purposes of Professional Codes

Why have professional codes of ethics? In the broad sense, these codes specify the moral role of the professional and the special obligations understood by the profession. "They tell professionals how to act *as a professional*, as understood by the professional group."[14]

Specifically, written codes of professional ethics have four major concerns. The first concern is to spell out *guidelines accepted collectively by peers*.

> The ethic of the professional is to be found in the dialectical interaction between the conscience of the individual professional and the collective conclusions of the profession as a whole, and the formulations of the "Professional Code," always provisional and continually being revised.[15]

Having guidelines protects professionals from possible errors and "keeps us from reinventing the wheel every time we make a decision."[16]

A second purpose of codes of ethics is *to protect the profession from incompetent practitioners*. Standards are established to protect the medical profession from "quacks" and the legal profession from shysters.

> Although it is not a virtue, competence is probably the most crucial of a professional's characteristics. Professionals have an ethical responsibility not to hold themselves out to do or accept work they are not competent to handle.[17]

Another purpose of the codes is *to support and protect individual members.*[18] The existence of a code protects the professional from social pressures to violate the code. An engineer can refuse to reveal corporate information simply by saying, "Sorry, my professional code of ethics forbids such disclosures." It also reminds the professional that personal actions represent to society the ethical convictions of colleagues and of the entire profession.[19]

A final purpose of professional codes is to *define the nature of the profession.*[20] Codes help to define the moral values of the group. Individuals considering entrance into a profession know from their written code what is the ethical tone of that particular vocation.

Karen Lebacqz has observed that if codes are simply guidelines for specific behavior in certain circumstances, they rapidly become either too vague to be helpful or too rigid to adapt to change. The ethics professor makes this proposal: "Rather than looking for specific guidelines for *action* in professional codes, they might be better understood as statements about the *image* of the profession and the *character* of professionals."[21]

Understood this way, codes are not simply rules for action. They identify the moral stress points within a profession and they present a model of a good professional.

Nature of Professional Codes

Professional ethics usually assumes the pattern of a code, contract, or covenant.[22] A contract involves a promise between people in which an obligation to perform is expected, followed by a reward when the action is accomplished. The covenant approach involves both codal and contractual elements, but it is based on a gift between two parties, resulting in a covenant promise and a change in the covenanted people because of this relationship (Gen. 17:1-22). The code approach is the most common criteria for evaluating professions, professionals, and their conduct.

In their classic study of the professions, Carr-Saunders and Wilson noted that most professional codes are characterized by positive prescriptions and negative sanctions.[23] These code rules usually try to balance the ethical concerns of the professionals, their clients, and the general public.

Do professionals live by different moral standards than the rest of society? Some debate that they do, believing higher standards give the professional a sense of mission to act appropriately. Others say that two sets of standards breed elitism, confuse the public, increase distrust of professionals, and put the nonprofessional in a vulnerable position.

The best understanding probably combines elements from both points of view. Ordinary morality governs all members of society, including professionals, but a profession's special ethical obligations are reflected in professional codes. These codes do not promote a unique system for an elite group, "but rather they utilize societal values to give the professional useful, specific direction."[24]

Structure of Professional Codes

Professional codes have a long history. The earliest known code was a medical code found on a stone pillar, dated 2250 B.C. Attributed to Hammurabi, the code mainly dealt with the physician-patient relationship. Hippocrates of Greece (350 B.C.) wrote the famous medical oath (which bears his name), to separate medicine from magic. Also called the "Doctor's Oath," it established a formal code of conduct for those physicians who treated disease. In the Middle Ages Maimonides, an Egyptian who practiced medicine (A.D. 1135-1204), wrote ethical guidelines that obligated physicians to treat any patient needing care, regardless of financial status.

Secular codes of ethics vary in content and structure. Most include basic categories of duties. The key ingredients of professional codes are: (1) private or personal obligations; (2) responsibilities to clients and special interest groups; (3) obligations to colleagues and to the profession; and (4) responsibilities to the community or society as a whole.

C. S. Calian surveyed eight codes from various professions and found a "large measure of commonality" in the spirit and purpose of their statements. He developed a list of fifteen items incorporating the main statements in most of the codes. Six of the fifteen items were obligations the professional personally assumed: a sense of calling or commitment, the value of knowledge and skill, the need for continuing education and improvement of skills, the derivation of primary income from the profession, the need to reduce or eliminate conflicts of interest, and the need to maintain good health.[25]

A major area covered by professional codes of ethics relates to *obligations between the professional and clients*. Calian's list of fifteen items of commonality in professional codes includes four that concern clients: questions about confidentiality, the primacy of service over remuneration, the duty to know one's limits and consult others, and the attitude of respect for the worth of every individual.

The duties a professional owes to his or her clients is a key chapter in Bayles' *Professional Ethics*. The university professor proposed the following obligations between the professional and client: trustworthiness, honesty, candor, competence, diligence, loyalty, fairness, and discretion. Bayles correctly added that clients also have unique responsibilities: to keep commitments, to be truthful, and not knowingly to request professionals to act unethically.[26]

A third area of responsibility contained in most professional codes covers *obligations of professionals to their profession and to their colleagues.* In the eight codes C. S. Calian reviewed, one item relating to fellow professionals made his list of fifteen: the need to cooperate with colleagues. Three specific duties professionals owe one another are respect, information concerning competence and character of applicants to the profession, and willingness to bear their fair share of the work in the profession's social role.[27]

Finally, what are the *obligations of professionals to their community or to society at large?* Calian listed three: to be sensitive to consumer's rights and well-being, to be discrete in publications and solicitations, and to example good citizenship.

The professional's responsibility for public good has at least three other facets. First, there is the role of social leadership, such as service with charitable organizations or governmental boards and agencies. A second facet of responsibility for public good is the improvement of professional knowledge and skills. A third facet is to preserve and enhance the social role of the profession itself, which ultimately benefits society.[28]

This overview of the structure of professional codes has revealed something important to the formation of a ministerial code of ethics. Secular codes typically outline the kinds of ethical dilemmas that professionals encounter, the loyalties expected of them, the duties they perform, and the conflicts their role creates. These obligations are not simply codes for action; as Lebacqz has stressed, they are statements that project the character of the professional.[29]

Enforcement of Professional Codes

Before we leave the subject of professional codes of ethics, it is necessary to explore one other issue, enforcement. In the past, professional groups have been self-regulating; most believe this is the best approach. The traditional method of professions for ensuring compliance has been selective admission and discipline of members, mainly through sanctions. Some ethicists believe a focus on sanctions is a mistake because there is no proof that adequate sanctions (whether blame or loss of license) deter misconduct by others.[30] William F. May strongly denounced using a code to solve the problem of professional discipline, preferring an approach that seeks to be remedial and inclusive, rather than codal and exclusive.[31]

Enforcement of codes of ethics poses many problems.[32] The basic problem of distribution is often overlooked. The regular distribution of a written code to members is not sufficient to ensure compliance. Simply posting an organization's code on a bulletin board will almost certainly encourage noncompliance. The assignment of accountability is also vital to enforcement. Experts contend enforcement committees should be composed of both professionals and laypersons to prevent in-house protectionism.

Enforcing of standards depends chiefly on the willingness of colleagues and the public to report violations. Once guilt has been determined, disciplinary action usually takes one of three forms: censure, suspension, or termination.

What then can be said about professional codes of ethics as they apply to ministerial ethics? Do they benefit the professions today?

It has become obvious in this summary that many people feel uncomfortable with a rules approach to morality, which the professional codes appear to be. This deontological bent downplays the role of character and overlooks the complex question of motives and consequences. As many note, the inner integrity of the professional may be assumed, but it is seldom encouraged in the codal approach to professional ethics.

Another concern about traditional professional ethics is its failure to consider the nature of social roles. Secular codes of ethics fail to recognize the "power gap" between the professional and the client. That may be the reason why the words *justice* and *liberation* do not appear in these codes of ethics.[33]

A third concern could be labeled self-interest. Lisa Newton attacks professional codes as "a code of Professional Manners oriented toward a Professional Image for the protection of Professional Compensation."[34] Her scathing critique notes that codes limit advertising, suppress competition, and forbid contradiction of professional judgments, which she terms "gentlemanly etiquette." Yale professor Gaylord Noyce agrees, stating that the codes of professional groups "are shot through with collusive self-interest."[35]

No doubt, the codes also have a serious problem with accountability. Because the authorship, instruction, and enforcement of the codes are conducted mainly within each professional organization, the perception is that professionals are more concerned with self-interest than ethical conduct. This obstacle is best overcome by including non-professionals, who have no vested interests, in all aspects of the code process.

In spite of these limitations, professional organizations continue to depend on codes of ethics to ensure standardized behavior. A report by the Business Roundtable found 84 percent of the Fortune 500 companies had a code of ethics in 1989.[36] Professional codes communicate the basic ethical expectations within an association of professionals. Codes of ethics will be expected to serve professionals, their clients, and the society at large for some time to come.

> "The code," then, is better understood as a process than a product, and can be originated by one person in an effort to raise moral consciousness as well as it can be the outcome of a collective desire for some kind of guiding law—i.e., it can be the function of the Code to create felt needs in the area of ethics, not only to respond to them.[37]

A Ministerial Code of Ethics

According to some, a code of ethics for ministers seems about as necessary as Reeboks for a jaguar. "After all, ministers live and breathe morality, don't they? Their job is *upholding* a community's ethics, isn't it? So why a code for pastors?"[38]

An early discussion of standards for ministers appeared in 1928 titled, *Ministerial Ethics and Etiquette: The Minister's Own Manual of Conduct—Practical Guidance for Specific Situations*. Like many early ministerial codes, "it is interesting as a period piece—but it is minimalism in ethics."[39] It has some discussion about relationships with colleagues, denomination, and community, but most of the lengthy admonitions concern personal life, finances, conducting worship, and appropriate dress. The focus is on professional etiquette, as the opening words of the author illustrate:

> It goes without saying that the minister is a Christian, and it goes with this saying that he is a gentleman. This is the base line of the code assembled in the following pages. It is accepted as an axiom that every minister is a Christian gentleman. . . . the true Christian will always know how to conduct himself everywhere."[40]

Since these words were penned, our expectations for an ethical ministry have increased. In recent days, moral lapses among many prominent ministers have alarmed parishioners and aroused the public. Recent studies claim 118 Southern Baptist ministers are terminated monthly.[41] Many of these losses are due to unethical conduct. Church leaders in every denomination are calling for a thorough study of ethical issues involving the clergy and seeking ways to increase moral accountability in the ministry.

After a Colorado district court awarded $1.2 million in damages to a woman who had an affair with an Episcopal cleric, Bishop Peter Lee of Virginia warned his priests:

Laity and others who turn to the clergy for pastoral counsel and prayer have every right to expect their most painful secrets to be safe, their most confusing thoughts to be heard, their hopes and their aspirations to be received with respectful concern. But some persons expect their clergy to provide the permanent tenderness of intimacy they missed as children or that eludes them now as spouses.[42]

His letter also cautioned the priests against offering themselves as "substitute objects" for the longings of their parishioners. Absent from the Bishop's communiqué, however, was any acknowledgment of clergy vulnerability or any plan for prevention.

This episode highlights one of the difficulties ministers share with the secular professions. Like them, we are self-protective.

Jürgen Moltmann reminds us that clergy protect the *status quo*. We fear we have much to lose if we examine our practice as clergy in the context of new understandings about our responsibilities; if we find ourselves wanting, we will have to change. We may have to give up established ways.[43]

As we have already observed, professional groups have traditionally regulated themselves (though not always with success), using codes of ethics and disciplining boards. The professions regularly examine their responsibilities to their constituencies, evaluate their behavior, compare codes, and work to improve ethical practice.

Should there be equivalent accountability among the clergy? It is indeed startling that these concerns are seldom raised by the ordained. Some think ministers do not need ethical reflection because ministry is a moral work, and, therefore, self-correcting. Others claim it is demeaning to approach ministry as you would a secular profession.

A major reason that codes of ethics for ministers are so rare, claims Paul Carmenish, is the clergy's dedication to "atypical moral commitment." Such a commitment is a significant part of the self-image of the minister and the public's expectations.

I would suggest that one reason the clergy has been slower than the other major professions to develop its own distinctive ethic is that this atypical moral commitment was assumed to be so central to the profession that many thought it insulting to suggest that specific rules and guidelines were needed to require it.[44]

Real differences do exist between professional and clergy codes. Due to separation of church and state in the United States, the public sector ordinarily does not regulate the standards of clergy as they do professionals, except in two areas: performing marriage ceremonies and counseling.[45] From an ethical perspective, differences like this should be no problem. Clergy standards should always be higher than legal codes.

In spite of this or any other variation, the question remains, "Does this difference free us from the accountability we expect of sisters and brothers working in other vineyards?"[46] We cannot presume that just because preachers proclaim justice, righteousness, and morality that we will be just, righteous, and moral.

Ministers are accountable for ethical behavior in their vocation not only because of professional expectations but also because of their commitment to Christian ethics. To be a moral example in ministry is biblical.[47] Ethical conduct based on theological convictions are the very soil in which the clergy work. Is it unreasonable, then, to expect ministers to be accountable for their ethical practices?

In developing a code of ethics for Christian counselors, the Christian Association for Psychological Studies (CAPS), cited six biblical "Building Blocks" which form a foundation for their proposed code.

> Conflicts, difficulties, power struggles, trials and tribulations are normal and to be expected, whether one is a Christian or not (John 16:33; Psalm 37:7; Romans 2:9).
> We are to grow and mature through the conflicts, problems, trials and tribulations, and discipline that we experience (James 1:2-4; 1 Thessalonians 5:18).
> We are to support and encourage each other (John 15:17; Ephesians 4:32; John 13:35).
> We are to admonish and, if necessary, discipline each other, especially those Christians in positions of leadership and trust. However, such discipline is to be constructive rather than judgmental, done in love, and with caution about our own shortcomings (Matthew 18:15-17; 1 Corinthians 5:11-13; Galatians 6:1).
> We are to demonstrate the lordship of Christ in our lives by servant-like leadership, a sense of community, and a life-style that reflects the will of God (Matthew 20:25-28; John 12:26; 1 Peter 4:8-11; Colossians 3:12-17).
> We are to reach out to others in love and concern (Matthew 25:31-40; Hebrews 13:16; 2 Corinthians 1:3-7).[48]

A ministerial code of ethics is supported by biblical principles, theological conclusions, professional standards, and practical considerations. That is why it is our deep conviction that a clergy code of ethics, properly developed, clearly written, and appropriately enforced can strengthen ministerial integrity.

Unlike professionals, we will probably never be driven by outside forces to begin this task. Nor should we be. Our own moral convictions and vocational expectations should motivate us to seek the highest ethical standards for ministry. Our calling from God, our personal character, and our commitment to Christian ministry will allow us to do no less.

Purposes of a Ministerial Code

The overarching purpose of a ministerial code of ethics is accountability. Clergy sometimes resist codes and regulations because they want to be answerable to no one except God. When questioned about financial accountability, televangelist Paul Crouch of Trinity Broadcasting Network declared publicly that "the Almighty [was] his only watchdog." An editorial in *Christianity Today* responded that eventually we all do get what is coming to us, but "in the meantime it helps to have structures that encourage us to behave."[49]

Professional codes were usually written to specify the moral obligations of the professional, as understood by the professional group. The preamble to the American Nurses' Association's "Code for Nurses" begins, "A code of ethics makes explicit the primary goals and values of the profession. When individuals become nurses, they make a moral commitment to uphold the values and special moral obligations expressed in their code."[50]

Likewise, a code of ethics for ministers should reflect how the ordained of God should conduct their ministry, as understood by their fellow ministers. In other words, the Christian minister is not only accountable to God but also to other members of the clergy. Codes are usually developed over many years and represent the combined experience of many people. As we shall see shortly, writing an adequate code is more than a personal enterprise.

The four major values of professional codes also apply to clergy codes. The first and foremost purpose of a ministerial code is to provide *guidelines* which reflect the values of ministry. Clergy ethics affirm that to be a Christian minister means assuming certain basic obligations common to all clergy. These norms guide those "called to serve" toward an ethical ministry, stressing those areas where the minister is uniquely vulnerable.

Archibald Hart of Fuller Seminary describes a strange paradox in Christian ministry:

> We can be supersensitive to sin and immoral behaviors, but we are often oblivious to the need for ethical boundaries. This partially accounts for the fall of upright, spiritual, and well-intentioned pastors.[51]

Hart concluded that the underlying problem is not so much a lack of morality as the lack of broad ethical guidelines to govern the practice of ministry.

Guidelines for the minister serve three functions.[52] First, they articulate significate personal ethical standards such as standards for financial and family responsibilities. Sometimes included are classic labor-management issues of work schedules, study habits, vacations, and sabbaticals. Second, as in most codes of ethics, guidelines discuss expectations for a minister's conduct in relation to colleagues, the congregation, and the community. Third, guidelines reach toward ministerial ideals. Like the best examples from professional codes, clergy norms should stretch toward a higher standard of behavior than is currently being practiced. The Disciples Code reads, "I will seek to be Christlike in my personal attitudes and conduct toward all people regardless of race, class or creed."[53]

Competency is a second purpose of a ministerial code. At first we may think this trait applies more to the secular professions than to the ministry. Doctors need to be well-trained and need to keep up with the latest medical discoveries. We confide in lawyers to protect our legal rights. Physicians and lawyers possess "threatening knowledge" which, if used carelessly or improperly, could be harmful.

Let us not forget that ministers also have threatening knowledge in the form of confidential information and in the knowledge they possess about God. For a pastor this knowledge requires at least two essentials: the need for ministry skills and the need for mental and spiritual health. Most ministerial codes require the clergy to grow "through comprehensive reading and careful study and by attending . . . conferences" and to cultivate their personal devotional life.[54]

A code of ethics can also serve to *support and protect* the individual minister. Under the topic "Financial Matters," the 1990 Eastern Oklahoma Presbyterian Code (appendix II) states, "Ministers and church professionals shall not use church funds, accounts, and/or resources . . . [or] parishioner funds, accounts, and/or resources for personal or private advantage." Such codified statements protect pastors by informing congregations of the minister's obligations in questionable areas.

Christian psychologist Archibald Hart compares morality to the edge of a precipice. On one side is safe ground (non-sin); on the other there is disaster (sin).

It's only one step from safety to falling off the cliff. A code of ethics is like a fence erected well back from the precipice edge. It warns all those who come close that this is dangerous territory: CAUTION! PASS HERE AT YOUR OWN RISK.[55]

Ministerial Ethics

A final purpose of an ethical code for ministers is to *define* the ministerial profession. For the person planning to become a minister as well as the layperson, a written code explains the ethical expectations of the pastoral vocation. An association of ministers in the United Church of Christ has just completed a policy on sexual ethics for their group. The document begins by explicitly defining sexual misconduct:

1) Sexual advances; welcome or unwelcomed
2) Requests for sexual favors
3) Inappropriate affection such as kissing, touching, bumping, patting
4) Any sexual contact related to terms of employment
5) Any sexual contact which exploits the vulnerability of a parishioner, client or employee
6) Dating of parishioners by religious professionals is a gray area filled with ambiguity. In such situations, consultation with colleagues is essential.[56]

There should be no doubt to this group of ministers, or their congregations, what is construed as sexual misconduct.

This fourfold purpose of ministerial codes should not mislead a person to view codes as a collection of moral rules to keep ministers out of trouble. It is true, in a sense, that:

> a professional code of ethics is simply an intensification of the ethical concerns of normal life, but an intensification needed because of the more specialized role, the intense knowledge in human situations of high risk and vulnerability, which are a part of functioning as an ordained pastor.[57]

As such, they are not just guidelines for how ministers are to act in certain situations. If so, they would always be too specific to adjust to change or too general to be helpful.

As Karen Lebacqz has explained, codes of ethics for ministers are better understood and used as statements about the "image of the profession and the character of the professionals."[58] Clergy codes of ethics reflect the virtues and values of the person called to minister in Christ's name. Simply put, a code paints the portrait of a good minister.

Structure of a Ministerial Code

A growing concern about the spiritual formation of seminary students and their readiness for ministry led the Association of Theological Schools (ATS) to conduct intensive research in the 1970s and

1980s. To develop a profile for ministry, the study group surveyed over 4000 clergy and laity representing all denominations affiliated with ATS. The results, along with recommendations, were published in the document *Clergy Assessment and Career Development*. One section of the report revealed some serious deficiencies in ministerial morality. These led the researchers to make three proposals: (1) that a more formal code of ethics be established to help regulate ministry relationships; (2) that the pastor set up an accountability system as a prevention strategy; and (3) that a minister know his or her personal limits and vulnerabilities.[59]

Let us assume a group of ministers took this charge seriously. Where would they begin? What topics should they address in a code? Should the document be composed of principles or of specific obligations? In particular, what categories should be covered in a ministerial code?

Due to the renewed interest in clergy ethics this past decade, a host of new publications have appeared. A survey of the literature uncovers several recurring themes, many focusing on the moral character of the cleric. According to these writers, the characteristics of a good minister include certain fundamental virtues: trustworthiness, prudence, faithfulness, truthfulness, and integrity.

When the conduct of the ordained is specifically described, certain issues keep rising to the surface. Presbyterian professors Wiest and Smith are most concerned with truth-telling, especially in relation to plagiarism, letters of recommendation, and theological differences. A philosophy professor writing about "Ethical Issues in the Practice of Religion," suggests that any discussion of the clergy/parishioner relationship should include clerical roles, truth-telling, confidentiality, paternalism, and behavior control.[60]

Another recently published text analyzes organized religion from a critical point of view. The book begins by looking at three central ethical issues: confidentiality, "risk taking," and "convert seeking." The author seems most concerned with religious groups that endanger the life and health of members or use coercive conversion techniques.[61]

Studies like these do help us pinpoint some of the more obvious and crucial issues in ministerial ethics. As you might expect, however, one of the best ways to analyze the structure of clergy codes is to study the existing ones.

During the early part of this century, several mainline denominations developed formal codes of ethics for their ministers (appendix I). In comparison to these early examples, the few denominational codes that remain in use today appear to be extensively updated (appendix II). The present trend is away from denominational documents and toward codes constructed by smaller associations of ministers, usually covering only one area of responsibility, such as clergy sexual ethics or counseling ethics (appendix III).

The analysis of these statements reveals a common structure and a similarity in content. One thing that is not apparent is the kind of language that best fits a clergy code. One Christian psychologist acknowledged that "some of the unique roles of the pastor don't easily lend themselves to ethical codes," therefore he preferred basic principles.[62] However, if a primary purpose of a code is to serve as a guideline, then specific obligations as well as guiding principles must be spelled out.

Another stated purpose of codes is ensuring competency. This intent does not surface in many of the present or past documents. Theological, pastoral, and spiritual qualifications for ministers need to be more clearly defined to endorse skills in ministry.

The practice of ministry also involves many unique roles and responsibilities. Most written codes address the major areas of ministerial vulnerability (such as sex, money, and power), as well as the unique pressure points (such as family, confidentiality, and plagiarism). Codal statements that cover these topics serve to support and protect the minister by clearly defining ethical boundaries.

Sometimes a code begins with an introductory paragraph, a preamble affirming the minister's sense of calling to the ministry and commitment to ethical integrity. The Disciples Code begins:

> I am a minister of the Lord Jesus Christ, called of God to proclaim the unsearchable riches of His love. Therefore, I voluntarily adopt the following principles in order that through dedication and self-discipline I may set a more worthy example for those whom I seek to lead and serve [appendix II].

As you have already discovered from the approach of this book, a clear definition of pastoral ethics can be arranged under four major areas of the minister's life: obligations to self and family, to congregation, to colleagues, and to the community. Most of the written clergy codes follow this format in one way or another. To lay the groundwork for a code of our own, let us look at each of these four worlds of the minister.

The *personal and family responsibilities* of the professional are often overlooked in other professional codes. Not so in codes of ethics for ministers. The personal integrity of the servant of God is at the heart of ministry. Guarding that integrity involves such obvious matters as life-style, which is why most denominations have written and unwritten codes defining "conduct unbecoming a minister." The codes cited by Harmon (appendix I) and current ones (appendix II) are specific: they require a minister keep physically fit, avoid debts, be scrupulously honest, pay bills before moving, and give ample time to family life. When pastoral needs collide with family needs, the minister must be sure that church duties do not become an idol before which spouse and children are sacrificed.

The personal integrity of the pastor is important because it affects credibility. As the "medium of the message," the life of the prophet of God must point to the truth of the gospel. Credibility in ministry includes such basic matters as the minister's covenant to cultivate a devotional life, to reserve study time, to refuse to plagiarize sermons (a besetting sin of preachers), and to keep in touch with the best religious thought.

Because ministers can never get it all done, we forever dangle between the weekly necessities (sermon preparation, newsletter articles, committee meetings), the unanticipated ministries (funerals, counseling, visiting the ill), and those hard-to-find creative moments (reading, growth conferences, spiritual disciplines). Meanwhile, the family waits at the dinner table. The busy church leader desperately wants to keep work and family life in proper balance. A well-written code can help a minister establish priorities and stick to them.

The second area to be guarded by a ministerial code is the *congregation*. Most difficult problems for professionals appear in relation to clients. Although the member of a congregation is a "client," several important differences exist between a typical professional-client association and a minister-congregation relationship.[63]

For one thing, the distinction between laity and clergy is not nearly so well-defined as it is for the client and other professionals. The authority of the minister is perceived very differently from that of a professional (and it should be). Another major disparity is that the minister's "clients" are an organized group; in fact, in many denominations the vote of the congregation determines employment, termination, and salary.

This reality imposes a vulnerability on the minister. No doctor worries about a disgruntled patient starting a campaign among clients to freeze his or her salary. Yet every time the pastor serves an individual member, the possible repercussions in the flock must be considered. Misperceptions could erupt into church conflict and cause the pastor's dismissal.

With this in mind, what ethical obligations do pastors have toward parishioners? One shepherding sin is almost universal in codes for ministers; this is "the unethical aspect of what we call 'sheep stealing' or proselytizing members from another community of faith."[64] This practice, perhaps influenced by the competitive nature of American business, undercuts the credibility of the pastoral office itself.

The limits of confidentiality is another issue with which all professionals wrestle. Many states now have legal codes that carefully prescribe "confessional privilege." Beyond what is legally required, the Christian pastor must untie the Gordian knot of when to disregard the normal expectations of confidentiality. The minister's obligation is often stated in codes as an absolute principle, "The confidential statements made to a minister by his parishioners are sacred and not to be divulged" (Presbyterian Code). It would be better to word the standard in a way that allows each minister to define the rare circumstances under which information may be divulged.[65]

Other responsibilities of ministers to their congregations covered in codes include service rather than salary as the primary motivation for ministry, integrity in preaching, fairness in dealing with factions, impartiality in administrative decisions, and the basic obligation to nurture the believing community.

Although ministers have a community of *colleagues*, they often lack structural unity. The ministry can be a lonely profession. Most ministers confess that they need support from their colleagues, including the need for moral discernment, empathetic understanding, encouragement, ministry resources, and general comradery. Too often the relationship between ministers is one of competition and conspiracy rather than mutual blessing.

Clergy can find many positive ways to build healthy relationships with other ministers and still uphold ethical standards. Almost all codes emphasize four basic obligations ministers owe to one another:

> I will not speak scornfully or in derogation of any colleague in public. In any private conversation critical of a colleague, I will speak responsibly and temperately. [UUMA Code]

> It is unethical for a minister to interfere directly or indirectly with the parish work of another minister. [Methodist Code]

> Except in emergencies, ministerial service should not be rendered to the members of another parish without the knowledge of the minister of the parish. [Presbyterian Code]

> If I am to share the ministry of a church with (an) other minister(s), I will earnestly seek clear delineation of responsibility, accountability, and channels of communication before responsibilities are assumed. [UUMA Code]

A variety of other collegial responsibilities appear in some of the current codes (appendix II). The Disciples Code adds a number of pledges: not to compete with other ministers for pulpits or honors; not to embarrass successors by "meddling in the affairs" of a former church; courtesy to predecessors; loyal support to one's pastor after retirement; and respect toward all ministers, regardless of the size or nature of their field.

The Eastern Oklahoma Presbytery Code (EOP) is thorough—twenty-five pages written in a narrative style. Under "Colleague Relationships" the authors present forty-four imperatives in nine categories. Most of these obligations cover the common ground of staff relationships, denominational duties, treatment of predecessors and successors, and the role of retired pastors. The document plows virgin soil, however, in two important areas overlooked in other codes: the responsibilities of the "minister-without-pastoral-charge" and proper relationships with other professionals.[66]

Are there limits to clergy collegiality? We all know ministers who destroy healthy congregations. Some are on the way out of ministry. Others are truly incompetent. A few have serious spiritual, moral, and emotional problems that will not change until they receive help. When such pastors fail and are forced to "move on," do we close ranks behind the flawed colleagues and try to find them another place of ministry?

Herein is a major ministerial dilemma. How can we be supportive to a comrade in the ministry and at the same time be honest in our responsibilities to other congregations? Truthfulness in letters of recommendation and "truth in love" to the guilty colleague is a starting point.[67] One current code reads, "Should I know that a colleague is engaged in practices that are damaging ... I will speak openly and frankly to her/him and endeavor to be of help" (UUMA Code).

The final statement of the Congregational Code summarizes for ministers their responsibility to each other: "As members of the same profession and brothers in the service of a common Master, the relation between ministers should be one of frankness, of comradeship, and of co-operation."

The final area usually covered by traditional ministerial codes is the cleric's *responsibility to the community*. This appears to be one of the weaker sections of most written codes. Three of the four early codes were silent on this subject. Only the Unitarian Code spoke to community obligations; the minister is "not under obligations to marry every couple that comes to him to be married," and as a citizen "he should, therefore, be faithful to his public obligations, and should respond to reasonable requests for assistance in community work."

More recent codes have more to say on the subject, but most of the counsel centers on the self-interests of the church, rather than service to the community. The concern of the Disciples Code seems to be a fear that the church or its ministers might be corrupted by the world; thus it warns its ministers "to be human . . . but never lower [your] ideals in order to appear 'a good fellow.'" It further cautions its clergy to avoid "funeral or marriage rackets" and beware of consuming the time of business and professional people with "unimportant matters."

A more positive word about church and community, as relates to the ministerial profession, comes from three different denominational groups. First is an obligation to be a moral and spiritual leader in the community: "I will maintain a prophetic pulpit, offering to the community religious and ethical leadership" (UUMA Code).

Second is a charge to remember that one's primary calling is to be the pastor of a congregation, the minister's primary community. This means on the one hand, "I consider that my first duty to my community is to be a conscientious pastor and leader of my congregation" (Disciples Code). On the other hand, "Ministers may assume outside commitments that do not detract from their pastoral responsibilities" (EOP Code). The statement in the Disciples document adds that this primary responsibility to the church should never be used "as an easy excuse to escape reasonable responsibilities that the community calls upon me to assume."

Only rarely do any of our gathered codes actually step into the world community to render beneficial service. Whereas professional codes emphasize that doctors, lawyers, and engineers have an obligation to be social leaders, assume community responsibilities, and work for the betterment of society, this concept is glaringly absent from ministerial codes.

One clergy code prohibits accepting "fees or gifts as payment for business or professional referrals" (EOP Code). Another encourages "sympathetic support to neighboring ministers or other religious bodies" (UUMA Code). The only time the codes of ethics for ministers really relate to the needs of the community is when they say, "I will encourage members' participation in efforts to solve community problems" (UUMA Code) and "Ministers shall support efforts to better that community" (EOP Code).

Obviously, the minister's responsibility to the citizenry is an area that needs serious thought. If the church is to be salt and light to the world (Matt. 5:13-16), the moral leader of the Christian community will surely have significant obligations to society.

What have we discovered then about the structure of ministerial codes? First, the language of the codes is dualistic, declaring both specific norms and general principles. Second, certain key issues, like confidentiality and truthfulness, appear in most codes. Third, the points at which a minister is most vulnerable ethically, such as sexual temptation and imbalanced work habits, receive a great deal of attention. Finally, most codes for ministers focus on the four major categories we have outlined above: self and family, congregation, colleagues, and the community.

Enforcement of a Ministerial Code

Earlier we noted three major difficulties in developing a code of ethics: authorship, instruction, and enforcement. The first two problems will be discussed when we consider how to write a code. Before us now is the issue of enforcement.

When the National Religious Broadcasters formally established its ethics and financial accountability code in January 1989, the organization told members that they must comply within three months or be dismissed. Before the year ended, officials admitted they had been overly optimistic about implementation and enforcement.[68] The variety of ways church groups have enforced their codes, or failed to do so, indicates the complexity of this issue.

By assumption of his role, the Christian minister is obligated to abide by certain codes of conduct, whether written or not. Formal clergy codes are based on this accountability. A ministerial code of ethics, by its very nature, assumes the acceptance of personal responsibility, the reporting of violations, and effective enforcement. Yet, this last matter of disciplining code-breakers has long troubled churches and denominations.

A Virginia minister who chairs an ethics guidelines committee in his religious body told of a recent dilemma. One of the denomination's prominent pastors became sexually involved with a married parishioner. After he expressed repentance for his failure, the erring cleric's church voted to restore him. Pastoral colleagues in the Ministers Association felt they also had an obligation to respond, as the group's code of ethics had been violated. After investigation by the association, the group sent a letter of admonition to the clergyman.

When church shepherds break their covenants to God and responsibilities to their congregation, what should be done? Should a minister report the sexual abuse of parishioners by another pastor, in the name of collegial support? What enforcement procedures should churches or denominations follow? What sanctions, if any, are appropriate? How should the laity and clergy relate to a fallen minister who needs healing and restoration?

As noted earlier, professional groups historically have been self-regulating. The importance of including both professionals and laypersons on enforcement committees, say the experts, cannot be overstressed. Another ingredient is the willingness of colleagues and the public to report problems. Key components in effective enforcement by committees are confidentiality, fair and just representation, and the release of committee members from legal liability.

Most ethics committees decide on all aspects of ethical behavior. As one regulatory board said, "We are the police, we are the prosecution, we are the grand jury, and the petit jury."[69]

To study the practice of churches and denominational groups whose ministers are accused of unethical behavior is a frustrating exercise. Most congregations have no established procedure. Most church groups act in a very informal way; they simply deal with offenses as they arise. When a pastor or other staff member is charged with some transgression, an established church authority (deacons, elders, or committee) usually investigates the accusation. They then either exonerate the falsely accused or sanction the guilty.

When you look beyond this general description for specific details, you discover no end to the ways religious bodies respond to ministerial misconduct. This obvious inconsistency among churches diminishes ministerial accountability. Why should the ordained seriously reflect on their ethical obligations if church and denominational expectations are lax or nonexistent?

The ministerial codes written during the first half of this century (appendix I) contain no instructions at all about enforcement. The documents seem to assume, with unrealistic optimism, that the ethical ideals contained in the codes would so motivate ministers, that no enforcement would be necessary.

The more recent pastoral codes (appendixes II and III) are not so naive. "A profession that will not police itself runs the danger of being policed by others," states the EOP Code. Newer documents evidence diversity, but all contain some procedure for compliance. At the same time, none of them outlines a method of distribution, and only one of them addresses the vital responsibility of reporting infractions.

The United Church of Christ statement on "Sexual Ethics in the Pastoral Relationship," framed by the Potomoc Association (appendix II), is a good example of a code created by a smaller group of ministers dealing with one ethical topic. The opening paragraph mentions that "specific incidents of sexual misconduct by religious professionals" have surfaced among their congregations. These incidents evidently precipitated the study and report. More than half of the document is devoted to spelling out procedural responsibilities to ensure compliance to the code.

The Potomoc group's Committee on Church and Ministry (composed of laity and clergy) has the primary responsibility for enforcement. The committee investigates allegations, appoints advocates, conducts hearings, and determines actions. Other procedures recommended in the code relate to appeals, timing, negotiated settlements, disciplinary reviews, and preventative strategies.

Two documents modeling a more complete procedure for enforcement are the Eastern Oklahoma Presbyterian (EOP) Code and the Universal Universalist Ministers Association (UUMA)[70] These two are also helpful because of the church traditions they represent—the limited hierarchical structure of the Presbyterians and the congregational ecclesiology of the Unitarian-Universalists.

In the EOP policy, a great deal of space is given to defining the responsibility of the governing authorities: Sessions, Presbyteries, Synods, the General Assembly, and the "Rules of Discipline" in the *Book of Order*.

Briefly described, the process follows this order: (1) allegations should be brought to an Elder; (2) the accused is confronted; (3) the Elder takes the accusation to Session; (4) the Session confronts the pastor and investigates; (5) if the charge is false, the accuser is disciplined; (6) if the allegation is true, the Committee on Ministry (COM) is contacted; (7) the COM may address the problem or assign it to a committee; (8) the investigation is done by a Special Disciplinary Committee, which decides on sanctions; and (9) the Presbytery may initiate its own investigation without a request.

The EOP report also included a policy regarding the immoral or unethical behavior of "Potential Members of Presbytery." This "front door" regulation determines the moral fitness of ministers who seek membership in the Presbytery.

Although the doctrines of the Unitarian-Universalist denomination are significantly different from most Christian churches, their government is basically congregational—one very similar to Baptist and Congregational churches, as well as many other evangelical denominations. UUMA ministers are called and ordained by a local congregation. If they plan to move to another church, they will need to receive ministerial credentials from a "Fellowship Committee," which is the gateway to membership in the Minister's Association.

An accusation against a UUMA minister is first handled by the local church. The *Guidelines* explain procedures for dismissing a faulty minister by vote of the congregation, along with the conditions of termination. Charges of immoral behavior could be taken to the "Fellowship Committee," who can themselves investigate the allegations. The Ministers Association also may initiate investigation, usually at the request of colleagues. A minister determined to be guilty by either group faces six possible sanctions: three levels of censure (caution, admonition, or reprimand) and three severe sanctions (probation, suspension, or removal from UUMA membership).[71]

The Christian Association for Psychological Studies (CAPS) is an organization for Christians in the helping professions, mainly counselors and mental health personnel. Although some CAPS members belong to other professional groups, many do not, and thus some members of the association had no code of ethics to guide them. This void led the Association to develop a prospective code for CAPS that was published in 1986 (appendix II).

Article 8 of the CAPS Code explains procedures to be followed when a member is guilty of unethical conduct. The guidelines urge five policies: confrontation according to biblical principles (8.1), adherence to civil law (8.2), investigations by an Ethics Committee that will recommend discipline (8.3), continued liason work by the Ethics Committee with an expelled member (8.4), and a disclaimer of legal liability (8.5).

A response to the proposed code was written by a CAPS member who directs counseling services in a Christian hospital. Dr. Housekamp expressed major criticism at the point of compliance.

> My concern comes out of formalizing a Code of Ethics which renders the organization responsible for following through on charges levied against a member in some formal way, including the possiblity of "discipline."[72]

Housekamp accurately pinpointed four main flaws in the enforcement procedures of this document: (1) the organization's lack of power and influence to discipline; (2) the failure to define the composition and function of the Ethics Committee; (3) the problem of insufficient evidence to deal with problems; and (4) the lack of financial and legal resources to face liability.

To their credit, professional codes of ethics over the years have developed carefully worded procedures prescribing enforcement of standards. To their detriment, however, ministerial codes of ethics seldom deal with compliance; few go beyond words of counsel about the censure or termination of ministers. Parachurch group codes are only slightly better.

What lessons can we learn from these limited attempts at enforcement of ethical standards by denominations, associations of ministers, and other Christian groups?

Should we begin by revealing the obvious, that ensuring compliance to a code is a difficult task with many risks? Perhaps that is why enforcement procedures are so rare among clergy codes. Nevertheless, since ministerial codes are based on accountability, there must be some group to which a minister is accountable.

A third lesson learned from this brief overview is the importance of a system for reporting violations, a system free from intimidation or coercion. Perhaps the most difficult aspect of enforcement is the one assigned to an authoritative group—the responsibility to investigate charges, determine actions, and apply sanctions. A committee adequate for this task must represent all involved, both laity and clergy.

To make certain that enforcement procedures are just and complete, a well-thought-out and clearly written policy is imperative. Of course, the church polity of a person's denomination will significantly influence the entire process.

In our discussion of a ministerial code of ethics, we have sought to understand the purpose, nature, and structure of codes, as well as their enforcement. Drawing insight from professional ethics models, we have analyzed several codes for ministers. In both the early and the contemporary examples, these documents have helped us to comprehend the strengths and the weaknesses of clergy codes in general. Now we wish to become more specific. As we approach our final assignment, that of writing a code of ethics suitable for today's minister, we will seek to apply what we have learned thus far to this practical conclusion.

How to Write a Code of Ethics

Voices from many sectors of the religious community are calling for a renewed appreciation for written codes of ethics for ministers. Earlier we discussed a study by the Association of Theological Schools that attempted to assess the correlation between readiness for ministry and seminary training. The published report contained many recommendations. In a section stressing the importance of personal growth for clergy, the authors noted with regret that ministers are "currently only loosely bound by a moral code that is subject to differing interpretations"; the AATS study proposed that "a more formal code of ethics be established to help regulate ministry relationships."[73]

The growing problem of pastoral abuse of women was the subject of a recent article in *Christian Century*. One suggestion by the author was the creation of "a new ethical code that accurately names and recognizes the problem."[74]

Another voice supporting codes of ethics for ministers is that of a psychology professor. Writing in support of a code for his own professional organization, Dr. H. Newton Maloney observed that clergy

malpractice issues are increasing and ministers have no accepted statement of ethics to which they can subscribe and be judged. He added,

> A recent national survey concluded that there is a dearth of concern for
> professional ethics among church bodies.... This lack of overt con-
> cern, coupled with denominational protectionism and the separation of
> church and state, leads me to say that the statement that there is no
> agreed upon code of ethics for clergy across denominations is not an
> exaggeration.[75]

Ministers, unlike other professionals, have no central organization
or single code of ethics to which they can turn for support. Even
among religious denominations, as we have just seen, there are
relatively few statements of ethical guidelines for the clergy. The two
major source books contain more than two hundred professional
codes, but not a single code for ministers.[76]

This void may be due to the nature of the ministerial profession and
to the existence of religious pluralism in the United States. American
religious diversity, however, does not prevent religious denominations or groups of ministers from creating a code for their own
constituency. Most certainly it does not hinder any single minister
from reflecting upon personal moral obligations and from writing a
code as a guide toward ethics in ministry.

Certainly a written code of ethics by itself does not guarantee
satisfactory moral performance. Nonetheless, a clear statement of
ministerial ethical standards, adequately authored, properly developed, and appropriately implemented can go a long way toward
strengthening ministerial integrity.

Authorship—The Who Question

Who should author codes, individuals or groups? Should authorship come from within the profession, or from without? As late as the
nineteenth century, single leaders in the professions produced codes
as the sole authors. Today, virtually no professional code has a single
author; "codes by committee" is the norm.[77]

The most common practice is for the members of a profession to
write the codes themselves. This is the pattern of most medical, legal,
and business codes. The obvious problem in this method is that the
documents might be written in the self-interest of the members, with
little regard for the clientele or society.[78] Proponents of internal authorship believe, however, that members of a profession can best
determine what policies are in society's best interest and that members are in a better position to relate these to society than a third party.

Those who argue for external authorship do so from one of two perspectives. One group believes that codes should be written entirely by outside sources. Since professions depend on society's willingness to promote them, only they can "provide a sufficient moral foundation."[79]

A second theory, and one that seems to be the best option, is that professionals should write codes in conjunction with laypersons. To do otherwise is to place too much importance on the work of either group. Not only does this cooperative effort offer great benefit from the outset, it also provides additional credibility at a later time when society may question certain practices.

How do these trends apply to the ministerial profession? The best code, the most comprehensive code, and the one most free from self-interest is undoubtedly the one produced by a committee composed of both laypersons and clergy. Since parishioners are the ones most affected by our ministries, they should be included in defining ethical standards and supervising implementation.

The committee chosen to author a clergy code should also be inclusive, representing male and female, young and old, and all ethnic groups within the larger body. A denomination, a church, or an association of ministers wanting to develop a code of ethics for its clergy would be wise to elect a committee so composed. This committee would provide perspectives and criteria quite different from one composed by ministers only; that difference could be an important distinction. If appropriate authorship is one of the key issues in writing a code, this proposal for inclusive committee representation seems to offer the best solution.

Does this mean a personal code authored by an individual minister is obsolete? Not at all. As an initial exercise in developing one's own ethical standards in ministry, writing a personal code of ethics is a good discipline. Every minister should at some time think through his or her own ethical conduct in ministry. What better way than by writing a personal code of ethics?

This document should be dynamic, allowing constant evaluation and updating. As ministers grow in ethical sensitivity, they should expand and adjust their moral guidelines. A personal code of ethics written by a minister could also be shared with the cleric's own congregation. Most churches would be pleased to learn of their spiritual leaders' ethical standards. Codes shared serve two main purposes: they support ministers by clearly defining ethical intentions and they hold ministers ethically accountable to a larger group, which is a central purpose of all ethical codes.

Procedure—The How Question

When a denomination, a church, or a group of ministers decide they need a code of ethics, how do they proceed? A typical approach might be as follows. The body approves a resolution authorizing a code committee to go to work. A representative committee is selected and begins by reviewing past and present clergy codes, comparing the recent codes of similar organizations, and studying helpful resources in the field of ministerial ethics. A preliminary draft of the new code is circulated to all members for feedback. When the responses have been assimilated, the committee puts the code in final form and sends it to the entire membership for study. The group of ministers then ratifies and adopts the document, and implementation begins.

What about the possibility of an individual minister's writing an explicit code of ethical behavior? A sole author of a clergy code, as a "committee of one," would need to follow a procedure similar to that outlined above. Without the aid of colleagues, however, a lone writer is like an Olympic weight lifter attempting to press a world record. The feat is possible, but it takes extraordinary work and discipline.

After wrestling with the key questions of ministerial ethics, you will need to reflect on the areas of clergy ethics to be covered by the code (see worksheet on p. 216). First, write a preamble statement. Follow this with those statements of obligation to self and family, congregation, colleagues, and community which you deem worthy of inclusion. The first draft could be reviewed by another minister and layperson to provide some perspective, as well as to prevent serious oversights. The final draft should become your working document as you mature in ministry.

Content: The What Question

We have come now to the "meat and potatoes" of a clergy code, the content. What subjects and statements should be included in an ethical code for ministers? Before we can unravel that question, a preliminary distinction must first be made.

Professional ethics scholars have called attention to differences between present and older codes. Modern Generation I codes, products of the early twentieth century, dealt with the etiquette of relationships—"do not speak ill of a colleague." Since the 1980s complex ethical questions have led to the era of Modern Generation II codes, which "deal with dilemmas rising out of new knowledge, new technology, and new social attitudes."[80]

In like manner, the older clergy codes printed by Harmon (appendix I) reflect *Ministerial Ethics and Etiquette* (the title of his book) —Modern Generation I codes. More recent codes (appendix II) reveal a more complex ministry in an increasingly complicated world— Modern Generation II codes.

A Ministerial Code of Ethics

One way to address the "what" question of ministerial codes would be to use the threefold division introduced by C. S. Lewis. His approach focuses on the major areas of the moral life itself: what do the codes have to say about the inner moral life of the practitioner, the relationships between individuals, and the purpose of human life as a whole?[81]

Whereas professional codes pay scant attention to the *inner life* of the practitioner, ministerial codes focus on the moral character of the clergy, as well they should. We say again, clergy codes are not just a Talmudic collection of rules to guide action. Laws will do little to promote ethical conduct unless the ministers who are to be guided are persons of character. Integrity is central to the ministry—it is not an option. An auto may lack air conditioning and still be a good car. Not so for the minister and moral character. "Losing integrity is like having your lungs cave in," writes Lewis Smedes, "everything else goes out with them."[82]

The individual or group who composes guidelines for ethics in ministry must underscore the centrality of character. Ministerial codes of conduct should point to the inner life of the one called of God to be an overseer of the church. Paul reminded Timothy that a pastoral overseer must be "blameless" (1 Tim. 3:2, NKJV). In personal life, family relationships, and spiritual leadership, the person set apart to minister must be "above reproach" (1 Tim. 3:1-7). Solomon, possibly reflecting upon his father's thumbprint on his own life, wrote, "The righteous walk in integrity—happy are the children who follow them" (Prov. 20:7, NRSV).

The shortcoming of most codes is that a set of rules fails to instill internal character. Many professional codes assume the integrity of their members and do not attempt to develop the inner life, which is the Achilles' heel of professionalism. Writers of codes for the clergy must not make this mistake. Though all pastors should be persons of good character, the code should contain statements that harmonize the inner life of church ministers with their personal ethical standards.

Far more coverage is given in the ministerial codes to the second area of the moral life, *relationships between persons*. The codes in the appendixes will reveal that most of the space is reserved for duties owed to parishioners, to fellow ministers, and to people in the community. Insofar as the clergy codes spell out in detail a cleric's obligations to others, they encourage enablement and minimize exploitative relationships.[83] Writers of codes need to give serious attention to stress points in the congregation, between colleagues, and among persons in the community, in relation to the church minister.

Self-interest is often overlooked. Ministers are no different from other professionals who often use their power to favor their own interest improperly. One illustration of this is seen in procedures outlined for reporting ministerial misconduct (EOP Code). A layperson is immediately disciplined if the accusation cannot be substantiated; a minister rightly charged is given numerous levels of appeal and a wide assortment of lesser sanctions. The system is weighed against the lay accuser.

In the third main area of ethics outlined by C.S. Lewis, that of the *purpose of human life*, most codes receive a low score. Many older codes, from Hippocrates in the fourth century B.C. to Florence Nightingale in the nineteenth century A.D. were explicitly religious. Modern American pluralism and secularism have put an end to that.

Codes of ethics for ministers should express in clear language a worldview based on Christian belief. The preamble is an appropriate place for the minister to state basic convictions about God, Jesus Christ, the church, the world, and the cleric's call and commitment to ministry. Statements of ministerial ideals that reach toward a higher standard of behavior than most are practicing should also appear in the code.[84] These ethical principles point to the moral will of God and provide a theological framework for clergy ethics.

The word that sums up the content of a ministerial code is the same word that characterizes ministerial ethics—*integrity*. What the clergy code envisions is an integrated moral life. The Hebrew word for it is *tom* meaning "whole, sound, unimpaired." Modern dictionary definitions of *integrity* explain the word to mean "soundness, adherence to a code of values, the quality or state of being complete or undivided."

In reality, no human being has arrived at "wholeness." The important thing, however, is direction. A code of ethics for ministers is intended to guide us on that journey.

> We have to check our intentions regularly and see whether we are still moving on the journey or whether, at some shadowed station, we left the train and went off to nowhere. For without integrity, anywhere is nowhere.[85]

Implementation: The When and Where Question

The mere existence of a professional code is no guarantee of ethical performance. Darrell Reeck observed that the code of the American Bar Association did not prevent lawyers surrounding President Nixon from committing unethical and illegal acts. The question now raised is this: What programs for implementing the code will make a difference?

A primary task is *distribution*. The first responsibility of any group producing a clergy code is to get copies printed and into the hands of every member. Simply publishing the code in a denominational journal is not enough. Every minister in the group must personally receive a copy. The newly ordained should receive copies of the code immediately after the "laying on of hands."

Common sense and informal evidence would lead a person to the conclusion that most ministers do not maintain a working knowledge of their respective codes. One of us assigned a seminary student to survey local pastors concerning their denomination's code of ethics. Most of the thirty quizzed were not sure if their ministers had a document, but eight of them claimed their religious body had a clergy code. Regrettably, not one of the group could find a copy or give any details about the statement's content.

Failure of *instruction* in the codes is a common weakness among all professions. A ministerial code of ethics will only be a document to frame and hang on the office wall (one denomination offers "a free copy beautifully printed in two colors"), unless responsible leaders provide training. Either someone within the group who worked with the code committee or, better, an authority on ethics from outside the profession could serve as teacher.

Instructional meetings should be scheduled immediately after the code is ratified. From that point forward, regular training sessions should be provided to teach new ministers about the code and to help longtime clergy maintain a working knowledge of their ethical guidelines. These regular gatherings would also provide a forum for dialogue, updating, and adaptation of the guidelines to changing needs.

A third responsibility of implementation is *organization*. Once the code is approved, ongoing structure is needed to ensure distribution, instruction, reporting, and enforcement. By assuming the ministerial role, a church shepherd is obligated to abide by the group's code of ethics. This first means personal responsibility, but it also means accountability to all members of the ministerial association, for misbehavior brings criticism to the entire body.

The best insights from other professions would lead a ministerial group to elect or appoint a standing committee to oversee enforcement, instruction, and other organizational responsibilities. As was true of the original code committee, this board should evidence gender, age, and ethnic inclusiveness.

Concerning *reporting* and *enforcement*, the standing committee should develop methods that encourage both colleagues and the public to share information about violations. Enforcement depends chiefly upon the willingness of others to report infractions. As we discussed at length in the previous section, the enforcement of a code is one of three major difficulties in developing a code. The enforcement committee could be a separate council, but for several practical reasons one standing committee would probably be adequate for most ministerial groups.

The toughest problem that any denomination or association of ministers faces is how to proscribe disciplinary action that is appropriate, fair, legal, and redemptive. The three most common options are censure, suspension, and termination, though the latter two might have to be enforced by the local congregation in denominations with autonomous churches.

In sum, then, does the writing of a clergy code of ethics, along with its implementation, enhance ministerial behavior? Our limited survey of past and present efforts suggests that the clergy profession has much work to do to make their codes a vital part of daily practice. Compared to ethical guidelines in the professions, codes for church leaders suffer many deficiencies in authorship, procedure, content, and implementation.

Despite this apparent failure, it is our conviction that a code of ethics for ministers has many values. The mere existence of a ministerial code exerts some influence. The fact that a church minister receives a copy and reads it at least once, along with the posssibility that in times of crisis he or she may refer to it for guidance, suggests a subtle but real indirect influence.[86]

At the beginning of this chapter, two questions were raised: Is a code a help or a hindrance? Is it possible to write such a document? By now we hope you realize that our answer to both questions is "Yes." We have tried to convince you that writing a code of ethics for ministers is not only possible—it is imperative! Ministers need the guidance and support a code gives. Laypersons need to understand the ethical commitments of their clergy. Ministers need to be accountable to one another.

Addressing the serious problem of sexual misconduct among the clergy, an associate minister concluded her appeal with several suggestions:

> [T]he most efficacious approach is clearly to work at prevention. Churches should encourage mutually supportive clergy marriages; develop clear professional ethical guidelines spelling out procedures and consequences for sexual misconduct; set limits on time, place, and circumstances of pastoral visits and counseling sessions; decrease pastoral stress factors . . . ; and put into place ministerial accountability (to the congregation, to denominational officials, and primarily, to God).[87]

We share this conviction about the need for guidelines and accountability. We also share a dream, a hope beyond just the reading or study of this text. From our perspective, the purpose of this book is

A Ministerial Code of Ethics

not fulfilled until you, the minister-reader, possess an ethical code to guide you in ministry. At the primary level, this may mean that you need to begin developing your own personal code of ethics. That is the reason for the worksheet at the close of this chapter.

At a second level, this may motivate you to initiate a code of ethics for a group of ministers to which you belong—a local association, a ministerial organization, or even a code developed within your church for all the ministers who serve there.

The denominational level is admittedly the most difficult. This is especially true in conventions like the one to which we both belong as ordained ministers. Baptists have strong convictions about congregational government and local church autonomy. At the same time, is it not possible for Baptists and similar religious bodies, who traditionally have produced confessions of faith that are accepted as doctrinal guides (although they may have no binding authority), also to develop a generic code of ethics for ministers? Further, could not each local church in those denominations adopt and support a denominationally approved code, or else write one of their own?

Why do we dream such dreams and see such visions? We believe, as the biblical prophets did, that such hope for integrity in ministry is not in vain. We pray that others agree.

Phillips Brooks, the renowned pastor of Holy Trinity Church in Boston, lived an exemplary and contagious Christian life. There was a saying that on gloomy days in Boston, when Brooks appeared in public, the sun came out. One day Josiah Royce, the Harvard philosopher, was asked by a student, "What is your definition of a Christian?" Royce walked to the window, peered over the campus, and pondered the question. After a moment of silence, he replied to the freshman, "I do not know what is the definition of a Christian, but there goes Phillips Brooks."[88]

Brooks preached by example, and, fellow ministers, so do we. May your code be your life, and may your life illustrate your code.

Suggested Readings

Bayles, Michael D. *Professional Ethics*, 2d ed. Belmont, CA: Wadsworth, 1989.

"Integrity," *Leadership* 9 (Spring, 1988): 12-133.

"Ministry Ethics," *Review & Expositor* 86 (Fall, 1989): 505-573.

Reasons, James A. "The Biblical Concept of Integrity and Professional Codes of Ethics in Ministerial Ethics" Ph.D. diss., Southwestern Baptist Theological Seminary, 1990.

Reeck, Darrell. *Ethics for the Professions: A Christian Perspective*. Minneapolis: Augsburg, 1982, 60-74.

Ministerial Ethics
MINISTERIAL CODE OF ETHICS WORKSHEET
Preamble (See p. 198)

_____
_____
_____
_____
_____
_____

Section I: Personal and Family Relationships (See 198-99 & Ch. 3)

_____
_____
_____
_____
_____
_____
_____
_____
_____

Section II: Congregational Relationships (See 199-200 & Ch. 4)

_____
_____
_____
_____
_____
_____
_____
_____
_____

Section III: Collegial Relationships (See 200-201 & Ch. 5)

_____
_____
_____
_____
_____
_____
_____
_____
_____

A Ministerial Code of Ethics
Section IV: Community Relationships (See 201-202 & Ch. 6)

_____

_____

_____

_____

_____

_____

_____

_____

Notes

[1]Dennis Campbell, *Doctors, Lawyers, Ministers: Christian Ethics in Professional Practice* (Nashville: Abingdon,1982), 23.

[2]Harmon's revised edition (1979), 201-208, listed Congregational, Disciples, Methodist, Presbyterian, and Unitarian codes of ethics.

[3]The Eastern Oklahoma Presbytery (PCUSA) adopted a code on February 13, 1990 (see appendix III).

[4]Arthur H. Becker, "Professional Ethics for Ministry," *Trinity Seminary Review* 9 (Fall, 1987): 69.

[5]James Allen Reasons, "The Biblical Concept of Integrity and Professional Codes of Ethics in Ministerial Ethics" (Ph.D. diss., Southwestern Baptist Theological Seminary, 1990), 1.

[6]James M. Alsdurf, review of *Is Nothing Sacred? When Sex Invades the Pastoral Relationship* by Marie Fortune, in *Christianity Today* 34 (16 July 1990), 53.

[7]Walter E. Wiest and Elwyn A. Smith, *Ethics in Ministry* (Minneapolis: Fortress Press, 1990), 12, who wrote such codes are "inherently legalistic" and "will not do."

[8]Reasons, 4.

[9]Raymond T. Stamm, *The Epistle to the Galatians*, vol. x in *The Interpreter's Bible* (New York: Abingdon: 1953), 517.

[10]Amitai Etzioni, "Money, Power and Fame," *Newsweek* (18 September 1989), 10.

[11]Alasdair MacIntyre, *A Short History of Ethics* (New York: MacMillan Co., 1966), 266.

[12]Jane A. Boyajian, ed., *Ethical Issues in the Practice of Ministry* (Minneapolis: United Theological Seminary, 1984), 82. For an example of a text used in training corporate executives, see Gordon F. Shea, *Practical Ethics* (New York: American Management Association, 1988).

[13]Michael Bayles, *Professional Ethics: Second Edition* (Belmont, CA: Woodsworth Publishing Co., 1989), 197.

[14]Karen Lebacqz, *Professional Ethics: Power and Paradox* (Nashville: Abingdon,1985), 66.

[15]Lisa Newton, "The Origin of Professionalism: Sociological Conclusions and Ethical Implications" *Business and Professional Ethics Journal* 1 (Summer, 1982), 40.

[16]Lebacqz, 18.

[17]Bayles, 84.

[18]David Reeck, *Ethics for the Professions: A Christian Perspective* (Minneapolis: Augsburg, 1982), 64.

[19]Reasons, 12-13.

[20]Campbell, 23. Darrell Reeck, 64, also notes many "unspoken purposes," such as to give an air of professionalism, to enhance public relations, and to enable bureaucritization.

[21]Lebacqz, 68.

[22]William F. May, "Code and Covenant or Philanthropy and Contract?", *Hastings Center Report* 5 (December, 1975): 29-38.

Ministerial Ethics

[23]A. M. Carr-Saunders and P. A. Wilson, *The Professions* (New York: Oxford University Press, 1933), 421.

[24]Reasons, 17.

[25]C. S. Calian, *Today's Pastor in Tomorrow's World* (New York: Hawthorne Books, 1977), 104-5. The list also appears in Lebacqz, 69.

[26]Bayles, 69-101.

[27]Ibid., 177.

[28]Ibid., 166-67.

[29]Lebacqz, 68.

[30]Bayles, 185.

[31]May, 38.

[32]Reasons, 46-54, provides a detailed discussion of this topic.

[33]Lebacqz, 135, who has made a unique contribution by emphasizing the significance of roles for professional ethics.

[34]Lisa H. Newton, "A Professional Ethic: A Proposal in Context," in John E. Thomas, ed., *Matters of Life and Death* (Toronto: Samuel Stevens, 1978), 264.

[35]Gaylord Noyce, *Pastoral Ethics* (Nashville: Abingdon, 1988), 198.

[36]Susan Bryant, "'Didn't mean it' is no excuse," *Richmond Times-Herald* (24 February 1992), B-5.

[37]Newton, "The Origin of Professionalism," 41.

[38]James D. Berkley, "Turning Points: Eight Ethical Choices," *Leadership* 9 (Spring, 1988): 32.

[39]Boyajian, 89.

[40]Nolan Harmon, *Ministerial Ethics and Etiquette* (Nashville: Abingdon, 1928), 9.

[41]"Minister Termination," *The Light* (September, 1990): 3.

[42]*Richmond Times-Dispatch* (19 October 1991), B-10.

[43]Boyajian, 85.

[44]James P. Wind, Russell Burk, Paul R. Carmenisch, and Dennis P. McCann, eds., *Clergy Ethics in a Changing Society* (Louisville: Westminster/John Knox, 1991), 125.

[45]Minnesota State Statue 148A requires all employers of counselors to make an inquiry of previous employers for the last five years to determine if there have been any occurrences of illegal sexual contact.

[46]Boyajian, 79.

[47]Henlee H. Barnette, "The Minister as a Moral Role Model," *Review and Expositor* (Fall, 1989): 505-516.

[48]Robert R. King, Jr., "Developing a Proposed Code of Ethics for the Christian Association for Psychological Studies," *Journal of Psychology and Christianity* 5 (Fall, 1986): 86.

[49]W. Ward Gasque, "God's Assistant Watchdog," *Christianity Today* 34 (5 November 1990), 19.

[50]Berkley, 32.

[51]Archibald D. Hart, "Being Moral Isn't Always Enough," *Leadership* 9 (Spring, 1988): 25.

[52]Boyajian, 90.

[53]Harmon, 202. Hereafter, references to codes will indicate their location in the appendixes.

[54]Noyce, 193. As previously noted, however, the minister's multiplicity of roles makes competency in all areas virtually impossible.

[55]Hart, 26.

[56]"Policy on Sexual Ethics in the Pastoral Relationship as Recommended to the Board of Directors of the Potomoc Association," unpublished document of the UCC in Virginia.

[57]Becker, 70.

[58]Lebacqz, 68.

[59]Richard A. Hunt, John E. Hinkle, Jr., and H. Newton Maloney, eds., *Clergy Assessment and Career Development* (Nashville: Abingdon, 1990), 40-41.

[60]M. Pabst Battin, "Professional Ethics and the Practice of Religion: A Philosopher's View," in *Ethical Issues in the Practice of Ministry*, ed. Jane Boyajian, 17-20.

A Ministerial Code of Ethics

[61]Margaret Battin, *Ethics in the Sanctuary: Examining the Practices of Organized Religion* (New Haven: Yale University Press, 1990), 3-4.

[62]Hart, 27-29, focuses on four principles: accountability, confidentiality, responsibility, and integrity.

[63]Reasons, 134-38.

[64]Becker, 75.

[65]Becker, 74, notes a Lutheran Council recommendation not to divulge "unless it is reasonably anticipated that such persons may do great harm to themselves or others." He also suggests pastors ought never agree to *secretiveness*, only confidentiality.

[66]"Report for the Task Force on Ministerial Ethics: Eastern Oklahoma Presbytery," adopted by Presbytery, February 13, 1990. Portions of this code are included in appendix II.

[67]In "When a Pastoral Colleague Falls," *Leadership* 11 (Winter, 1991): 102-11, an unnamed author admits he failed "to gently but firmly hold a ministry colleague accountable."

[68]"NRB Moves Slowly to Enforce Ethics Code," *Christianity Today* (9 March 1992), 59.

[69]Robert Spanier, "Anti-Board Sentiment Rouses Mass. Physicians," *American College of Physicians Observer* 9 (December, 1989): 7.

[70]Rudolph W. Nemser, "Guidelines for the Unitarian Universalist Ministry: A History," in Boyajian, 70-75, which explains the function of these *Guidelines*.

[71]Rev. Wayne Arnason of Charlottesville, Va., interview by author, 14 February 1992, and UUMA *Guidelines*, 28 (C).

[72]Richard E. Houskamp, "Comments on Proposed Code of Ethics," *Journal of Psychology and Christianity* 5 (Fall, 1986): 92.

[73]Hunt, Hinkle, and Maloney, 40.

[74]Pamela Cooper-White, "Soul-Stealing: Power Relations in Pastoral Sexual Abuse," *The Christian Century* 108 (19 February 1991): 199.

[75]H. Newton Malony, "Codes of Ethics: A Comparison," *Journal of Psychology and Christianity* 5 (Fall, 1986): 94.

[76]Jane Clapp, *Professional Ethics and Insignia* (Metuchen, NJ: The Scarecrow Press, 1974), and Rena A. Gorlin, ed., *Codes of Professional Responsibility*, 2d. ed. (Washington, D.C.: Bureau of National Affairs, 1990).

[77]Reeck, 61-62.

[78]Arthur L. Caplan, "Cracking Codes," *The Hastings Center Report* 8 (August, 1978): 18.

[79]Reasons, 40-41.

[80]Reeck, 61.

[81]C. S. Lewis, *Mere Christianity* (New York: Macmillan, 1960), 71.

[82]Lewis Smedes, *A Pretty Good Person* (San Francisco: Harper & Row, 1990), 86.

[83]Reeck, 66.

[84]James D. Berkley, 32-41, discusses eight areas of ethical concern for pastors who construct their own codes: Beliefs, Service, Morality, Competence, Compensation, Colleagues, Confidentiality, and Friendships.

[85]Smedes, 86.

[86]Reeck, 72.

[87]Joy Jordan-Lake, "Conduct Unbecoming a Preacher," *Christianity Today* (February 10, 1992), 30.

[88]Richard Spann, *The Ministry* (New York: Abingdon-Cokesbury Press, 1959), 44-48.

Appendixes

Appendix I

Early Denominational Codes

The Congregational Code[1]

I. The Minister and His Work

1. As a minister controls his own time, he should make it a point of honor to give full service to his parish.

2. Part of the minister's service as a leader of his people is to reserve sufficient time for serious study in order thoroughly to apprehend his message, keep abreast of current thought, and develop his intellectual and spiritual capacities.

3. It is equally the minister's duty to keep physically fit. A weekly holiday and an annual vacation should be taken and used for rest and improvement.

4. As a public interpreter of divine revelation and human duty, the minister should tell the truth as he sees it and present it tactfully and constructively.

5. It is unethical for the minister to use sermon material prepared by another without acknowledging the source from which it comes.

6. As an ethical leader in the community, it is incumbent on the minster to be scrupulously honest, avoid debts, and meet his bills promptly.

7. The minister should be careful not to bring reproach on his calling by joining in marriage improper persons.

II. The Minister's Relations with His Parish

1. It is unethical for a minister to break his contract made with the church.

2. As a professional man the minister should make his service primary and the remuneration secondary. His efficiency, however, demands that he should receive a salary adequate to the work he is expected to do and commensurate with the scale of living in that parish which he serves.

3. It is unethical for the minister to engage in other lines of remunerative work without the knowledge and consent of the church or its official board.

4. The confidential statements made to a minister by his parishioners are privileged and should never be divulged without the consent of those making them.

5. It is unethical for a minister to take sides with factions in his parish.

6. The minister recognizes himself to be the servant of the community in which he resides. Fees which are offered should be accepted only in the light of this principle.

Appendix I

III. The Minister's Relations with the Profession

1. It is unethical for a minister to interfere directly or indirectly with the parish work of another minister; especially should he be careful to avoid the charge of proselyting.

2. Ministerial service should not be rendered to the members of another parish without consulting the minister of that parish.

3. It is unethical for a minister to make overtures to or consider overtures from a church whose pastor has not yet resigned.

4. It is unethical for a minister to speak ill of the character or work of another minister, especially of his predecessor or successor. It is the duty of a minister, however, in flagrant cases of unethical conduct, to bring the matter before the proper body.

5. As members of the same profession and brothers in the service of a common Master, the relation between ministers should be one of frankness and cooperation.

Methodist Ministers' Ethical Code[2]

When a Methodist minister becomes a member of the conference he promises to employ all of his time in the work of God. We again call attention to the fact that he is thus honor bound to give full service to his parish.

Part of the minister's service as a leader of his people is to reserve sufficient time for serious study in order thoroughly to appreciate his message, keep abreast of current thought, and develop his intellectual and spiritual capacities.

It is equally the minister's duty to keep physically fit. A weekly holiday and an annual vaction should be taken and used for rest and improvement.

As a public interpreter of divine revelation and human duty, the minister should tell the truth as he sees it and present it tactfully and constructively.

It is unethical for the minister to use sermon material prepared by another without acknowledging the source from which it comes.

As an ethical leader in the community, it is incumbent on the minister to be scrupulously honest, avoid debts, and meet his bills promptly.

The minister should be careful not to bring reproach upon his calling by joining in marriage improper persons.

As a professional man the minister should make his service primary and the remuneration secondary. This implies a salary, paid regularly, and adequate to the work he is expected to do and commensurate with the scale of living in that parish where he serves.

The confidential statements made to a minister by his parishioners are privileged and should never be divulged without the consent of those making them.

In the making of conference reports, it is unethical for a minister to report other than the actual salary received.

The minister recognizes himself to be the servant of the community in which he resides. Fees which are offered should be accepted only in the light of this principle.

It is unethical for a minister to interfere directly or indirectly with the parish work of another minister; especially should he be careful to avoid the charge of proselyting.

Ministerial service should not be rendered to the members of another parish without consulting the minister of the parish, or by invitation from him.

Ministerial Ethics

It is unethical for a minister to speak ill of the character or work of another minister, especially of his predecessor or successor. It is the duty of a minister, however, in flagrant cases of unethical conduct, to bring the matter before the proper body.

It is unethical for a minister on leaving a charge to leave the parsonage property in other than in first-class condition, with all dirt, rubbish, etc., removed. Common courtesy to his successor demands the observance of the golden rule.

As members of the same profession and brothers in the service of a common Master, the relation between ministers should be one of frankness, of comradeship, and of co-operation.

The Presbyterian Code[3]

I. Personal Standards

1. As a minister controls his own time, he should make it a point of honor to give full service to his parish.

2. Part of a minister's service as a leader of his people is to reserve sufficient time for serious study in order to thoroughly apprehend his message, keep abreast of current thought, and develop his intellectual and spiritual capacities.

3. It is equally the minister's duty to keep physically fit. A weekly holiday and an annual vacation should be taken and used for rest and improvement.

4. It is unethical for a minister to use sermon material prepared by another, without acknowledging the source from which it comes.

5. As an ethical leader in the community, it is incumbent on the minister to be scrupulously honest, avoid debts, and meet his bills promptly.

II. Relations with the Parish

1. In accepting a pastorate, a minister assumes obligations which he should faithfully perform until released in the constitutional manner.

2. As a professional man, the minister should make his service primary and the remuneration secondary.

3. A minister should not regularly engage in other kinds of remunerative work, except with the knowledge and consent of the official board of the Church.

4. The confidential statements made to a minister by his parishioners are sacred and not to be divulged.

5. As a minister is especially charged to study the peace and unity of the Church, it is unwise as well as unethical for a minister to take sides with any faction in his Church, in any but exceptional cases.

6. The minister is the servant of the community and not only of his Church, and should find in the opportunity for general ministerial service a means of evidencing the Christian spirit.

III. Relations with the Profession

1. It is unethical for a minister to interfere directly or indirectly with the parish work of another minister; especially should he be careful to avoid the charge of proselyting from a sister Church.

2. Except in emergencies, ministerial service should not be rendered to

the members of another parish without the knowledge of the minister of the parish.

3. A minister should not make overtures to or consider overtures from a Church whose pastor has not yet resigned.

4. It is unethical for a minister to speak ill of the character or work of another minister, especially of his predecessor or successor. It is the duty of a minister, however, in cases of flagrant misconduct to bring the matter before the proper body.

5. A minister should be very careful to protect his brother ministers from imposition by unworthy applicants for aid, and should refer such cases to established charitable agencies rather than to send them to other Churches.

6. A minister should be scrupulously careful in giving endorsements to agencies or individuals unless he has a thorough knowledge and approval of their work lest such endorsements be used to influence others unduly.

7. As members of the same profession and brothers in the service of a common Master, the relation between ministers should be one of frankness and co-operation.

Unitarian Ministers' Code of Ethics[4]

I. The Minister and His Task

1. The minister should always place service above profit, avoiding the suspicion of an inordinate love of money, and never measuring his work by his salary.

2. He should be conscientious in giving full time and strength to the work of his church, engaging in avocations and other occupations in such a way and to such a degree as not to infringe unduly upon that work unless some definite arrangement for part-time service is made with his church.

3. The minister should count it a most important part of his work to keep in touch with the best religious thought of his day, and should make it a point of honor to set aside sufficient time for reading and study.

4. It is the minister's duty to keep himself in as good physical condition as possible.

5. The minister should set a high moral standard of speech and conduct. He should be scrupulous in the prompt payment of bills, and careful in the incurring of financial obligations.

6. The minister should never speak disparagingly of his church or his profession.

II. The Minister and His Church Officials

1. The minister's relation to his parish is a sacred contract, which should not be terminated by him, or broken by his resignation, without at least three months' notice, except by special agreement.

2. The minister is the recognized leader of the parish, but he should not assume authority in church affairs which is not expressly granted to him by the terms of his contract, or the usage of his office, or the vote of his church.

3. The minister rightfully controls his own pulpit, but he should not invite persons into it who are not generally acceptable to the parish, and he should

be ready to accede to all reasonable requests by responsible church officials for its use.

III. The Minister and His Parishioners

1. The minister should remember that he is pastor of all his people. He should avoid the display of preferences, and the cultivation of intimacies within the parish which may be construed as evidence of partiality. He should not attach himself to any social set either in the church or in the community. He should not allow personal feelings to interfere with the impartial nature of his ministrations.

2. In the case of parish controversy, the minister should maintain an attitude of good will to all, even when he himself is the subject of controversy.

3. It is unethical to divulge the confidences of parishioners without their consent.

4. Professional service should be gladly rendered to all, without regard to compensation, except for necessary expenses incurred.

IV. The Minister and His Brother Ministers

1. It is unethical for a minister to render professional service within the parish of another minister, or to occupy another minister's pulpit, without the consent of that minister, whenever obtainable, and this consent should be given readily.

2. He should be very careful not to proselytize among the members of another church.

3. He should discourage all overtures from a church whose minister has not yet resigned.

4. He should always speak with good will of another minister, especially of the minister who has preceded or followed him in a parish. It may be his duty, however, to bring to the attention of the responsible officials of the fellowship any instance of gross professional or personal misconduct that may injure the good name of the ministry.

5. The minister should be very generous in responding to reasonable requests for assistance from his brother ministers and his denominational officials, remembering that he is one of a larger fellowship.

6. It is his duty to show a friendly and co-operative interest in his brethren, attending the group meetings of the ministers, assisting his brother ministers with labors of love, defending them against injustice, and following them with kindly concern in their hours of need or distress.

7. He should never accept from a brother minister fees for professional services at christenings, weddings, and funerals.

V. The Minister and His Community

1. The minister is not under obligations to marry every couple that comes to him to be married. The power of refusal, however, should be exercised with great discretion.

2. The minister's responsibility to the state is that of a citizen. He should, therefore, be faithful to his public obligations, and should respond to reasonable requests for assistance in community work.

Appendix I

Notes

[1]Harmon, 201, states the code was adopted by the New Haven, CT, Association for Congregational Ministers and published in *Church Administration* by Cokesbury Press in 1931.

[2]Harmon, 204, states this code was adopted "by a group of Methodist ministers meeting in conference at Rockford, Illinois," and it was published in the *Christian Century* (16 December 1926).

[3]Harmon, 205, notes this code was adopted by the New York Presbytery and quoted in an article by William H. Leach in *The Methodist Quarterly Review* (July, 1927).

[4]Harmon, 206, indicates this code was adopted by the Unitarian Ministerial Union and quoted in *Church Management* (August, 1926).

Appendix II

Contemporary Denominational Codes

The Disciples Code[1]

My Ministerial Code of Ethics

I am a minister of the Lord Jesus Christ, called of God to proclaim the unsearchable riches of His love. Therefore, I voluntarily adopt the following principles in order that through dedication and self-discipline I may set a more worthy example for those whom I seek to lead and serve.

I. My Personal Conduct

I will cultivate my devotional life, continuing steadfastly in reading the Bible, meditation and prayer.

I will endeavor to keep physically and emotionally fit for my work.

I will be fair to my family and will endeavor to give them the time and consideration to which they are entitled.

I will endeavor to live within my income and will not carelessly leave unpaid debts behind me.

I will strive to grow in my work through comprehensive reading and careful study and by attending conventions and conferences.

I will be honest in my stewardship of money.

I will not plagiarize.

I will seek to be Christlike in my personal attitudes and conduct toward all people regardless of race, class or creed.

II. My Relationship to the Church Which I Serve

I will dedicate my time and energy to my Christian ministry and will maintain strict standards of discipline.

In my preaching I will exalt the Bible and will be true to my convictions, proclaiming the same in love.

I will maintain a Christian attitude toward other members of the church staff and will not expect the unreasonable of them.

I will not seek special gratuities.

In my pastoral calling, I will have respect for every home I enter for I am a representative of Christ and the Church.

In my administrative and pastoral duties I will be impartial so no one can truthfully say that I am pastor of only one group in the church.

I will strive with evangelistic zeal to build up my church, but will maintain

Appendix II

a Christian attitude at all times toward members of other religious bodies.

I will under no circumstance violate confidences that come to me as a minister.

I will strive to strengthen the congregation when leaving a pastorate regardless of the circumstances.

III. My Relationship to Fellow Ministers

I will refuse to enter into unfair competition with other ministers in order to secure a pulpit or place of honor.

I will seek to serve my fellow ministers and their families in every way possible and in no instance will I accept fees for such services.

I will refrain from speaking disparagingly about the work of either my predecessor or my successor.

I will refrain from frequent visits to a former field and if, in exceptional cases, I am called back for a funeral or a wedding, I will request that the resident minister be invited to participate in the service.

I will never embarrass my successor by meddling in the affairs of the church I formerly served.

I will be courteous to any predecessor of mine when he returns to the field, and will be thoughtful of any retired minister.

I will, upon my retirement from the active ministry, give my pastor loyal support.

I will not gossip about other ministers.

I will hold in sincere respect any minister whose work is well done, regardless of the size or the nature of the field he serves.

I will consider all ministers my co-laborers in the work of Christ and even though I may differ from them I shall respect their Christian earnestness and sincerity.

IV. My Relationship to the Community

I will strive to be human in all my relationships to the community but will never lower my ideals in order to appear "a good fellow."

I will not be a party to funeral or marriage rackets.

I will be considerate of the working hours of business and professional men and will not consume their time with unimportant matters.

I consider that my first duty to my community is to be a conscientious pastor and leader of my own congregation, but I will not use this fact as an easy excuse to escape reasonable responsibilities that the community calls upon me to assume.

V. My Relationship to My Communion

I will at all times recognize that I am a part of a fellowship that has made large contributions to my church, my education, and my ministry. In view of this fact I acknowledge a debt of loyalty to my communion and will strive to fulfill my obligations by co-operating in its efforts to extend the Realm[2] of God.

VI. My Relationship to the Church Universal

I will give attention, sympathy and, when possible, support to the Ecumenical Church, recognizing that my church is a part of the Church Universal.

Ministerial Ethics

Eastern Oklahoma Presbyterian Code[3]

II. Principles of Ethical Conduct[4]

Fundamental Principles

In all matters, Ministers of the Word and Sacrament, Elders, Deacons, and staff maintain practices that give glory to Christ, advance the goals of the Church, and nurture, challenge, and protect the welfare of church members, parishioners, clients, and the public.

B. Ministers, Elders, Deacons, and staff act in a manner to uphold and enhance the honor, integrity, morality, and dignity of the Faith.

C. Ministers and staff limit their practice to those positions and responsibilities for which they are qualified.

D. Ministers, Elders, Deacons, and staff conduct all matters in a manner that assures security and confidentiality and avoids conflicts of interest.

E. Ministers and staff demonstrate respect, honesty, and fairness when interacting with clergy-colleagues and persons in related professions.

F. Ministers and staff maintain professional competency throughout their careers.

G. In personal as well as professional relationships Ministers, Elders, Deacons, and staff have honest and sincere motives, upholding the peace, unity, and purity of the Church, and sharing faith, hope, and love with all people.

H. Ministers, Elders, Deacons and staff maintain the sexual standard of fidelity and chastity.

I. Ministers, Elders, Deacons, and staff respect and are sensitive to the vulnerability of others and avoid all exploitation.

III. Professional Practices

Preface

Professional practices are based upon the standards of personal integrity and respect for others. These standards concern not just sexual practices and financial practices, but also even suggest the inappropriateness of an ethnic slur and the importance of tithing.

A. Representation of Qualifications

Ministers and church professionals shall accurately represent their professional qualifications in education, training, and experience in all communications with the church and the public sector:

    —in composition of dossiers
    —in materials prepared for publications
    —in information issued for speaking engagements
    —in announcements of professional services offered

  1. Such communications shall be objective and truthful.

  2. Ministers and other professionals are responsible for correcting any misrepresentations promptly.

B. The Focus of Professional Practice

Ministers and church professionals shall work for the benefit of their congregations or institutions.

  1. Personal benefit shall not be the goal of professional endeavor.

Appendix II

2. The purpose and pattern of leadership shall be understood in terms of service rendered rather than power gained.

3. To further the peace and unity of the church, the believing community (the congregation) shall be accepted as it is. From that point, church professionals shall nurture it toward faithful membership in Christ's body through growth in worship, mission (service), evangelism, stewardship, and education.

4. To strengthen the total life of the believing community, individuals of the community shall be nourished with energy, intelligence, imagination, and love.

C. Practice and Personal Expertise

Ministers and church professionals shall work within their personal and professional qualifications and limitations.

1. God-given talents and professional expertise, natural and acquired, shall be shared for the integrity, unity, and health of the believing community.

2. Medical, financial, and psychological counseling needs beyond the expertise of the church professional shall be referred to qualified professionals.

D. Financial Matters

Ministers of the Word and Sacrament shall be financially responsible.

1. Those who serve congregations shall provide their services to members of their believing community(ies) without additional compensation.

2. Ministers of the Word and Sacrament shall stand ready to render professional service to individuals and communities in crisis without financial remuneration.

3. Financial arrangement for professional services provided for non-members shall be determined in advance.

4. Ministers and church professionals shall not use church funds, accounts, and/or resources for personal or private advantage.

5. Ministers and church professionals shall be prudent and responsible in personal financial matters.

E. Confidentiality

Church professionals shall conduct all professional matters in a manner that assures confidentiality and seeks to avoid conflict of interest.

1. Personnel records (written and taped) of staff members, members of the congregation, and/or non-member clients shall be stored where security and confidentiality are assured.

2. Critical confidential information shall not be shared except when written permission is given by the person involved.

3. Privileged information shall not be used for personal gain.

F. Speech and Conduct

Ministers and church professionals shall shape their speech and conduct as Scripture counsels in Ephesians 4 and Philippians 4.

1. Ministers and church professionals shall speak the truth in love, but make judgments with understanding, tact, and discretion.

2. All persons shall be treated with a sense of respect, a spirit of fairness, decency, and concern for Christian equality.

3. Disparagement of clergy and persons in other professions is unacceptable.

4. Faith, hope, and love in all relationships shall be shared.

Ministerial Ethics

IV. Colleague Relationships

Preface

There are practices in all human relationships that make possible greater harmony, reduce points of tension, and in the calling to ministry within the church, lead to confidence and trust among those who are charged with representative leadership (Elders, Deacons, Ministers of the Word and Sacrament) as well as those who have taken vows of membership. The assumptions that are held in the larger society of correct behavior are not always shaped by Gospel norms. There are ecclesiastical and religious traditions that have established certain norms and practices of their own that are not in accord with those in the Presbyterian and Reformed Tradition. Therefore, we find it necessary and desirable to remind the continuing members of Eastern Oklahoma Presbytery, members of its Sessions, congregational staffs, boards, and members of the conduct that is expected in collegiality as they pursue their callings among us.

A. Relationships with Staff

Staff members must be given equal respect without regard to age, gender, race, ethnic origin, disability, marital status, or job description. Staff positions include Ministers of the Word and Sacrament, other professionals, and support staff: secretarial, custodial employees, and volunteers.

Staff members accept each other as persons of worth who are dear to God, know each other's position descriptions and responsibilities, respect one another's competencies, offer constructive suggestions to one another, forgive misunderstandings, and are tolerant of differences of opinion and style of operation.

1. Staff members shall not aspire to succeed other persons on the staff.

2. Staff members shall avoid innuendo and gossip. Staff should loyally support one another in every way that is appropriate. In the interests of staff peace and unity, staff should speak openly and frankly about differences and problems to the person involved.

3. Clear and well-defined supervisory roles must be in place with free and open communication being maintained among staff members.

4. Staff members who feel unable to Minister and work on a staff in a creative, effective, and harmonious manner should consult with the head of the staff and/or the personnel committee. If there is no resolution, the staff member should give serious consideration to relocating for the sake of the ministry of the congregation.

5. Termination of staff members is an ethical matter and should be done only in accordance with Equal Employment Opportunity and General Assembly guidelines.

B. Relationships with Parish, Congregation, Session and Presbytery

Ministers called as pastors have unique responsibilities to that congregation as well as to the Presbytery of their membership.

1. Pastors shall devote time and energy Ministering to the people of their parish and to the activities of their congregation.

2. Pastors shall be active in the work of Presbytery.

3. Terms of call concerning vacations and study-leave shall be strictly observed.

4. Staff members who experience conflict in their relationships with other

members on staff should attempt to resolve them or learn how to manage the conflict.

5. In administrative and pastoral duties, pastors should strive earnestly for impartiality.

6. Confidences, either verbal or in writing, shall not be violated. Necessary records of a confidential nature shall be kept secure.

7. Honoraria shall not be considered a substitute for adequate compensation of pastors. Honoraria shall not be sought from members of the congregations served. Care should be exercised in accepting inappropriate honoraria or gifts.

8. Congregational funds, other than budgeted salaries and allowances, shall not be used for the personal or private advantage of pastor or staff.

9. Requests for reimbursement for allowable professional expenses shall be accompanied by appropriate documentation.

10. Pastors and Sessions shall not encourage persons to transfer membership from neighboring congregations, Presbyterian or other. Care must be taken to give no hint of proselyting persons in vulnerable situations.

C. Leaving a Congregation

When pastoral relationships with congregations are dissolved, certain ethical behavior is required in order to preserve the peace and unity of the church.

1. Pastors shall announce publicly that they are no longer available for pastoral services, except with an invitation from the successor (pastor, stated supply, interim) or Session, and that new pastoral relationships need to be established.

2. Former pastors shall refer requests for pastoral services to the current pastor or the Clerk of Session when such requests come from members of a former congregation.

3. Pastors shall exercise great care to have no further influence on the former congregation and its members by conversation, correspondence, or other action.

4. Former pastors shall exercise no part in the selection of a Pastor Nominating Committee or in the selection of a successor (pastor, interim, stated supply).

5. Interim pastors and stated supplies shall not encourage personal loyalties because their tenure is temporary and their function is intended to prepare the congregation for the calling and installation of a new pastor.

D. Pastor and Predecessor

Ministers of the Word and Sacrament who become pastors of congregations from which Ministers have been called, retired, or resigned have responsibilities toward the former pastor(s).

1. The relationship shall be marked by courtesy.

2. The relationship shall be marked by refusal to discuss former ministries except in the exercise of necessary administrative, liturgical, or pastoral duties.

3. The relationship shall be marked by awareness of loyalties that have been in place. Courtesy and wisdom should unite to cause the currently installed pastor to be sensitive to those loyalties. It may be appropriate in some cases to invite former pastors to participate in events that have great meaning for members of the congregation. The same sensitivities and courtesies shall be exercised by Ministers who are interims or stated supplies.

Ministerial Ethics

E. Pastor and Successor

Ministers who have resigned, retired, or accepted another call shall behave in a manner that affirms the ministry of the successor.

1. Ministers shall treat successors with courtesy.

2. Ministers shall refrain from commenting on or voicing judgments about the ministry of a successor.

3. Ministers shall make no professional contacts with persons in former parishes.

4. Ministers making social visits with members of former congregations shall take care that professional matters do not intrude.

F. Specialized Ministries

Ministers-without-pastoral-charge are faced with unique responsibilities.

1. Ministers shall establish a relationship of service and a relationship for worship with a local congregation.

2. Ministers are encouraged to be available as Parish Associate of a congregation.

3. Intrusion into the pastoral functions of Ministers serving a parish is unacceptable.

4. Invitations to preside at weddings or funerals shall be accepted only when extended by the current pastor or, for congregations without an installed pastor, the Clerk of Session.

5. The sacraments of Baptism and Holy Communion shall be celebrated only at the invitation of a pastor or a Session or by the permission of Presbytery.

6. Counseling or advising members of a congregation having a pastor is not usually acceptable unless the counselee is referred by their pastor.

7. Service as temporary or occasional supply for vacant pulpits due to vacation, sickness, emergencies, is expected.

G. Retired Pastor

When pastoral relationships with congregations are dissolved through retirement, special sensitivity is required to preserve the peace and unity of the church.

1. The status of Honorably Retired or the title of Pastor Emeritus does not give retirees authority or the right to engage in pastoral activities or exercise influence in former congregations except by specific invitation of the current pastors or Sessions.

2. Retired pastors who are residents in the community of most recent service shall avoid formal and informal participation in and comment on the work of the Pastor Nominating Committee.

3. In all community contacts, retired pastors shall be cautious that their views are not attributed to former congregations.

H. Relationships with Related Professions

Pastors and Ministers-without-pastoral-charge are often called upon to work closely with professionals in related fields (health care, social services, legal services). These professionals include persons who have a variety of faith commitments or those with no faith commitment. In each situation Presbyterian Ministers shall conduct themselves in such a way that vital concerns for persons are maintained. Respect and support shall be given to peer professionals. In many cases, Ministers will be closely dependent upon them for the carrying out of their ministry. Confidentiality shall be protected. In every

Appendix II

relationship the integrity of the Presbyterian Minister shall be above reproach.

I. Relationships with the Public Community

Ministers are members of a public community that may have conflicting demands and purposes.

1. Ministers shall strive to be human in all relationships within the community.

2. Ministers shall support efforts to better that community.

3. Ministers shall not accept fees or gifts as payment for business or professional referrals.

4. Ministers shall pay just debts as promptly as possible.

5. Ministers shall live within their financial means.

6. Ministers shall be considerate of the responsibilities and working hours of business and professional people.

7. Ministers may assume outside commitments that do not detract from their pastoral responsibilities. Session concurrence shall be secured for remunerative activities.

8. Ministers shall not proselyte from other faith communities.

V. Pastor/Counselee Relationships

Professionalism in the counseling vocations is the art of being helpful to those who need and seek assistance in living. Behavior that hinders healing and eventual wholeness in a client is ethically and morally wrong.

Basic guidelines for healthy, ethical pastor/counselee relationships.

1. Pastors must not allow personal problems, desires, and issues to invade the relationship that comes to exist between themselves and counselees. Every pastor is subject to the danger of becoming inappropriately involved in the life of a person being counseled. When pastors become aware that they have inappropriate feelings, they shall immediately seek the advice of a trusted colleague or another professional counselor.

2. Pastors must learn to deal with their own feelings in ways that will not be detrimental to the counseling relationship. However, the personal dynamics present in the counseling relationship should not be denied, but must be treated in a way that will harm neither the counselee nor the counselor.

3. Knowing when to refer a counselee is imperative. Most pastors and many pastoral counselors are not equipped to deal with mental illness and, therefore, should limit their work to spiritual and behavioral issues. However, some kinds of behavioral problems are beyond the expertise of the parish pastor who has had training at the Master of Divinity level. Pastors and pastoral counselors must become knowledgeable about community resources and be willing to refer to other professionals. Illnesses that demand medication or hospitalization require the care of a licensed physician.

4. Professional ethics demand that the pastor shall not use information obtained in counseling inappropriately. Disclosures made by the counselee shall be treated with confidentiality. Counselees must have full confidence that what has been said in the counseling session will remain confidential and will be used by the pastor only for therapeutic purposes.

5. Pastors may be called on to help counselees make decisions that pertain to business transactions. In such instances, pastors shall not use their association with the counselee to benefit their own causes.

Ministerial Ethics

6. If payment is to be received for counseling services performed by a pastor outside the congregation, the pastor shall make full disclosure to Session concerning fee schedules and time involvement.

7. Pastors shall maintain the highest standards in the counseling relationship in order that healing and comfort may be experienced by the counselees who come with expectations that they will be treated with respect.

8. It is essential that if a pastor/counselee relationship results in abuse or inappropriate behavior, it must be referred to the Committee on Ministry for appropriate action.

VI. Sexual Conduct

A. Issues of Trust

The relationship between Minister and people is based upon trust. When, in the most difficult and tender times of life, members of a congregation turn to a Minister for comfort, support, guidance, and assurance, they expect that person to act as pastor, shepherd, counselor, and friend. There is trust that the Minister will not harm them when they are most vulnerable, neither will they be taken advantage of nor manipulated when the ability to care for themselves is lacking.

The psychodynamics in the pastor/parishioner relationship have been explored and discussed in a number of articles and books over the last two decades. It behooves pastors and church leaders to be aware of the scope of the literature. It is not our purpose to address these psychodynamics in depth, but to remind pastors of the issues.

We are becoming increasingly aware that pastors struggle with their feelings when they are engaged in close relationships with those to whom they Minister. Educational programs that help pastors recognize and deal with their feelings have been established by our seminaries. Clinical Pastoral Education encourages students to examine pastoral identity and the societal pressures placed on Ministers.

Pastors are encouraged to deal with their feelings about the demands and temptations confronting them and to learn how to cope in a trustworthy and responsible manner. For example, it is expected that when a person is seductive and acting out of a need to control, the pastor must know how to recognize the behavior, know the reason for the advances, and reject the advances in a compassionate, caring, and direct manner. Pastors need to know when it is necessary or appropriate to refer that person for psychological help. Pastors must never take advantage of a situation in order to fulfill their own emotional needs.

B. The Congregation as Family

The relationship existing between pastor and parishioners may be characterized as a family. How pastors relate to those in the congregation they serve is summed up in the advice to Timothy: "Do not rebuke an older man but exhort him as you would a father; treat younger men like brothers, older women like mothers, younger women like sisters, in all purity" (1 Tim. 5:1,2). With that as the paradigm for the pastor/parishioner relationship, any illicit or compromising sexual behavior between the pastor and those of the congregation is incestuous. It affects the very foundation of the congregation. Just as a biological family is dysfunctional when a parent enters into a sexual relation-

Appendix II

ship with the children or when siblings engage in sexual acts among themselves, so too does a congregation become ineffective as a family when the head of the congregational family becomes sexually involved with a member.

Code of Professional Practice[5]

As Revised at the UUMA Annual Meetings of June 1987 and June 1988

Statement of Purpose

We, the members of the Unitarian Universalist Ministers Association, give full assent to this code of professional life as a statement of our serious intent, and as an expression of the lines and directions that bind us in a life of common concern, shared hopes and firm loyalties.

1. SELF

Because the religious life is a growing life, I will respect and protect my own needs for spiritual growth, ethical integrity, and continuing education in order to deepen and strengthen myself and my ministry.

I commit myself to honest work, believing that the honor of my profession begins with the honest use of my own mind and skills.

I will sustain a respect for the ministry. Because my private life is woven into my practice of the ministry, I will refrain from private as well as public words or actions degrading to the ministry or destructive of congregational life.

As a sexual being, I will recognize the power that ministry gives me and refrain from practices which are harmful to others and which endanger my integrity or my professional effectiveness. Such practices include sexual activity with any child or with an unwilling adult, with a counselee, with the spouse or partner of a person in the congregation, with interns, or any other such exploitative relationship.

Because the demands of others upon me will be many and unceasing, I will try to keep especially aware of the rights and needs of my family and my relation to them as spouse, parent and friend.

2. COLLEAGUES

I will stand in a supportive relation to my colleagues and keep for them an open mind and heart.

I will strictly respect confidences given me by colleagues and expect them to keep mine.

Should I know that a colleague is engaged in practices that are damaging, as defined in our Code of Professional Practice, I will speak openly and frankly to her/him and endeavor to be of help. If necessary, I will bring such matters to the attention of the UUMA Board.

I will not speak scornfully or in derogation of any colleague in public. In any private conversation critical of a colleague, I will speak responsibly and temperately.

I will inform my colleague in advance of any public engagement I may accept in his or her community or church, which might bear upon local issues or policies. I will accept no request for my services in the office of the ministry within my colleague's congregation without his or her explicit invitation or permission. I will inform my colleague of any request for advice or counsel from members of his or her congregation, and I will consider with respect any objection to my meeting such a request. When in doubt I will err on the side of deference to the prerogatives of my colleague's call.

If I am to share the ministry of a church with (an)other minister(s), I will earnestly seek clear delineation of responsibility, accountability, and channels of communication before responsibilities are assumed. I will thereafter work in cooperation and consultation with them, taking care that changing roles and relations are re-negotiated with clarity, respect and honesty.

If I am a member of a colleague's congregation, I will in all ways honor the priority of his or her call to the ministry of that congregation, and I will carefully shun inappropriate influence which other members may tend to yield to me. I will be generous toward a colleague who is a member of my congregation.

I will share and support the concerns of the Unitarian Universalist Ministers Association, especially as reflected in these *Guidelines*.

I will keep my collegial relationships alive by attending UUMA Chapter meetings whenever possible and by thoughtfully considering matters of mutual professional interest.

3. CONGREGATION

I will uphold the practices of congregational polity including both those of local self-government and those of counsel and cooperation within our Association. I will only serve regularly a congregation(s) issuing a call in the manner prescribed by the Bylaws of the congregation(s) or under a program instituted by the UUA or its member groups. Throughout my ministry I will teach the history, meaning and methods of congregational polity, recognizing informed and faithful adherence to these practices as the bond preserving and reforming our free corporate religious life.

I will respect the traditions of the congregation, enriching and improving these in consultation with the members.

I will hold to a single standard of respect and help for all members of the church community of whatever age or position.

I will respect absolutely the confidentiality of private communications of members.

I will remember that a congregation places special trust in its professional leadership and that the members of the congregation allow a minister to become a part of their lives on the basis of that trust. I will not abuse or exploit that trust for my own gratification.

I will not invade the private and intimate bonds of others' lives, nor will I trespass on those bonds for my own advantage or need when they are disturbed. In any relationship of intimate confidentiality, I will not exploit the needs of another person for my own.

I will not engage in sexual activities with a member of the congregation who is not my spouse or partner, if I am married or in a committed relationship. If I am single, before becoming sexually involved with a person in the congregation, I will take special care to examine my commitment, motives, intentionality, and the nature of such activity and its consequence for myself, the other person, and the congregation.

I will exercise a responsible freedom of the pulpit with respect for all persons, including those who may disagree with me.

Appendix II

I will encourage by my example an inclusive, loyal, generous, and critical church leadership.

I will take responsibility for encouraging clear delineation of responsibility, accountability and channels of communication for the minister(s) and other staff.

I will take responsibility for encouraging adequate and sensible standards of financial and other support for minister and staff.

Prior to sabbatical or other leave, I will clearly negotiote a minimum amount of time to serve as minister to the congregation upon my return before making myself available as a candidate for another pulpit.

I will inform the Board of the congregation immediately when I have accepted a call to another position.

4. MOVEMENT AND ASSOCIATION

I will encourage the growth of our congregations and the spread of the ideals of the Unitarian Universalist tradition and fellowship.

I will participate and encourage lay participation in meetings and activities of our Association.

I will encourage financial support of the Unitarian Universalist Association and its associated programs.

I will inform myself of the established candidating procedures of the Unitarian Universalist Association and I will strictly observe them.

I will make myself a candidate for a pulpit only with serious intent.

5. COMMUNITY

In word and deed I will live and speak in ways representing the best Unitarian Universalist tradition and leadership in the larger community.

I will maintain a prophetic pulpit, offering to the community religious and ethical leadership.

I will encourage members' participation in efforts to solve community problems.

I will offer sympathetic support to neighboring ministers of other religious bodies.

The Pastor's Code of Ethics[6]
[United Church of Christ]

As a minister of the Lord Jesus Christ, called to God to proclaim the Gospel of his love, I subscribe to the following principles in order that I may set a more worthy example for those whom I seek to lead and serve:

My Personal Conduct

I will observe times of quietness for reading the scriptures, meditation and prayer.

I will endeavor to keep physically and emotionally fit.

I will remember my obligations to the members of my family to give them the time and consideration to which they are entitled.

I will endeavor to be a student at all times, through comprehensive reading and study and attendance at conferences and institutes.

I will be honest and responsible in my stewardship of money.

I will seek to be Christlike in my attitudes and conduct toward all people.

Ministerial Ethics

My Relationship to the Church I Serve

I will remember that a minister is also a servant. I will love the people I serve with the love of Christ, exercising conviction with patience, guidance with understanding.

In preaching, I will be diligent in my preparation, scriptural in my presentation, speaking the truth in love.

I will be diligent in the discharge of my responsibilities as pastor, preacher, and teacher, observing proper work habits and responsible schedules.

I will strive with evangelistic zeal to build up the church I serve, but will not proselyte the members of other religious groups.

I will not violate confidences which come to me as a minister.

I will not seek special gratuities or privileges as a clergyman.

My Relationship to My Fellow Ministers

I will endeavor to be a brother in Christ to my fellow ministers, and to offer and receive counsel in times of difficulty.

I will not speak disparagingly about the work of either my predecessor or my successor, nor encourage members in their real or imagined grievances.

I will refrain from visits to a former field for professional services, such as baptisms, weddings, funerals and anniversaries, except upon invitation of the resident pastor.

I will, upon retirement from the active ministry, give my pastor my loyal support.

My Relationship to the Community

I will consider my primary duty to be the pastor, but will also accept reasonable responsibilities which the community may call upon me to assume.

I will not set aside convictions and ideals to win popular favor.

My Relationship to My Denomination

I will recognize that I am a part of the larger fellowship which is the United Church of Christ and will strive to fulfill my obligations to it, accepting my responsibility both to support and to constructively criticize its efforts to extend the Kingdom of God.

My Relationship to the Church Universal

Recognizing that the United Church of Christ is a part of the Church Universal, I will participate in the work of the Ecumenical Church, supporting, as my convictions and energy permit, whatever measures may be proposed toward the strengthening of the fellowship of Christians everywhere.

The Covenant and Code of Ethics
for Professional Church Leaders
of the American Baptist Churches in the U.S.A.[7]

Having accepted God's call to leadership in Christ's Church, I covenant with God to serve Christ and the Church with God's help, to deepen my

Appendix II

obedience to the Two Great Commandments; to love the Lord our God with all my heart, soul, mind and strength, and to love my neighbor as myself.

In affirmation of this commitment, I will abide by the Code of Ethics of the Ministers Council of the American Baptist Churches and I will faithfully support its purposes and ideals. As further affirmation of my commitment, I covenant with my colleagues in ministry that we will hold one another accountable for fulfillment of all the public actions set forth in our Code of Ethics.

+ I will hold in trust the traditions and practices of our American Baptist Churches; I will not accept a position in the American Baptist family unless I am in accord with those traditions and practices; nor will I use my influence to alienate my congregation/constituents or any part thereof from its relationship and support of the denomination. If my convictions change, I will resign my position.

+ I will respect and recognize the variety of calls to ministry among my American Baptist colleagues, and other Christians.

+ I will seek to support all colleagues in ministry by building constructive relationships wherever I serve, both with the staff where I work and with colleagues in neighboring churches.

+ I will advocate adequate compensation for my profession. I will help lay persons and colleagues to understand that professional church leaders should not expect or require fees for pastoral services from constituents they serve, when these constituents are helping pay their salaries.

+ I will not seek personal favors or discounts on the basis of my professional status.

+ I will maintain a disciplined ministry in such ways as keeping hours of prayer and devotion, endeavoring to maintain wholesome family relationships, sexual integrity, financial responsibility, regularly engaging in educational and recreational activities for professional and personal development. I will seek to maintain good health habits.

+ I will recognize my primary obligation to the church or employing group to which I have been called, and will accept added responsibilities only if they do not interfere with the overall effectiveness of my ministry.

+ I will personally and publically support my colleagues who experience discrimination on the basis of gender, race, age, marital status, national origin, physical impairment or disability.

+ I will, upon my resignation or retirement, sever my professional church leadership relations with my former constituents, and will not make professional contacts in the field of another professional church leader without his/her request and/or consent.

+ I will hold in confidence any privileged communication received by me during the conduct of my ministry. I will not disclose confidential communications in private or public except when in my practice of ministry I am convinced that the sanctity of confidentiality is outweighed by my well-founded belief that the parishioner/client will cause imminent, life-threatening or substantial harm to self or others, or unless the privilege is waived by those giving the information.

Ministerial Ethics

+ I will not proselytize from other Christian churches.

+ I will show my personal love for God as revealed in Jesus Christ in my life and ministry, as I strive together with my colleagues to preserve the dignity, maintain the discipline and promote the integrity of the vocation to which we have been called.

Signed _____

Code of Ethics for
Ordained and Licensed Ministers and Lay Speakers
in the Church of the Brethren[8]

We believe that we have been called by God, through the church, to the set-apart ministry in the Church of the Brethren. It is our calling, and our function, to lead and facilitate the church in its mission to obey and serve Christ and to witness to the good news of the gospel. We are committed to fulfilling the trust the church has place in us by maintaining a high standard of Christian conviction, by sincerity of purpose, by nurturing and sharing our gifts, and by integrity of our character. We are dedicated to upholding the dignity and worth of every person who seeks or is reached by our care and proclamation. In order to uphold our standards we, as ministers in the Church of the Brethren, covenant to accept the following disciplines:

1. We will be true to the Judeo-Christian scriptures in our preaching, teaching, and conversation.

2. We will be true to Christian convictions as revealed in the Bible and interpreted, taught to, and nurtured in us by the church under the guidance of the Holy Spirit.

3. We will live lives of integrity, upholding the commitments we make to God, to others, to the church, and to ourselves.

4. We will exercise lifestyles consistent with the teachings of Christ, giving serious attention to relevant Annual Conference statements.

5. We will treat members of our family with Christian love and respect.

6. We will not misuse the trust placed in us and the unique power inherent in our function by exploiting in any way those who seek our help or care. We will guard against violating the emotional, spiritual, and physical well-being of people who come to us for help or over whom we have any kind of authority. We will not use our authority to defame, manipulate either individual or congregational decisions, or to create or cultivate dependencies. We will avoid situations and relationships which could impair our professional judgment, compromise the integrity of our ministry, and/or use the situation or relationship for our own gain.

7. We will avoid all forms of sexual exploitation or harassment in our professional and social relationships, even when others invite such behavior or involvement.[9] We will not seek sexual favors from volunteers or employees of the church as a condition of their participation or employment.

8. We will not engage in any form of child abuse, sexual, physical or emotional.

9. We will not use our office or authority to apply influence upon a parishioner or others in order to get bequests, gifts, or loans that would personally benefit us.

Appendix II

10. We will act with financial integrity in all our dealings, professionally and personally.

11. We will endeavor to manage our affairs in order to live within our income and neither expect nor specify financial favors, fees, or gratuities because of our position.

12. We will be responsible and honest in the managemnt of all resources and funds entrusted to our care in the course of our employment.

13. We will give credit for all sources quoted or extensively paraphrased in sermons and prepared papers. We will honor all copyrights.

14. We will respect the privacy of individuals and will not divulge information obtained in confidence. We will share confidences revealed by others without their consent only where such information may need to be revealed for legal reasons or for professional consultations.

15. We will neither exchange nor tolerate scandalous, malicious, or inaccurate information with or about other persons.

16. We will, wherever possible, maintain a friendly, courteous, and cooperative relationship with other ministers, both within our denomination and in the larger Christian community. We will not proselytize people from other churches. We will not render professional service in the congregation being served by another pastor without the knowledge and consent of that pastor, except in emergencies.

17. We will not perform professional services in former parishes, unless invited to do so by the present pastor. We consider it unethical to be involved in the pastoral affairs of a congregation after leaving it or upon retirement, or to cultivate such relationships with former parishioners as may hinder the ministry of the new pastor.

18. We will assume responsibility for our physical and emotional health and for our spiritual growth and enrichment. We will strive to maintain reasonable expectations for ourselves and not allow others' unreasonable expectations for us to endanger our well-being.

Notes

[1]"My Ministerial Code of Ethics," (Indianapolis, IN: Department of Homeland Ministries—Christian Church (Disciples of Christ), 1990. An executive states in the foreword, "Since its publication in 1944, more than thirty thousand copies of the code have been distributed. . . . With each successive reprint, a general committee was given the possibilities of change in the code. When all the suggestions were received, it was determined that they were sufficient only to effect editorial changes. The code has stood well the test of time and is commended to all ministers as a high code of professional conduct."

[2]Comparing this contemporary Disciples Code with the one printed in Harmon, 202-204, reveals only one word change, "*Kingdom* of God" to "*Realm* of God."

[3]"Report from the Task Force on Ministerial Ethics," Eastern Oklahoma Presbytery, adopted by Presbytery (February 13, 1990), 3-14.

[4]Included are eleven of the twenty-five pages of the code, the sections which deal with personal, collegial and congregational relationships.

[5]As published in the *Guidelines: Unitarian Universalist Ministers Association* (Boston: September, 1988), 11-14.

[6]Provided by the First Congregational Church, Chesterfield, Virginia, affiliated with the United Church of Christ. Similarities to the Disciples Code are quite obvious.

[7]Provided by Harley D. Hunt, Executive Director of the Ministers Council, American Baptist Churches, USA, and dated May, 1991. Also available is "A Process for Review of

Ministerial Ethics

Ministerial Standing" adopted by the National Commission on the Ministry, January 18, 1991, which defines the procedures for handling allegations and enforcing the code.

[8]*Ethics in Ministry Relations—1992*, approved by 1992 Annual Conference of the Church of the Brethren (Elgin, IL: September, 1992), 10-11. The twenty-three page document also includes an excellent section titled "A Theology of Ministerial Ethics" (4-9) and one on "Process for Dealing With Allegations of Sexual Misconduct" (11-18).

[9]Sexual exploitation is defined as, but not limited to, all forms of overt and covert seduction, speech, gestures, and behavoir. Harassment is defined as, but not limited to, repeated unwelcome comments, gestures or physical contacts of a sexual nature.

Appendix III

Ministerial and Parachurch Group Codes

Potomoc Association Sexual Ethics Code[1]

Because of increased awareness of sexual misconduct by clergy and religious professionals in general and because of specific incidents surfacing within the Central Atlantic Conference regarding sexual misconduct of religious professionals, the Church and Ministry Committee of the Potomac Association has been urged to study the procedures for dealing with problems of professional sexual misconduct.

Statement of Policy

In all cases involving complaint, the person charged will be considered innocent until proven guilty *beyond a reasonable doubt*.

Sexual contact as described below is a violation of the trust necessary for effective pastoral care and constitutes unethical behavior.

The professional is *always* responsible for protecting the spiritual, emotional, and physical well-being of those who seek counsel and help. Sexual contact *always* undermines that well-being.

The complainant, the accused, and the church or organization are entitled to fair and just treatment and due process, are to be accorded respect, and are to be assured of the church's intent to seek justice, reconciliation, and healing.

Theological Foundation

Human sexuality is a gift of God given to all creatures as a way by which partnership with God in the development of God's creative intent for human life is enabled. Through human sexuality love and mutuality is built, our connection and link with the whole created order is affirmed, the continuity of human life is assured, and the development and evolution of new life is empowered.

Because human life has been endowed with freedom, human sexuality can be used to undermine and corrupt God's creative intent. Sexual expression may express hostility and anger as well as love. It may seek to exert dominance and exploit vulnerability as well as express mutuality. It can become an agent of addiction by which meaning and esteem is [sic] sought in an exclusively sexual context. As such, sex is elevated to a level of meaning and importance it is not capable of providing. The result is sexual addiction and abuse of self and others, undermining God's creative intent for us.

Ministerial Ethics

When God's creative intent has become distorted our faith reminds us that God calls us to engage in the work of justice, reconciliation and healing. Justice is, in the eyes of faith, restoring life to its original purpose and intent; it means restoring right relationships, the root meaning of the word righteousness. Repentence, restitution, and restoration are involved in the work of justice. The presence of justice is the foundation for human *reconciliation*. While a state of absolute justice is impossible to fully achieve, a maximum state of relative justice is essential if reconciliation between people is possible. Reconciliation is the establishment of conditions in which alienated and injured parties have the optimum opportunity to heal personally. Healing occurs when the possibilities of justice and reconciliation are realized.

The purpose in cases of sexual misconduct is to commit ourselves to the work of healing by establishing standards of justice and remaining open to possibilities of reconciliation.

Definitions of Terms Regarding Sexual Misconduct or Inappropriate Sexual Behavior in the Pastoral Relationship

Sexual misconduct is a broad term that includes the following behaviors:
1. Sexual advances; welcomed or unwelcomed.
2. Requests for sexual favors.
3. Inappropriate affection such as kissing, touching, bumping, patting.
4. Any sexual contact related to terms of employment.
5. Any sexual contact which exploits the vulnerability of a parishioner, client or employee.
6. Dating of parishioners by religious professionals is a gray area filled with ambiguity. In such situations, consultation with colleagues is essential.

The term "religious professional" in this document applies to the following people: all licensed, commissioned, or ordained ministers; Directors of Christian Education; church musicians with the exception of paid church soloists and others contracted for limited services; pastoral counselor and others in specialized ministries involving licensing, commissioning or ordination.

Responsibilities in Dealing with Sexual Misconduct

Investigations of complaints regarding sexual misconduct of religious professionals may be appropriately initiated by local church leaders, the professional, professional colleagues, the ACM or Conference Minister for cause, or the Committee on Church and Ministry of the Potomac Association.

It shall be the responsibility of the initiating party to seek pastoral intervention by the ACM, or their designee. The purpose of pastoral intervention is to hear complaints and allegations; to assess need for further action; and to inform complainants and the professional of due process procedures if necessary.

The Committee on Church and Ministry in consultation with the ACM shall appoint advocates for the professional, the complainant, and the church or organization. Advocates will seek to understand their clients' needs, help them through the due process procedures, and provide a non-judgmental presence through the whole process.

The advocate for the complainant will arrange for the following ministries of support.

a. counseling to meet the initial trauma
b. explanation of the procedures to be used in dealing with the complaint
c. advocacy if fair and just treatment seems questionable
d. determining ways, in co-operation with the church advocates, for complainant's community of faith to understand the complainant's feelings and views
e. referring the complainant to appropriate resources for on-going treatment and healing
f. advocating before the Association and Conference for a just share of meeting financial expenses incurred.

The Committee on Church and Ministry shall determine the necessity for special or disciplinary reviews and conduct all necessary hearings, and make the initial determination of action.

If appeal is made the Board of Directors will review the Committee on Church and Ministry findings and will confirm or reverse the commitee's [sic] action.

An ecclesiastical council may be called by the complainant, professional, or church to review actions by the Board. The ecclesiastical council's decision is final.

Procedures

All complaints must be submitted in writing by complaining parties to the ACM.

The ACM informs the Chair of the Committee on Church and Ministry of the complaint and the steps to be taken regarding pastoral intervention. *TIME IS OF THE ESSENCE. RESPONSE TO COMPLAINTS SHOULD OCCUR WITHIN 72 HOURS OF RECEIPT.*

The ACM or designee will make pastoral intervention. The purpose of pastoral intervention is to determine the depth and dimensions of the problems, to assess the possibility of resolution, to inform all parties of the procedures of due process.

Within two weeks the ACM, or designee will report to the Committee on Church and Ministry regarding the results of the pastoral intervention.

The Committee determines whether a negotiated settlement is possible. If so the procedures for Special Review as outlined in the *Manual on the Ministry* are begun. This involves 1) a meeting individually with the complainant, the professional and church or other organizational leaders 2) convening a meeting with all parties to explore options [and] 3) assess the possibility of settlement.

If the process of Special review brings no resolution or if the Committee on Church and Ministry determines negotiated settlement is not possible or desirable, procedures for Disciplinary Review are initiated according to the Procedures outlined in the *Manual on the Ministry*. It should be noted that in matters of sexual misconduct disciplinary review is almost always necessary.

The following procedures for Disciplinary Review shall be instituted by the Committee on Church and Ministry[:]

1. Advocates will be assigned to the complainant, the professional, and the church.
2. Charges shall be set out in writing—presented to the professional and to the Committee on Church and Ministry.

Ministerial Ethics

3. The Committee will seek response from the professional to the charges.
4. A hearing will be scheduled. It shall be closed and confidential unless otherwise requested by the professional and agreed to by the Committee on Church and Ministry.
5. The hearing will be conducted as follows:
    a. statement of the role of the Church and Ministry Committee
    b. introduction of all persons present and statement of their roles
    c. statement about how the hearing will be conducted
    d. prayer for guidance
    e. reading of the charges against the minister in question
    f. presentation of evidence supporting the charges against the minister in question, generally through the testimony of witnesses or use of documents
    g. presentation of evidence refuting charges against the minister in question, again through the testimony of witnesses or use of documents
    h. opportunity for the presenter to respond to the minister in question's evidence
    i. opportunity for the minister in question to respond to the evidence against him or her
    j. closing statement by the presenter
    k. closing statement by the minister in question
    l. prayer for continued guidance and comfort
6. The Committee on Church and Ministry will determine the outcome.
7. Appeal of the outcome maybe [sic] made to the Board of Directors of the Potomac Association by the Church, the complainant, or the professional.
8. Appeal of the decision of the Board of Directors will result in a call for Ecclesiastical Council whose decision is final.

The office of Church Life and Leadership of the United Church of Christ will act as a consultant in the proceeding as deemed necessary.

Possible Outcomes

1. The charges are unfouded.
2. If the charges are judged unfounded the Association, through its Committee on the Ministry will make a public declaration both through the mail and at an appropriately called congregational meeting.
3. Educative response is made in situations where nothing unethical has occurred but poor judgement has been shown.
4. Warnings may be given where behavior is inappropriate and unwise but not unethical.
5. Censure may be given where behavior is unethical but consequences are minor.
6. Rehabilitation treatment and supervision may be ordered where unethical behavior is determined.
7. Temporary leaves and removal from pastoral responsibilities may be recommended by the committee for the purpose of treatment.
8. Termination of employment may be recommended.
9. Termination of authorization to practice may be recommended.
10. Termination of Ministerial standing may be determined and enacted.

Appendix III

Timing

In case of sexual misconduct, time is of the essence: 1) pastoral intervention should occur within 72 hours; 2) reports of the intervention and determination of further procedures within 2 weeks; 3) disciplinary review and conclusions within 3 months; 4) board review within 5 months; 6) ecclesiastical council within 6 months. In cases where legal procedures have been instituted this time line will need to be revised and extended depending on circumstances.

Appendix: Preventative Strategies

While stress and external pressures cannot be used as an excuse for sexual misconduct by a religious professional, it is believed and substantiated that proper support and education of religious professionals greatly reduces the incidence of such behavior. Therefore, the following preventative steps, while not exhaustive, may serve as guidelines to Conference, Association, and local church leaders in working to prevent incidence of sexual misconduct.

A. Support strategies to religious professionals and their families.

1. The role of the Conference and Association in advocating for fair and just professional compensation for all religious professionals should be extended to include more than ordained ministers in parish settings. Fiscal security is both an affirmation of worth and a reducer of stress.

2. Association and Conference leadership need to work with local churches in supporting the religious professionals' need for adequate rest, relaxation, privacy, and both educational and spiritual renewal.

3. The Association and Conference structures need to provide opportunities for professional and personal growth of religious professionals.

4. The Association and Conference need to provide a list of resources available for help to families of religious professionals who face personal and family crisis. Such resources should be separate from Conference and Association connections in order to insure [sic] objectivity and confidentiality.

B. Educational strategies regarding sexual misconduct of religious professionals.

1. Seminaries and other training institutions should provide a course in ministerial ethics in general and the dynamics of sexual misconduct in particular.

2. Associations should provide workshops on sexual misconduct and this policy.

3. This policy should be a point of conversation at every periodic review with clergy and should be a point of conversation at every change of pastorate with both clergy and representatives of the calling body.

4. The Committee on the Ministry of the Potomac Association should orient in-care students to the issues of sexual misconduct in general and this policy in particular.

5. The Association should request opportunities to present the issues of sexual misconduct to the leaders and members of each local church in the Potomac Association and to orient them to this policy.

C. Continuing the Process.

It is quite clear that a policy of such personal and intimate dimensions with such public and social impact needs constant monitoring and adjustment in the light of further experience and changing conditions. Therefore, it is recommended that periodic reviews of this policy be conducted by the Committee on Church and Ministry upon request by the Potomac Association through its Board of Directors.

Christian Association of Psychologists and Counselors[2]

Applicability of the Code

This Code of Ethics (hereinafter referred to as the "Code") is applicable to all current dues-paid Members and Associate Members of the Christian Association for Psychological Studies (CAPS). While CAPS is not a licensing or accrediting agency, it does desire that members who provide mental health, pastoral or other personal services do so with the highest possible level of Christian and service or ministry ethics, whether professional, layperson or student. Further, even though CAPS is not a licensing or accrediting agency, it does have the authority to set and monitor qualifications for membership in good standing. Thus, the Board of Directors urges each member to consider carefully and prayerfully the Code and to adopt it personally.

Biblical Foundation

Note: Each of the biblical blocks of the foundation that follows has one or more references. The references are not exhaustive, nor are they meant to be convenient "proof-texting." Rather, the Scriptures cited are meant to be representative of the many biblical references that build the foundation of this Code. The complete foundation is the total message of the Gospel of Jesus Christ. Also, it is recognized that each believer in Christ has the capacity—even the privilege and duty—to explore the depths of God's Word and discover personal guidance for daily living. This Code could not hope to explore all the richness of the Bible as it relates to ethical conduct.

Biblical "Building Blocks" of the Foundation

Conflicts, difficulties, power struggles, trials and tribulations are normal and to be expected, whether one is a Christian or not (John 16:33; Psalm 37:7; Romans 2:9).

We are to grow and mature through the conflicts, problems, trials and tribulations, and discipline that we experience (James 1:2-4; 1 Thessalonians 5:18).

We are to support and encourage each other (John 15:17; Ephesians 4:32; John 13:35).

We are to admonish and, if necessary, discipline each other, especially those Christians in positions of leadership and trust. However, such discipline is to be constructive rather than judgmental, done in love, and with caution about our own shortcomings (Matthew 18:15-17; 1 Corinthians 5:11-13; Galatians 6:1).

We are to demonstrate the lordship of Christ in our lives by servant-like leadership, a sense of community, and a life-style that reflects the will of God (Matthew 20:25-28; John 12:26; 1 Peter 4:8-11; Colossians 3:12-17).

We are to reach out to others in love and concern (Matthew 25:31-40; Hebrews 13:16; 2 Corinthians 1:3-7).

Appendix III

Basic Criteria and Principles of the Code

1. The Code includes a broad range of morality, yet it is specific enough in certain areas to offer guidance for ethical conduct in a variety of situations. It is intended to be universal without being platitudinous. On the other hand, it aims to be functional without being legalistic.

2. The Code calls for commitment to a distinctively Christian code of ethical behavior in our helping professions. Yet it recognizes that ethical behavior is certainly not the hallmark only of Christians, thus there is no implication of judging persons of different faiths or value systems.

3. The Code is not a credo or doctrinal statement of CAPS. Article II of the CAPS Constitution and By-Laws contains the basis for our association:

> The basis of this organization is belief in God, the Father, who creates and sustains us; Jesus Christ, the Son, who redeems and rules us; and the Holy Spirit, who guides us personally and professionally, through God's inspired Word, the Bible, our infallible guide of faith and conduct, and through the communion of Christians.

4. The Code is not a position paper on major social issues. While CAPS has genuine interest in social issues, it has traditionally encouraged members to become involved personally, as led by God, rather than as prescribed by CAPS. Also, CAPS has traditionally encouraged the free exchange of ideas among members, rather than defining "truth" or a partisan viewpoint for its members.

5. All humans are created in the image of God. We are holistic in our being and thus most descriptions of our parts, such as mind, body, soul, spirit, personality or whatever, are primarily to make it easier to discuss and evaluate our nature. Much of being created in the image of God is still a mystery to us. However, it does mean that we and those persons we serve have basic dignity and worth, along with basic human rights and essential human responsibilities. Also, we are to glorify God in worship, service and stewardship.

6. The family is the basic unit of our culture; it merits honor, encouragement and protection. In addition, "family" to the Christian includes our "neighbor" (Luke 10:29-37). Thus, our "circle of love" embraces God, neighbor and self (Luke 10:27). Not only that, we are to love our enemies (Matthew 5:43). Also, our influence, our activities in the helping professions, are to be "salt and light" in this world (Matthew 5:13, 14).

7. Scientific and humanistic activities in the helping professions are good, even excellent, but not good enough. While love without professional standards can become mere sentimentality, scientific observations and professional standards without love and Godly ethics can become mere clinical experiments. Thus, the Christian is called to maximize helping others by integrating the distinctives of Christian commitment—including prayer—with professional education, training and, if appropriate, licensing.

8. The world as we know it is a temporal place of human existence with the ever-present contrasts or polarities such as good and evil, order and disorder, joy and sorrow, generosity and selfishness, love and apathy, abundance and scarcity. Further, we do not necessarily know the reasons for any particular situation, event or relationship.

9. Exploiting or manipulating another person for our own or yet another's pleasure or aggrandizement is unethical and sinful.

Ministerial Ethics

10. Pretending to have expertise beyond our abilities or practicing beyond the scope of our licensure is unethical, very likely illegal, and does not value the person who needs help, nor does it glorify God.

11. Attempting to do for others what they are able and responsible to do for themselves, especially those persons who are seeking counsel, tends to create dependency and is thus unethical.

12. Some persons—such as children, for example—are more dependent than others and thus merit a greater degree of protection from persons who would thoughtlessly or selfishly take advantage of or manipulate them.

13. Each of us, whether helper or the person being helped, is a fallible human being who has limits that are universal in human nature yet unique in magnitude and proportion within each individual.

14. The helping professions are both art and science, with much to be learned. Also, each of us who serves, whether as professional or layperson, needs to be competent enough in what we do and of sufficient personal stability and integrity that what we do promotes healing rather than disorder and harm.

Articles of the Code of Ethics

Note: In an effort to avoid awkward and lengthy descriptions of persons we serve, the somewhat neutral word "client" is used. According to the perspective of members, words such as "peer," "parishioner," communicant," "patient," "helpee," "counselee" or even "prisoner" may be used.

Also, the word "service" or "serving" is used frequently in the Code to describe what we do. Again, according to the perspective of members, words such as "helping ministries," "helping professions," "counseling," "ministering" or "pastoring," for examples, may be substituted. Admittedly, no word is neutral, since language shapes (and reflects) our reality. Thus, the word "service" or its derivatives is meant to reflect Christ's statement that He came to serve, rather than to be served.

1. *Personal Commitment as a Christian*

1.1 I agree with the basis of CAPS, as quoted earlier in this Code, stated in the Constitution and By-Laws.

1.2 I commit my service, whether as professional or layperson, to God as a special calling.

1.3 I pledge to integrate all that I do in service with Christian values, principles and guidelines.

1.4 I commit myself to Christ as Lord as well as Savior. Thus, direction and wisdom from God will be sought, while accepting responsibility for my own actions and statements.

1.5 I view my body as the temple of the Holy Spirit and will treat it lovingly and respectfully. Balance in my priorities will be prayerfully sought.

2. *Loving Concern for Clients*

2.1 Clients will be accepted regardless of race, religion, gender, income, education, ethnic background, value system, etc., unless such a factor would interfere appreciably with my ability to be of service.

2.2 I value human life, the sanctity of personhood, personal freedom and responsibility, and the privilege of free choice in matters of belief and action.

2.3 I will avoid exploiting or manipulating any client to satisfy my own needs.

Appendix III

2.4 I will abstain from undue invasion of privacy.

2.5 I will take appropriate actions to help, even protect, those persons who are relatively dependent on other persons for their survival and well being.

2.6 Sexual intimacy with any client will be scrupulously avoided.

3. *Confidentiality*

3.1 I will demonstrate utmost respect for the confidentiality of the client and other persons in the helping relationship.

3.2 The limits of confidentiality, such as those based on civil laws, regulations and judicial precedent, will be explained to the client.

3.3 I will carefully protect the identity of clients and their problems. Thus, I will avoid divulging information about clients, whether privately or publicly, unless I have informed consent of the client, given by express, written permission, and the release of such information would be appropriate to the situation.

3.4 All records of counseling will be handled in a way that protects the clients and the nature of their problems from disclosure.

4. *Competency in Services Provided*

4.1 I pledge to be well-trained and competent in providing services.

4.2 I will refrain from implying that I have qualifications, experiences and capabilities which are in fact lacking.

4.3 I will comply with applicable state and local laws and regulations regarding the helping professions.

4.4 I will avoid using any legal exemptions from counseling competency afforded in certain states to churches and other non-profit organizations as a means of providing services that are beyond my training and expertise.

4.5 I will diligently pursue additional education, experience, professional consultation and spiritual growth in order to improve my effectiveness in serving persons in need.

5. *My Human Limitations*

5.1 I will do my best to be aware of my human limitations and biases, and openly admit that I do not have scientific objectivity or spiritual maturity, insofar as my subjective viewpoint will permit.

5.2 I will avoid fostering any misconception a client could have that I am omnipotent, or that I have all the answers.

5.3 I will refer clients whom I am not capable of counseling, whether by lack of available time or expertise, or even because of subjective, personal reasons. The referral will be done compassionately, clearly and completely, insofar as feasible.

5.4 I will resist efforts of any clients or colleagues to place demands for services on me that exceed my qualifications and/or the time available to minister, or that would impose unduly on my relationships with my own family.

6. *Advertising and Promotional Activities*

6.1 I will advertise or promote my services by Christian and professional standards, rather than commercial standards.

6.2 Personal aggrandizement will be omitted from advertising and promotional activities.

7. *Research*

7.1 Any research conducted will be done openly and will not jeopardize the welfare of any persons who are research, i.e., test, subjects. Further, clients will not be used as publicly identifiable test subjects.

8. *Unethical Conduct, Confrontation, and Malpractice*

8.1 If I have sufficient reason to believe a Christian colleague in CAPS has been practicing or ministering in a way that is probably damaging to the client or the helping ministries, I will confront that person. The principles and procedures specified in Matthew 18:15-17 will be followed in confronting the person who appears to be behaving unethically. In addition, the more stringent actions against pastors specified in 1 Timothy 5:19-20 will be considered, if relevant.

8.2 In addition to the confrontation procedures based on Scriptural guidance, civil law will be followed if relevant or applicable.

8.3 If the CAPS Board becomes aware that a member has been accused of unethical conduct, the Ethics Committee (either standing or ad hoc) will investigate the situation and recommend ethical discipline, including expulsion from membership, if appropriate.

8.4 Since ethical concerns may be complex and/or have legal implications, the consultation provided will be primarily in helping think through a situation, without assuming responsibility for the case.

8.5 The value of malpractice insurance will be carefully considered, especially if a lawsuit—whether justified or not—would possibly drain financial resources of the ministry organization with which I am associated, or of my family.

9. *General Prudential Rule*

9.1 Recognizing that no code of ethics is complete, I will make day-to-day decisions based on the criteria and principles stated at the beginning of this Code. Even more important, I will do my best to serve and live in a way that is congruent with the stated basic principles of this Code and with my faith as a Christian.

Revisions to the Code

Any suggestions for improving the Code would be welcome and should be addressed to any current Board member, whether CAPS or regional, or to the Regional Director for your CAPS region.

Approval of any suggested revision would require a two-thirds majority vote of the CAPS Board.

Notes

[1]"Policy on Sexual Ethics in the Pastoral Relationship as Recommended to the Board of Directors of the Potomac Association," unpublished copy of the Potomoc Association Church and Ministry Committee of the Central Atlantic Conference of the United Church of Christ, provided by Rev. Jerry Moore, St. John's United Church of Christ, Richmond, VA, February, 1992.

[2]Published in *The Journal of Psychology and Christianity* 5 (Fall, 1985), 86-90. (This issue also contains an analysis and responses to the code by members.) The code is also found in Gary R. Collins, *Excellence and Ethics in Christian Counseling* (Waco, TX: Word Books, 1991), 179.

Appendix IV

Sample Codes of Ethics[1]

Pastor or Senior Minister Code
(Includes basic obligations for all ministers)

Preamble
As a minister of Jesus Christ, called by God to proclaim the gospel and gifted by the Spirit to pastor the church, I dedicate myself to conduct my ministry according to the ethical guidelines and principles set forth in this code of ethics, in order that my ministry be acceptable to God, my service be beneficial to the Christian community, and my life be a witness to the world.

Responsibilities to Self
1. I will maintain my physical and emotional health through regular exercise, good eating habits, and the proper care of my body.
2. I will nurture my devotional life through a regular time of prayer, reading of the Scriptures, and meditation.
3. I will continue to grow intellectually through personal study, comprehensive reading, and attending growth conferences.
4. I will manage my time well by properly balancing personal obligations, church duties, and family responsibilities, and by observing a weekly day off and an annual vacation.
5. I will be honest and responsible in my finances by paying all debts on time, never seeking special gratuities or privileges, giving generously to worthwhile causes, and living a Christian lifestyle.
6. I will be truthful in my speech, never plagiarizing another's work, exaggerating the facts, misusing personal experiences, or communicating gossip.
7. I will seek to be Christlike in attitude and action toward all persons regardless of race, social class, religious beliefs, or position of influence within the church and community.

Responsibilities to Family
1. I will be fair to every member of my family, giving them the time, love, and consideration they need.
2. I will understand the unique role of my spouse, recognizing his or her primary reponsibility is as marital partner and parent to the children, and secondarily as church worker and assistant to the pastor.
3. I will regard my children as a gift from God and seek to meet their individual needs without imposing undue expections upon them.

Ministerial Ethics

Responsibilities to the Congregation

1. I will seek to be a servant-minister of the church by following the example of Christ in faith, love, wisdom, courage, and integrity.
2. I will faithfully discharge my time and energies as pastor, teacher, preacher, and administrator through proper work habits and reasonable schedules.
3. In my administrative and pastoral duties, I will be impartial and fair to all members.
4. In my preaching responsibilities, I will give adequate time to prayer and preparation, so that my presentation will be biblically based, theologically correct, and clearly communicated.
5. In my pastoral counseling, I will maintain strict confidentiality, except in cases where disclosure is necessary to prevent harm to persons and/or is required by law.
6. In my evangelistic responsibilities, I will seek to lead persons to salvation and to church membership without manipulating converts, proselytizing members of other churches, or demeaning other religious faiths.
7. In my visitation and counseling practices, I will never be alone with a person of another sex unless another church member is present nearby.
8. I will not charge fees to church members for weddings or funerals; for nonmembers I will establish policies based on ministry opportunities, time constraints, and theological beliefs.
9. As a full-time minister, I will not accept any other remunerative work without the expressed consent of the church.
10. In leaving a congregation, I will seek to strengthen the church through proper timing, verbal affirmation, and an appropriate closure of my ministry.

Responsibilities to Colleagues

1. I will endeavor to relate to all ministers, especially those with whom I serve in my church, as partners in the work of God, respecting their ministry and cooperating with them.
2. I will seek to serve my minister colleagues and their families with counsel, support, and personal assistance.
3. I will refuse to treat other ministers as competition in order to gain a church, receive an honor, or achieve statistical success.
4. I will refrain from speaking disparagingly about the person or work of any other minister, especially my predecessor or successor.
5. I will enhance the ministry of my successor by refusing to interfere in any way with the church I formerly served.
6. I will return to a former church field for professional services, such as weddings and funerals, only if invited by the resident pastor.
7. I will treat with respect and courtesy any predecessor who returns to my church field.
8. I will be thoughtful and respectful to all retired ministers and, upon my retirement, I will support and love my pastor.
9. I will be honest and kind in my recommendations of other ministers to church positions or other inquiries.
10. If aware of serious misconduct by a minister, I will contact responsible officials of that minister's church body and inform them of the incident.

Responsibility to the Community

1. I will consider my primary responsibility is to be pastor of my congrega-

Appendix IV

tion and will never neglect ministerial duties in order to serve in the community.

2. I will accept reasonable responsibilities for community service, recognizing the minister has a public ministry.
3. I will support public morality in the community through responsible prophetic witness and social action.
4. I will obey the laws of my government unless they require my disobedience to the law of God.
5. I will practice Christian citizenship without engaging in partisan politics or political activities that are unethical, unbiblical, or unwise.

Responsibilities to my Denomination
1. I will love, support and cooperate with the faith community of which I am a part, recognizing the debt I owe to my denomination for its contribution to my life, my ministry, and my church.
2. I will work to improve my denomination in its efforts to expand and extend the kingdom of God.

Associate Minister Code[2]
(Education/Music/Youth/Etc.)

I will be supportive and loyal to the senior pastor or, if unable to do so, will seek another place of service.

I will be supportive and loyal to my fellow staff ministers, never criticizing them or undermining their ministry.

I will recognize my role and responsibility on the church staff and will not feel threatened or in competition with any other minister of the church.

I will maintain good relationships with other ministers of my special area of ministry.

If single, I will be discreet in my dating practices, especially in relation to members of my congregation.

Pastoral Counselor Code[3]

I will have a pastor/counselor to whom I can turn for counseling and advice.

I will be aware of my own needs and vulnerabilities, never seeking to meet my own needs through my counselees.

I will recognize the power I hold over counselees and never take advantage of their vulnerability through exploitation or manipulation.

I will never become sexually or romantically involved with a client, or engage in any form of erotic or romantic contact.

I will demonstrate unconditional acceptance and love toward all counselees, regardless of their standards, beliefs, attitudes, or actions.

If I am unable to benefit a client, I will refer him or her to another professional who can provide appropriate therapy.

I will maintain good relationships with other counselors and therapists, informing and confering with them about mutual concerns.

I will keep confidential all matters discussed in a counseling setting, unless the information is hazardous for the client, for another person, or is required by law.

I will offer my assistance and services to fellow ministers and their families whenever needed.

Ministerial Ethics

I will support and contribute to the ministry of my church through personal counseling, seminars, lectures, workshops, and group therapy.

I will seek to support the policies and beliefs of my church without unduly imposing them upon any counselee.

Military Chaplain Code[4]

I will be an ethical example of a Christian lifestyle in a military setting.

I will perform my service duties according to the military codes of conduct, recognizing my ultimate allegiance is to God.

I will be truthful in my reports to my senior officers without divulging unnecessary confidential information.

Notes

[1]These sample codes are generic examples of numerous ministerial codes and they have been edited to include the most significant emphases, both principles and specific guidelines, in each category. To write a code, a minister should evaluate his or her own ministry obligations in light of the text discussions, then utilize these sample codes as broad statements of possibilities for a personal code of ministerial ethics.

[2]The "Sample Codes" of the associate ministers and others which follow will include only those obligations in addition to the Senior Minister Code, which uniquely apply to each special ministerial role.

[3]See appendix III for the Code of the Christian Association of Psychologists and Counselors, which, although it has many obvious weaknesses, does deal with the primary issues facing pastoral counselors.

[4]These statements have been suggested by military chaplains as additions to the basic code for ministers.